A LIST OF THE EARLY

SETTLERS OF GEORGIA

A LIST OF THE EARLY SETTLERS OF GEORGIA

Edited by

E. MERTON COULTER

and

ALBERT B. SAYE

The University of Georgia Press

Athens

Copyright 1949
The University of Georgia Press

Second Printing 1967

Printed in the United States of America

To

WYMBERLEY WORMSLOE DeRENNE

CONTENTS

INTRODUCTION ix

PART I 1

    Persons Who Went from Europe to Georgia at the Trustees' Charge

PART II 61

    Persons Who Went from Europe to Georgia on Their Own Account

APPENDIX 105

    A List of the First Shipload of Georgia Settlers
    Edited by E. Merton Coulter

INTRODUCTION

This list of the settlers of Georgia to 1741 is taken from a manuscript volume entitled *A List of Persons Who Went from Europe to Georgia on Their Own Account, or at the Trustees' Charge, or who Joyned the Colony or were Born in It, Distinguishing Such as Had Grants there or were only Inmates* (serial no. 14220), purchased together with twenty other volumes of manuscripts on early Georgia history by the University of Georgia in 1947. The manuscripts, sold at auction by Sotheby's in London, had formerly constituted a part of the library of Sir Thomas Phillipps, Bt., of Middle Hill, Worcestershire, and Thirlestaine House, Cheltenham, and were reported to have originally belonged to the Earl of Egmont, first President of the Trustees for Establishing the Colony of Georgia in America. Much of the material in the Egmont manuscripts is familiar to students who have used the official records of the Trustees in the British Public Record Office, from which source 26 volumes have been published by the State of Georgia as *The Colonial Records of the State of Georgia* (Allen D. Candler, Ed., Atlanta, 1904-13) and 13 more volumes have been collected and are available at the Georgia Department of Archives and History. Yet there are items of great interest that have never been used by historians, notably the list of the early settlers and the *Journal* of William Stephens from October, 1741, to September, 1743.

The list of settlers in the Egmont manuscripts is given under two headings: first, those who went from Europe to Georgia at the Trustees' charge and, second, those who went on their own account. The settlers are listed in roughly alphabetical order, followed by parallel columns with the following headings: age, occupation, date of embarcation, date of arrival, lots in Savannah, lots in Frederica, and "Dead, Quitted, Run Away." Footnotes give additional information concerning most of the persons listed. The division of the colonists into two lists based upon the payment of their passage has been followed in the present publication, but for convenience in printing, the parallel columns and footnotes have been abandoned and the information concerning each colonist quoted directly after his name. Except for this change in arrangement, an attempt has been made to reproduce all of the information in the same form as it appears in the original manuscript.

A summary statement at the opening of the manuscript shows that from June 9, 1732, to September 29, 1741, a total of 1,810 persons were sent to Georgia at the expense of the Trustees, that 1,021 joined the Colony at their own expense, that 142 children were born in the Colony, and that "the total supposedly in the Colony on March 4, 1743" was 2,092. The total of 1,810 persons sent to Georgia on charity from 1732 to 1741 compares closely with the figure 1,847 shown by the record of Benjamin Martyn quoted below, preserved in the British Public Record Office (C.O. 5/671), as the number of persons sent on charity to June 9, 1742.

Number of Persons Sent to Georgia on the Charity[1]

		Persons	Foreign Protestants	British
In the 1st year to the 9th of June,	1733	152	11	141
In the 2nd year	1734	341	104	237
In the 3rd year	1735	81	58	23
In the 4th year	1736	470	129	341
In the 5th year	1737	32	---	32
In the 6th year	1738	298	163	135
In the 7th year	1739	9	7	2
In the 8th year	1740	138	134	4
In the 9th year	1741	6	3	3
In the 10th year	1742	320	230	90
		1,847	839	1,008

These figures show that of the settlers sent to Georgia on charity during the first ten years 45.4% were "Foreign Protestants." In the present list of settlers sent on charity 319 are specifically described as Palatine Trust Servants, 47 as Palatines, 222 as Salzburgers, 142 as Swiss, 34 as Germans, 13 as German Trust Servants, 29 as Moravians, 33 as Scots, and 2 as Italians. No Jews were included in this list, but 92 of the settlers in the list of those who paid their own passage are identified as Jews. This list, which manifestly is incomplete, shows 1,675 people coming at the expense of the Trustees, and 1,304, on their own charge. It will be noted that compared with the statistics given above, the list falls short in the first classification and is in excess of the latter. Undoubtedly the compiler worked from imperfect and incomplete information. It is not evident why his sums total vary so widely from his lists; but undoubtedly he did not secure his totals from

---
[1]. Albert B. Saye, *New Viewpoints in Georgia History* (Athens, 1943), 32.

adding up his lists, as is indicated from the fact that the sums total are recorded on a separate piece of paper inserted and bound with the uniform sheets of the lists.

Occupations listed are of the widest variety—butchers, bakers, and candlestick makers, musicians and writers, vinedressers and brewers, ministers and teachers, seamen and soldiers, merchants and farmers, glaziers and graziers, and a host of others, including two attorneys, Will. Aglionby "who made much mischief in Savannah," and Will Williamson. The leading occupations in numbers were servants, husbandmen, farmers, labourers, carpenters, and weavers. The 827 settlers in the list sent on charity whose occupations were indicated are classified in contemporary terminology as follows: accompts, 3; alehouse keepers, 1; apothecaries, 5; apprentices, 14; bakers, 8; basket makers, 1; blacksmiths, 4; blockmakers, 1; bookbinders, 2; bookkeepers, 1; book sellers, 1; braziers, 2; brewers, 2; bricklayers, 4; brokers, 1; butchers, 2; cabinet makers, 4; calendars, 1; calico printers, 1; carpenters, 38; carvers, 1; chairmen, 1; clerks, 5; clogmakers, 1; cloth workers, 1; coachmakers, 1; coal sellers, 1; cooks, 1; coopers, 4; cord wainers, 2; cow herders, 5; cyder merchants, 1; drumers, 1; dyers, 6; farmers, 41; fishermen, 2; flax dressers, 3; gardiners, 8; gentlemen, 1; glaziers, 2; glovers, 1; goldsmiths, 1; graziers, 1; grocers, 1; gunsmiths, 1; half pay officers, 1; hatters, 4; heel makers, 1; hosiers, 1; hunters, 1; huntsmen, 1; husbandmen, 49; Indian traders, 1; inn holders, 1; iron mongers, 1; joyners, 2; labourers, 41; leather dressers, 1; linen drapers, 2; linen weavers, 1; locksmiths, 5; masons, 6; mercers, 3; merchants, 2; midwives, 2; millers, 8; millwrights, 5; miners, 5; ministers, 10; missioners to Indians, 1; musicians, 1; oil men, 1; Palatin servants, 18; Palatin trust servants, 61; peruke makers, 5; potash makers, 1; potters, 1; recorders, 1; rope makers, 4; salters, 1; saltpeter men, 1; saw makers, 1; saw mill wrights, 1; sawyers, 6; schoolmasters, 7; schoolmistresses, 1; seamen, 3; secretaries, 1; scriveners, 1; servants, 153; shipwrights, 1; shoemakers, 13; shopkeepers, 1; silk men, 3; silk throwsters, 1; silk weavers, 1; silversmiths, 1; smiths, 6; soldiers, 1; stockingmakers, 1; stockingweavers, 4; storekeepers, 2; surgeons, 8; tallow chandlers, 3; tanners, 6; taylors, 18; teachers of agriculture, 1; traders in goods, 1; trust servants, 90; turners, 3; upholsterers, 3; vine dressers, 4; vintagers, 2; vintners, 1; vitualers, 1; watchmakers, 2; weavers, 23; wheelwrights, 3; wine coopers, 1; wood cutters, 3; woodmen, 1; woolcombers, 1; writers, 3; writing masters, 1; wyre drawers, 1.

The 528 colonists in the list of those who paid their own passage whose occupations are indicated may be classified as follows: apothecaries, 3; attorneys 2; bailiffs, 1; bakers 1; blacksmiths, 4; bricklayers, 4; butchers, 1; carpenters, 3; cheesemongers, 1; clerks, 2; coopers, 2; farmers, 28; fort employees, 1; gentlemen, 11; haberdashers, 1; Indian interpreters 1; Indian traders, 9; engineers and surveyors of land, 1; joyners, 1; labourers, 21; masons, 1; masters of periagua, 2; masters of scout boat, 2; merchants, 1; millers, 1; ministers, 2; periagua employees, 1; planters, 1; plasterers, 1; potters, 1; pylots, 1; sailors, 4; sawyers, 1; servants, 360; shipwrights, 1; shoemakers, 3; soldiers, 8; speakers, 1; storekeepers, 4; surgeons, 2; taylors, 5; tinkers, 1; trust servants, 21; upholsterers, 1; victuallers, 1; weavers, 3.

What varied skills these early Georgians had! But, of course, there was no chance for them to engage in such occupations in their new home.

A notable feature of the information contained in this list of settlers is a record of pathos. Of the 114 colonists who sailed in November, 1732, on the *Ann*, 29, or 25.4%, died within the first year. Within the first ten years, 47 of the first 114 colonists died, and 20 others left the Colony either to return to England or to go to Carolina.

An effort to identify the authorship of the manuscript list of settlers has resulted in the conclusion that it was written by the First Earl of Egmont, original President of the Georgia Corporation. Comparison of penmanship definitely eliminated Benjamin Martyn, Secretary of the Georgia Trustees, a likely suspect as the author. Mr. H. B. Fant, Archivist, Executive and Courts Section, National Archives, took to England a photostatic copy of several pages from the manuscript list of settlers. In a letter dated London, 17 October 1948, he reported: "I am of the opinion that the photostats you furnished me definitely represent the handwriting of the Earl of Egmont. He was a very meticulous soul, and the List is made up in his own hand, just as he indexed certain of his own volumes personally. When in a hurry, as he frequently was when writing down his diary entries, his handwriting is not always as clear or uniform as is the handwriting in the photostatic specimens furnished me. But when he had plenty of time and when he was indexing or putting in marginal notations or interlineations he used the identical calligraphy. The numerals, the capital letters, the words, the long dashes, and above all the crosses for 'died,' are distinctively those of the 1st Earl of Egmont."

Through the coöperation of R. L. Atkinson, Esq., Secretary of the Historical Manuscripts Commission, photostatic copies were secured in December, 1948, of a number of pages from the known writings of the First Earl of Egmont. From our own comparison of handwriting, we concluded that the finding of Mr. Fant was correct. This conclusion was sustained by the Division of Manuscripts of the Library of Congress. In a letter of March 21, 1949, Dr. Leslie W. Dunlap, Assistant Chief, Division of Manuscripts, reported: "The photostats of the two eighteenth century English manuscripts which you sent have been examined by three members of the staff of this Division. They report that comparison of many individual letters, such as final 'g' and double 'ss,' the formation of capitals, and the general appearance indicate identity of handwriting of the two manuscripts, and that it is reasonable to conclude that the 'list of settlers' was written by the Earl of Egmont known to be the writer of the second manuscript. This is not to be considered a report of handwriting experts, but an opinion based on experience in the reading of early English manuscripts."

One of the introductory pages in the manuscript list of settlers is headed, "Mem.d for Georgia 4 March 1742/3," and contains a summary of the number of settlers who went over, the number of those who died, deserted the colony, etc. Though this memorandum suggests 1743 as the date of composition of the manuscript, additions were made as late as 1747, as may be seen by noting names in Part I, numbered 202-206, and elsewhere. The fact that many of the dates in the manuscript are written in a style devised to prevent confusion of Old and New Style reckoning, for example, the entry "10 Jan. 1735-6," cannot be regarded as evidence that the manuscript was written after 1752, the year in which England officially adopted the New Style Calendar. Replying to an inquiry on this point, Dr. St. George L. Sioussat, Chief, Division of Manuscripts, Library of Congress, stated in a letter of February 26, 1948: "It is not possible to state any established rule as to use of double dates. I may say, however, that certainly, many manuscripts written prior to 1752 carry double dates." The *Handbook of British Chronology* edited by F. M. Powicke and others (Royal Historical Society. Guides and Handbooks. No. 2. London, 1939. Pp. 377-78) contains the following pertinent statement: "The adoption of the Gregorian calendar of course affected the month-date, according to the point at which superfluous days were omitted, and also the year-date if the events concerned happened between 1 January and 25 March. Because the adoption had not synchronized in all countries, there came into being, as the late Deputy Keeper of the Public Records has well said, *'one of the most dangerous traps for students using original documents,' to be avoided only by careful consideration of the origin of any document in use and the habits of its writer."* [Italics added.] That the Earl of Egmont was one of those who used the double-date style of reckoning before the adoption of the Gregorian calendar is borne out by his diary and other known writings, the original manuscripts of which are preserved in the Public Record Office.

The publication of this list will, we hope, stimulate further research in the colonial history of Georgia. We express appreciation to Dr. George Hugh Boyd, Dean of the Graduate School of the University of Georgia, for encouragement in the work, to the Faculty Advisory Council of the University Center in Georgia for financial assistance, and to Miss Birdie Bondurant, Mrs. Lucy Wester and Mrs. Joan Burns for technical assistance in editing the manuscript.

E. M. C.
A. B. S.

Athens, Georgia
April 5, 1949

PART I

Persons Who Went from Europe to Georgia at the Trustees' Charge

1. Abbot, Will—Wood cutter; embark'd 14 Oct. 1735; arrived Feb. 1735-6; lot 8N. in Frederica. Appointed 2nd constable of Frederica in case of vacancy, 26 Sept. 1735.
2. Abraham, Eliz.—Widow; servt. to Peter Gordon; embark'd 31 Oct. 1734; arrived 2 Dec. 1734.
3. Adde, Solomon—Age 30; shoemaker; Palatin; embark'd July 1738; arrived 7 Oct. 1738. Adde and his family carry'd over by Capt. Thompson at his own risk, but Col. Oglethorpe charged the Trustees with their passage (which they disapproved) and gave them to the Saltsburgers.
4. ——, Margaret, w.—Age 32; embark'd July 1738; arrived 7 Oct. 1738.
5. ——, John, son—Age 3; embark'd July 1738; arrived 7 Oct. 1738.
6. Addison, Edwd.—Miller; embark'd 14 Oct. 1735; arrived Feb. 1735-6; lot 15N. in Frederica. Third Bailif of Frederica—removed abt. 1739. Went to settle with his family in Carolina Dec. 1740. Quitted Dec. 1740.
7. ——, Mary, w.—Went with her husband to Carolina Dec., 1740.
8. ——, Edwd., son—Went with his father to Carolina Dec., 1740.
9. ——, Mary, d.—Quitted Dec., 1740.
10. Aigel [or Argel] Geo.—Age 40; husbandman, Saltsburgr.; embark'd 22 Sept. 1741; arrived 2 Dec. 1741.
11. ——, Ursula, w.—Age 41.
12. ——, Anna Maria, d.—Age 6.
13. ——, Anna Teresa, d.—Age 10.
14. ——, Jo. Franz, son—Age 3.
15. ——, Laurentz, son—Age 5.
16. ——, Ludwig, son—Age 9.
17. ——, Saml., son—Age 1½.
18. Allen, John—Servt. to Hen. Fletcher; embark'd 4 April, 1733; arrived 21 July, 1733.
19. Allen, Will—Baker; embark'd 14 Oct. 1735; arrived Feb. 1735-6; lot 6S. in Frederica. Appointed Tithing man of Frederica 26 Sept. 1735; quitted May 1741 and went to Carolina. Quitted May 1741.
20. ——, Eliz., w.—Quitted May 1741.
21. Amatis, Nics.—Italian silk man; emmark'd 4 April 1733; arrived 21 July 1733. Brother to Paul; brought from Piedmont for the same purpose, but proved an idle troublesome fellow and quitted the Colony. In Aug. 1735 his brother discharged him. Quitted Aug. 1735.
22. ——, Paul—Italian silk man—embark'd 6 Nov. 1732; arrived 1 Feb.

1

1732-3; lot 14 in Savannah. Brought from Piedmont to introduce silk in Georgia, but took a disgust and settled chiefly at Charlestown, where he died. Dead Dec. 1736.

23. Amble, John—Palatin Tr. servt.; arrived 20 Dec. 1737.
24. Ambrose, Jo—Embark'd 21 Sept. 1733; arrived 12 Jan. 1733-4; lot 134 in Savannah. Fyn'd for selling Rum 2.0.0. 23 May 1735. Lot vacant Feb. 1738-9. Dead 7 July 1735.
25. ——, Eliz., w.—Dead 15 June 1734.
26. ——, Eliz., d.—She marry'd Elisha Baker and her father's lot was granted him, but they both quitted Savannah to settle in Carolina: and the lot is supposed vacant they not having perform'd the Covenants required on penalty of forfeiture. Quitted since Dec. 1738.
27. Anderly, Henry—Settled at Vernonberg; arrived 1746. In the Colony the end of the year 1746.
28. ——, [?], w.—Settled at Vernonberg. In the Colony the end of the year 1746.
29. ——, [?], Child—Settled at Vernonberg. In the Colony the end of the year 1746.
30. Andrews, Will—Cabinet maker; embark'd 20 Sept. 1733; arrived 14. Jan. 1733-4; dead 13 Feb. 1733-4.
31. ——, Eliz., w.—Re-marry'd to George Roan 10 Aug. 1734.
32. ——, Ja., son—Dead 1740.
33. ——, Jo, son—Dead 15 March 1733-4.
34. ——, Will, son—Dead 6 March, 1733-4.
35. Antrobus, Tho.—Embark'd 11 Sept. 1733; arrived 16 Dec. 1733. Re-marry'd the Wid. Eliz. Taylor 1 Dec. 1734 & settled on her lot in Savannah No. 137. He was before seated at Abercorn which he totally abandon'd, and never cultivated land. Absent in Carolina. Dead.
36. ——, Margt. w.—Dead April 1734.
37. ——, Eliz., d.—Quitted.
38. ——, Ellen, d.—Dead 13 April 1734.
39. ——, Margaret, d.—Became servt. to Ja. Burnside 1737.
40. ——, Mary, d.—Became servt. to Ste. Terryan 1737.
41. Armsdorf, J. Pet.—Saltsburger. Settled at Ebenezar. Living 13 March 1738/9.
42. Arnold, Sarah—Servt. to —— Delgrass; embark'd 14 Oct. 1735; arrived Feb. 1735-6.
43. Arnstein, Anna Maria, w.—Age 28; her husbd. (Caspar Arnstein, a German Swiss taylor) pd. his own passage; embark'd 21 Sept. 1741; arrived 4 Dec. 1741. Settled with her husband Caspar Armstein [Arnstein ?] on a grant S. E. of Hampstead.
44. Attwell, Tho.—Carpenter; embark'd 15 June 1733; arrived 29 Aug. 1733; lot 96 in Savannah. Fyn'd for assault and wounding 0.13.4. 11 May 1734. Went to Carolina but was expected to return. Quitted Jan. 1737/8.
45. ——, Mary, w.—Dead 1739.
46. Auchtenleck, Jo.—Writer & accompt.; embark'd 20 Oct. 1735; arrived Feb. 1735-6.
47. Avery, Walter—Apprentice to Geo. Spencer; embark'd 20 Oct. 1735; arrived Feb. 1735-6.
48. Bach, Gabriel—Husband-man; embark'd 31 Oct. 1734; arrived 28 Dec. 1734. Saltsburger. Settled at Ebenezar.
49. Bacher, Balthovar—Age 26; carpenter; Saltsburger; embark'd 21 Sept. 1741; arrived 2 Dec. 1741.
50. ——, Anna Maria, w.—Age 32.
51. Bacher, Gabriel—Husband-man & miner; embark'd 31 Oct. 1734; ar-

rived 28 Dec. 1734. Saltsburger. Settled at Ebenezar.
52. ——, Maria, w.—Saltsburger. Settled at Ebenezar.
53. ——, Apolonia, d.—Saltsburger. Settled at Ebenezar.
54. ——, Maria, d.—Saltsburger. Settled at Ebenezar.
55. Bacher, Mathias—Age 55; husbandman; Saltsburger; embark'd 21 Sept. 1741; arrived 2 Dec. 1741.
56. ——, Christina, w.—Age 48.
57. Bailey, Tho.—Smith; embark'd 28 Sept. 1733; arrived 14 Jan. 1733-4; lot 128 in Savannah. Found guilty of assault 20 Feb. 1734-5. He marry'd the widow Cadman 15 July 1735.
58. Baillou, Ja.—Storekeeper; embark'd 17 Dec. 1733; arrived 12 Mar. 1733-4; lot 142 in Savannah. An industrious man, and in 1736 had thoroughly cultivated his 5 acre lot. The formost in planting vines. April 1741.
59. ——, Mary, w.—Dead 29 Aug. 1742.
60. ——, Isaac, son.
61. Baillou, Pet.—Vine dresser & hatter; embark'd 18 June 1733; arrived 29 Aug. 1733; lot 119 in Savannah. Fyn'd 3 Oct. 1734 & 7 July 1737 for seducing servants to run away. His lot is swamp overflow'd.
62. Bain, Jo, of Lochain—Age 45; Tr. servant; embark'd 20 Oct. 1735; arrived 10 Jan. 1735-6.
63. Baldwyn, Eliz.—Embark'd 20 Oct. 1735; arrived Feb. 1735-6.
64. Bandley, Agatha—Trust. servt. for 5 years; embark'd 14 May 1735. German mother in law to G. Schumaker.
65. Barber, Amos—Servt. to Will Bradley; embark'd 20 Oct. 1735; arrived Feb. 1735-6.
66. Barbo, Will—Servt. to Jo. Brownfeild; embark'd 14 Oct. 1735; arrived Feb. 1735-6; out of his time.
67. Barisch, Math.—Husband man; embark'd 14 Oct. 1735; arrived Feb. 1735-6. Moravian. The Trustees advanced the passage of the Moravians, which was some years honestly repaid by them.
68. Barker, Jo.—Servt. to Will Bradley; embark'd 20 Oct. 1735; arrived Feb. 1735-6.
69. ——, [?], w.
70. ——, [?], child.
71. Barnes, Jo.—Dyer; embark'd 15 June 1733; arrived 29 Aug. 1733. Settled at Tybee 4 April 1734. On 11 June 1733 a grant of 2800 acres was past to him, Hen. Parker and Joseph Sacheveril in Trust. But to whom the same was parcel'd out I know not. Dead 5 Oct. 1734.
72. Bauer, Andreas—Labourer; embark'd 20 Oct. 1735; arrived Feb. 1735-6. Saltsburger settled at Ebenezar.
73. Bell, Joseph—Servt. to Hen. Loyd; embark'd 31 Oct. 1734; arrived 28 Dec. 1734.
74. Bellie, Jo.—Age 30; Palatin Tr. servt; arrived 20 Dec. 1737.
75. ——, Anne, w.—Age 23.
76. ——, Anna Barbara, d.—Age 4.
77. Belts, Hans Ulric—Age 30; weaver; German Swiss; embark'd 21 Sept. 1741; arrived 4 Dec. 1741. Settled on a grant S.E. of Hampstead with his family.
78. ——, Marg., w.—Age 23.
79. ——, Eliz., d.—Age 2.
80. Bender, Christ.—Age 46; Taylor. Tr. servt.; embark'd July 1738; arrived 7 Oct. 1738. German Palatines. Appointed to work on the lands for Religious uses under Mr. Habershams directions. In the Colony the end of the year 1746.
81. ——, Eliz., niece—Age 24; Tr. servt.; arrived 7 Oct. 1738. German Palatines. Appointed to work on the lands

for Religious uses under M. Habershams directions. Supposed dead Oct. 1740.
82. Bennet, Levi—Inn holder; embark'd 20 Oct. 1735; arrived Feb. 1735-6; lot 9N. in Frederica; deserted and died 1738.
83. ———, Anne, w.—Inmate for a time at Savannah, then settled at Frederica & kept a good Publick house there, but on her husband's death she marry'd —— Lee, who is an idle fellow and her business is almost lost.
84. ———, Jo., son.
85. Beon, Gilbert—Baker; embark'd 14 Dec. 1733; arrived 12 Mar. 1733-4. Saltsburger settled at Ebenezar.
86. Berenberger, Margt.—Spinster; embark'd 29 Mar. 1739. Settled at Ebenezar; a Saltsburger.
87. Berrier, John—Age 39; weaver, Palatin Tr. servt.; arrived 20 Dec. 1737.
88. ———, Maria Magdalen, w.—Age 28.
89. ———, Anna Christina, d.—Age 2.
90. ———, Hiero, son—Age 12; supposed dead July 1741 or before.
91. ———, Jo. Divolt, son—Age 10.
92. ———, Jo. Peter, son—Age 4.
93. ———, Margt, d.—Age 7.
94. Billinghurst, Ja.—Embark'd 14 Oct. 1735; arrived Feb. 1735-6.
95. Binker, J. Frederick—Age 35; Palatin servt.; embark'd July 1738; arrived 7 Oct. 1738. Binker & his children; delivered Andrew Walser Qur. Master to Col. Oglethorpes Regiment, & their passage to be repaid the Trustees by his bond for the same.
96. ———, Christians, d.—Age 10.
97. ———, J. Urich, son—Age 7.
98. Binks, Anthony—Servt. to Will Stephens, Esq.; embark'd 16 Aug. 1737; arrived 31 Oct. 1737.
99. Bishop, Hen.—Servt. to Mr. Boltzius; embark'd 31 Oct. 1734; arrived 28 Dec. 1734. He was schoolmaster at Ebenezar to teach the children English. He marry'd a German in 1740, and took a lot 6 miles from Ebenezar to settle on, Col. Oglethorpe giving him his freedome.
100. Bishoven, widow—Age 39; Palatine servt.; embark'd July 1738; arrived 7 Oct. 1738. German Palatines. Appointed to work on the lands for Religious uses under M. Habershams directions. Passage paid by the Trustees, to Capt. Thompson, to be repaid by Col. Stephens who took her.
101. Bland, [?]—Wid.; embark'd Feb. 1734-5.
102. ———, Ja., son—Lot 224 in Savannah. A minor, gone none knows where. In May 1737 he belong'd to the Compy. Settled at Fort Arguile. Run away.
103. Blinne, Valentine—Blacksmith. Palat. Tr. servt.; arrived 20 Dec. 1737. He marry'd Dorothy Rheinstetler at his embarkation for Georgia, Oct. 1737.
104. Bliss, Anne—Wid.; embark'd 14 May 1735.
105. Blithman, Will.—Carpenter; embark'd 15 June 1733; arrived 29 Aug. 1733; lot 89 in Savannah. Settled at Tybee 2 April 1734. But held lot 89 in Savannah. Dead.
106. ———, Martha, w.—Dead 7 Feb. 1733-4.
107. ———, Will., son—Became servt. to Tho. Trip. a minor, & succeeded to William his father's lot tho a servt. to Tho. Trip.
108. Boltschauster, Jacob—Age 45; carpenter; German Swiss; embark'd 21 Sept. 1741; died in the passage.
109. ———, Ursula, w.—Age 45.
110. ———, Elias, son—Age 6.
111. ———, Hans Jacob, son—Age 5.
112. ———, Hen., son—Age 4.
113. Boltzius, Jo. Martin—Saltsburg Ministr: embark'd 14 Dec. 1733; arrived

12 Mar. 1733-4. Minister & chief Director of the Saltsburgers at Ebenezar. He marry'd Gertrude Rhomoriseen 5th Aug. 1735. In the colony the end of the year 1746.
114. Bosomworth, [?]—Went to be clerk to Col. Stephens; embark'd 21 Sept. 1741; arrived 4 Dec. 1741; quitted, ret. to England Nov. 1742.
115. Bowen, Lewis—Bookseller; embark'd 15 June 1733; arrived 29 Aug. 1733. I don't find he took a lot. He went to Charlestown and there died; he went thither to buy goods, and to return with them to Georgia. Dead Aug. 1734.
116. Bowler, Cha.—Apprentice to Will Brownjohn; embark'd 15 June 1733; arrived 29 Aug. 1733; lot 157 in Savannah. This lot was granted him after his service under Will Brownjohn, but he deserted the Colony. Quitted Dec. 1736.
117. Bowling, Tim.—Age 38; potash maker; embark'd 6 Nov. 1732; arrived 1 Feb. 1732-3; lot 35 in Savannah; dead 5 Nov. 1733.
118. ——, Eliz., w.—embark'd 25 May 1733; arrived 23 Sept. 1733. She lives on her husband's lot.
119. ——, Mary, d.
120. Box, Will.—Hatter; embark'd 11 Sept. 1733; arrived 16 Dec. 1733; dead 16 April 1734. Settled at Abercorn; succeed'd in his lot there 1737 by Geo. Thompson.
121. ——, Mary, w.—Re-marr'd to Tho. Young of Savannah July 1734 & removed to his lot there.
122. ——, Ja., son—Inmate with his father in law Tho. Young.
123. ——, Phil., son—Inmate with his father in law Tho. Young.
124. Boynell, Simon—Gardiner; embark'd 28 Sept. 1733; arrived 14 Jan. 1733-4. Settled at Highgate. Dead 9 Sept. 1734.
125. ——, Simon Peter, son—Dead 21 Aug. 1734.
126. Bradford, Isaac.—Servt. to Tho Upton. A notorious thief; ran away to Carolina and was there taken May 1739.
127. Bradley, Will.—Was sent to teach agricultr.: embark'd 20 Oct. 1735; arrived Feb. 1735-6. He had a grant of 500 acres 17 Nov. 1735. The Trustees sent him over to instruct the Inhabitants in Agriculture, and are now (1739) calling him to account for malversation. The Trust servants were put under his care, but were taken from him 1739, lives Inmate in Savannah on lot 37. A Rioter in open Court 20 Oct. 1735; & convicted of stealing a calf & hog 2 Nov. 1737 which he confest. He since put his own mark on the Trustees cattle, & killed others impunedly which is felony. He took possession of his 500 acres 26 April 1739. He stole out of the Colony to avoid settling his account 28 May 1740 & ran to Carolina. Run away 28 May 1740.
128. ——, Eliz., w.—Dead 13 June 1737.
129. ——, Jas., son—Lot 56 in Savannah. An infant. This lot was granted him in 1736. But he lives with his father on lot 37 an Inmate.
130. ——, Jane, d.
131. ——, Martha, d.
132. ——, Ri., son.
133. ——, Robt., son.
134. ——, Will., son—Lot 186 in Savannah. He lives not on his lot but with his father.
135. Brandner, Mathias — Husbandman; embark'd 31 Oct. 1734; arrived 28 Dec. 1734. Saltsburger settled at Ebenezer living 13 March 1738/9.
136. ——, Mary, w.—Saltsburger settled

at Ebenezar living 13 March 1738/9.
137. Breath, Alex.—Age 17; Trust. servt.; embark'd 24 June 1737; arrived 20 Nov. 1737.
138. Breman, Maria—Widow. Palatin Tr. servant; arrived 20 Dec. 1737.
139. ——, Maria Magdalene, d.—Palatin Tr. servt.; arrived 20 Dec. 1737.
140. Brewin, Robt.—Sawyer; embark'd 28 Sept. 1733; arrived 14 Jan. 1733-4; lot 159 in Savannah; run away 1736.
141. Bright, Humfrey—Iron monger; embark'd 11 April 1734; arrived 21 Aug. 1734; lot 141 in Savannah; run away 1737. He ran away to Carolina before 16 Jan. 1737-8.
142. Brooks, Fra.—Embarked 14 Oct. 1735; arrived Feb. 1735-6; lot 174 in Savannah; shot by the Spaniards Feb. 1739-40. He marry'd Anne d. of Tho. Mouse of Skidaway; had been servant to Col. Oglethorpe; left a widow & 2 children.
143. ——, Anne Mouse, w.
144. Brown, Math.—Arrived 10 Jan. 1735-6. On the 10 Dec. 1735, an order past that he and his servant should go from Bristol on the poor acct.
145. Brownberger, Math.—Miller, embark'd 14 Dec. 1733; arrived 12 Mar. 1733-34; dead 17 Oct. 1734. Saltsburger settled at Ebenezar.
146. Brownfeild, Eliz.—Sister to John Brownfeild; embark'd 22 March 1736/7; arrived 4 June 1737. Marry'd to John Pye Recorder of Savannah. Went to Carolina for fear of the Spaniards. Quitted 30 Aug. 1740.
147. Brownfeild, Jo.—Embark'd 14 Oct. 1735; arrived Feb. 1735-6; lot 175 in Savannah. Had been servant to Col. Oglethorpe, and was made Register & Naval Officer 7 October 1735 but tis said gave it up in 1739. He was negligent in that office, and troublesome to the magistrates, and is factor for some English merchants. Afterwards he profest great zeal to perform his office, but absolutely neglected. of different religions 1: of the Chch. England; 2. a follower of Whitfeild; 3. of Wesley; & 4. a Moravian. Dead 24 March 1737/8.
148. ——, [?], w.—Dead 13 Aug. 1738.
149. Brownjohn, Benj.—Age 15; brother of William; embark'd 2 Dec. 1735; arrived 2 Feb. 1735/6; lot 197 in Savannah; quitted to England 1738.
150. Brownjohn, Will—Gardiner; embark'd 15 June 1733; arrived 29 Aug. 1733; lot 100 in Savannah.
151. ——, Anne, w.—Dead.
152. Bruchner, Geo.—Husb. man & locksmith; embark'd 31 Oct. 1734; arrived 28 Dec. 1734. Saltsburger settled at Ebenezar living 13 March 1738/9.
153. Bruchlin, Barbara—Age 23; single woman; Saltsburger; embark'd 21 Sept. 1741; arrived 2 Dec. 1741.
154. Buckley, Hen.—Embark'd 20 Oct. 1735; arrived Feb. 1735-6; lot 39N. in Frederica. Incapable of work. Deserted before Apr. 1740.
155. Buner, Jo.—Joyner; embark'd 14 Oct. 1735; arrived Feb. 1735-6. Moravian.
156. Bunyon, Robt.—Carpenter; embark'd 11 Sept. 1733; arrived 16 Dec. 1733. Settled at Abercorn, boat builder, and skilfull.
157. ——, Constant, w.
158. ——, Anne, d.
159. ——, Constant, d.
160. Burchard, Adrian—Age 43; farmer; German Swiss. He paid his own and his wife's passage; embark'd 21 Sept. 1741; arrived 4 Dec. 1741.
161. ——, Cath., w.—Age 38.
162. ——, Adrian, son—Age 12.
163. ——, Hans Jacob, son—Age 11.
164. ——, Susanna, d.—Age 7.

165. Burchard, Anna Maria—Sister of Hary and Jo.; age 17.
166. ——, Hary—Age 18; farmer; German Swiss; embark'd 21 Sept. 1741; arrived 4 Dec. 1741.
167. ——, Jo.—His brother; age 11.
168. Burgemeister, Christ.—Age 32; silk weaver; German Swiss; embark'd 21 Sept. 1741; arrived 4 Dec. 1741. Settled on a grant S.E. of Hampstead with his family.
169. ——, Eliz., w.—Age 34.
170. ——, Christr., son—Age 4.
171. ——, Hans Mric., son—Age 1.
172. ——, Martin, son—Age 6; dead soon after landing.
173. Burgi, Rudolf—Age 50; woodman; Swiss; embark'd 21 Sept. 1741; arrived 4 Dec. 1741. Settled on a grant S.E. of Hampstead with his family. Dead soon after landing.
174. ——, Esther, w.—Age 50; dead soon after landing.
175. ——, Anna, d.—Age 13. Settled on a grant S.E. of Hampstead with her family.
176. ——, Anne Marg. d.—Age 11; dead in the passage.
177. ——, Esther, d.—Age 6; dead in the passage.
178. ——, Hans Unroth, son—Age 10; dead in the passage.
179. ——, Rudolf, son—Age 19. Settled on a grant S.E. of Hampstead with his family.
180. Burgsteiner, Mathias—Husbandman; embark'd 31 Oct. 1734; arrived 28 Dec. 1734. Saltsburger settled at Ebenezar, living 13 March 1738/9.
181. ——, Agatha, w.—Saltsburger settled at Ebenezar, living 13 March 1738/9.
182. Burnside, Ja.—Writing master; embark'd 11 Sept. 1733; arrived 16 Dec. 1733; lot 191 in Savannah. His lot was granted in 1736: But he left it to settle on a Country lot at Rotton Possum without leave of the Trust. He marry'd Margt. Bovey 12 March 1736-7. A Rioter in open court 20 Oct. 1737. Turned with his wife Moravian. Run away to Carolina Aug. 1742; returned.
183. Bush, Edwd.—Gunsmith; embark'd 17 Dec. 1733; arrived 12 Mar. 1733-1734; lot 150 in Savannah. Convicted of assault 20 Feb. 1734-5. In 1736 he had 5 acres thoroughly cultivated which produced 30 bushels of Indian corn, and 6 of rice. In 1739 he had leave to dispose of his lot by will to one of his daughters. Run away to Carolina Aug. 1742.
184. ——, Eliz., w.—Arrived 21 Oct. 1734. In 1737 she let a house for a girls school at 7.4.0 p. ann.
185. Cadman, Jo.—Farmer; embark'd 15 June 1733; arrived 29 Aug. 1733. Settled at Tybee. Dead 23 June 1735.
186. ——, Hannah, w.—Re-marry'd to Tho. Bailie 15 July 1735.
187. Calder, Will.—Age 20; Tr. servt. for 4 years; embark'd 20 Oct. 1735; arrived 10 Jan. 1735-6. Made by Col. Oglethorpe at the expiration of his service a soldier of the highland Independt. Compy. & as such returned 6 May 1741.
188. Callifer, Anne—Age 22; single woman; Germ. Swiss; embark'd 21 Sept. 1741; arrived 2 Dec. 1741.
189. Calliser, Hans Caspar—Age 24; a conductor of his countrymen; rope maker; German Swiss; embark'd 21 Sept. 1741; arrived 2 Dec. 1741.
190. Calloway, Will—Wine cooper; embark'd 31 Oct. 1734; arrived 28 Dec. 1734; lot 202 in Savannah. His wife was in England when he died. Quitted if she be living. Dead 4 June 1735.
191. ——, Susanna, w.—Lot 202 in Sa-

vannah; in Engld. when her husband died.

192. Calvert, Will.—Age 44; trader in goods; embark'd 6 Nov. 1732; arrived 1 Feb. 1732-3; lot 77 in Savannah. Said to be a landholder at Fort Arguile, 16 Jan. 1737-8, but I don't find him in the list. Would have denyd a note of hand to Ja. Dormer but was cast 7 July, 1737.

193. ——, Mary, w.—Age 42; dead 4 July 1733.

194. Calwell, Jo.—Tallow chandler; embark'd 20 Oct. 1735; arrived Feb. 1735-6; lot 4N. in Frederica. Made Tything Man 26 Sept. 1735 and Deputy Surveyor of lands to Ausperger, and 3d Bailif of Frederica 1739. on 9 Oct. 1738 & 22 Nov. following Col. Oglethorp advanc'd him 2.2.4 to help him to follow his trade, wch. is charged to the Trustees.

195. ——, Constance, w.

196. Cameron, Jannet—Age 26; servt. for 4 yrs.; embark'd 19 Nov. 1737; arrived 14 Jan. 1737-8. Hired & carry'd at Capt. Thompson the owners risk, but the Planters unable to pay for her, Mr. Causton without orders took her on the Trustees Acct. and certified the same which made us lyable to the charge.

197. Cameron, Jo.—Age 18; Tr. servt.; embark'd 24 June 1737; arrived 20 Nov. 1737.

198. Cameron, John—Age 20; Tr. servt.; embark'd 24 June 1737; arrived 20 Nov. 1737. Made a Ranger by Col. Oglethorpe at the expiration of his service, and as such return'd living 6 May 1741.

199. Cameron, John—Age 27; servt. for 4 yrs.; embark'd 19 Nov. 1737; arrived 14 Jan. 1737-8. Hired & carry'd at Capt. Thompson the owners risk, but the Planters unable to pay for him, Mr. Causton without orders took him on the Trustees Acct. and certified the same which made us lyable to the charge.

200. Cameron, Ri.—Age 35; servt. to Fra. Scot; embark'd 6 Nov. 1732; arrived 1 Feb. 1732-3; abst. at Palocholas.

201. Campbell, Jo.—Age 24; wood cutter; Scotch; embark'd 21 Sept. 1741; arrived 2 Dec. 1741.

202. Camuse, Jacob—Servt. to Nic. Amatis; embark'd 4 April 1733; arrived 21 July 1733; lot 10 in Savannah. After his Master went away he and his wife became the principal Managers of the Silk. In the Colony at the end of the year 1746.

203. ——, Jane Mary, w.—In the Colony at the end of the year 1746.

204. ——, Fra. Ant., son—In the Colony at the end of the year 1746.

205. ——, Jeffry, son—In the Colony at the end of the year 1746.

206. ——, Jo Bapt., son—In the Colony at the end of the year 1746.

207. Cannon, Danl.—Carpenter; embark'd 20 Oct. 1735; arrived Feb. 1735-6; lot 6N. in Frederica. Appointed 2d Bailif of Frederica in case of vacancy 26 Sept. 1735.

208. ——, Danl., son.

209. ——, Joseph, son—Quitted 1740.

210. Cannon, Ri.—Age 36; calendar; embark'd 6 Nov. 1732; arrived 1 Feb. 1732-3; lot 5 in Savannah. He marry'd to his 2d. wife the widow of Daniel Preston 24 Oct. 1734. Dead 27 May 1735.

211. ——, Mary, w.—Age 33; dead 22 July 1733.

212. ——, Clementine, d.—Age 3.

213. ——, James, son—Age 1; dead in the passage.

214. ——, Marmaduke, son—Age 9; afterwd. servt. to Tho. Causton.

215. Carpenter, Nic.—Tr. servt. for 11 years; embark'd 14 May 1735.
216. Carter, Cha.—Tr. servt.; embark'd 14 Oct. 1735; arrived Feb. 1735-6. Indented to the Trust 24 Sept. 1735.
217. Carteriades, Ja.—Hatter; embark'd 17 Dec. 1733; arrived 12 Mar. 1733-4. Als. Carder and settled at Highgate. Dead 27 Aug. 1734.
218. ——, Magdalene, w.
219. Carwell, Ja.—Age 35; peruke maker; embark'd 6 Nov. 1732; arrived 1 Feb. 1732-3; lot 4 in Savannah. Keeper of the work house 1737 but of very bad character. In July 1739 Mr. Oglethorpe appointed him Provost Marshal and Jailer at Savannah wth. a sallary of 20£ p ann.
220. ——, Margt., w.—Age 32; dead 7 Sept. 1733.
221. Causton, Tho.—Age 40; calico printer; embark'd 6 Nov. 1732; arrived 1 Feb. 1732-3; lot 24 in Savannah. At first appointed 3d. Bailif, then 2d. & lastly 1st. Bailif in 1734. He was also Publick Store Keeper on Hughes death 30 Sept. 1733, but turn'd out of both offices 1739 for abusing his Trust.
222. ——, Martha, w.—Embark'd 25 May 1733; arrived 23 Sept. 1733; dead 10 Oct. 1740.
223. ——, Tho., inft. son—Arrived 23 Sept. 1733; lot 161 in Savannah. This lot was granted him 1736. He lives at Oxstead with his father late 1 Bailif. Dead 1 Oct. 1740.
224. Cawtrey, Jo.—Embark'd 14 Oct. 1735; arrived 4 Feb. 1735-6.
225. Chance, Will.—Tr. Servt. afterwd. to T. Causton; embark'd 14 Oct. 1735; arrived Feb. 1735-6.
226. Charles, Jacob—Weaver; embark'd 11 Sept. 1733; arrived 16 Dec. 1733; lot 138 in Savannah. Fyn'd for defamation—0.6.8. 7 Aug. 1734. Also try'd for cheating 22 May 1736. Run away for debt 1737.
227. ——, Anne, w.—Fyn'd for the same 0.6.8. Same time she ran away for England wth. the Revd. Mr. John Wesley, and took her two sons with her, 1737. Run away 1737.
228. ——, Gideon, son.
229. ——, Jo., son.
230. Cheeswright, Paul—Sawyer; embark'd 24 Jan. 1732-3; lot 42 in Savannah; dead 1736.
231. ——, Rebecka, w.—Embark'd 24 Jan. 1732-3. Sentenc'd 60 lashes for barborously cutting an infant down the back with a knyfe 28 July 1735 and afterwards ran away to England December 1736. Run away Dec. 1736.
232. Cheney, Goodwin—Tr. servt. oil man; embark'd 28 Sept. 1733; arrived 14 Jan. 1733-4. Settled at Skidaway.
233. Chensack, John—Weaver; embark'd 11 Sept. 1733; arrived 16 Dec. 1733. Settled at Highgate.
234. ——, Anne, w.
235. ——, James, son—Dead 6 July 1734.
236. Chewter, Tho.—Upholster; embark'd 15 June 1733; arrived 29 Aug. 1733; dead 13 Dec. 1733.
237. Christe, Jo. Gotfred—Labourer & taylor; embark'd 20 Oct. 1735; arrived Feb. 1735-6. Saltsburger settled at Ebenezar.
238. Christer, H. Fred—Tr. servt. for 5 years; embark'd 14 May 1735. German.
239. ——, Maria, w.—Tr. servt. for 5 years. German.
240. Christie, Tho.—Age 32; mercht.; embark'd 6 Nov. 1732; arrived 1 Feb. 1732-3; lot 19 in Savannah. Recorder of Savannah till made 1st Bailif in Hen. Parkers room 20 June 1739. But removed 25 March 1740 by letter from the Trustees & likewise suspended from being Recorder till an

acct. he has made with the stores be made up. He lives on in open adultery with Turners' wife and is guilty of other faults. Abt. April 1740 he left Georgia, & in June following came for England, where he proposed to stay, but returned. Quitted April 1740 but to return.

241. Clark, Hen.—Farmer; embark'd 15 June 1733; arrived 29 Aug. 1733; dead 30 Dec. 1733.
242. ——, Anne, w.—Dead 24 Sept. 1733.
243. ——, Anne, d.—Became servt. to Jos. Hethrington. Mr. Whitfeild brought her to England 30 Dec. 1740. Quitted to Engld. Dec. 1740.
244. ——, Hen., son.
245. ——, Tho., son.
246. Clark, Isaac King—Apothecary; embark'd 11 Sept. 1733; arrived 16 Dec. 1733; lot 123 in Savannah. He went away to Carolina. Quitted 1738.
247. ——, Eliz., w.—Rendt. at Darien 6 May 1741.
248. Clarke, Robt.—Age 37; taylor; embark'd 6 Nov. 1732; arrived 1 Feb. 1732-3; lot 22 in Savannah; dead 18 April 1734.
249. ——, Judith, w.—Age 29. Re-marry'd to Tho. Cross 29 June 1734 and quitted the Colony with him. Quitted Dec. 1738.
250. ——, Cha., son—Age 11; dead.
251. ——, James, son—Age 1; dead in the passage.
252. ——, John, son—Age 4.
253. ——, Peter, son—Age 3.
254. Clause, Leopold—Age 35; taylor; Palatin; Tr. servt.; embark'd Oct. 1737; arrived 20 Dec. 1737.
255. ——, Anne Cath., w.—Age 33.
256. ——, Jo. Michl. Simon, son—Age 4.
257. Cleaness, Alexr.—Age 24; Tr. servt.; embark'd 24 June 1737; arrived 20 Nov. 1737. Living at Darien, & still a servant 6 May 1741.
258. Clement, Eliz.—Niece of Hen. Parker; embark'd 15 June 1733; arrived 29 Aug. 1733.
259. Clements, [?], widow—Age 35; Palatin; embark'd July 1738; arrived 7 Oct. 1738. Widow Clements. Settled at Vilage Bluff on St. Simons. Gave bond to repay her passage to the Trust.
260. Close, Hen.—Age 42; cloth worker; embark'd 6 Nov. 1732; arrived 1 Feb. 1732-3; lot 40 in Savannah. His lot was swamp overflow'd. Dead 14 Dec. 1733.
261. ——, Hannah, w.—Age 32. Re-marry'd to Ja. Smith a Carolinian 8 Feb. 1733-4 who lives with her on her lot. Abt. May 1740 they both left the Colony to settle in Scotland on an estate, and sold their lot to Capt. Thompson for 20£. Quitted May 1740.
262. ——, Anne, d.—Age 2; dead 2 April 1734.
263. Cluer, Eliz.—Age 33; Palatin; servant; embark'd July 1738; arrived 7 Oct. 1738. Eliz. Cluer: Deliver'd to Tho. Walker of Frederica, who gave bond to repay the Trustees her passage.
264. Clyat, Tho.—Apprentice to Tho. Hird; embark'd 14 Oct. 1735; arrived Feb. 1735-6.
265. Coates, Jo.—Turner; embark'd 11 Sept. 1733; arrived 16 Dec. 1733; lot 121 in Savannah. He was constable when he deserted to Carolina for debt. A riotous fellow in open court at the Tryal of Watson 20 Oct. 1737. He died there Sept. 1739. Run away 3 Dec. 1737; dead Sept. 1739.
266. ——, Sarah, w.—Dead 1 Aug. 1734.
267. ——, Sarah, d.—Inmate after her fathers running away on lot 29.
*268. Coglar, Geo.—Carpenter; embark'd 31 Oct. 1734; arrived 28 Dec. 1734; Saltsburger settled at Ebenezar.

---

* Same as Koglar, p. 28, no. 795.

269. Coguch, Jo.—Age 33; labourer & Cow heard; Scotch; embark'd 21 Sept. 1741; arrived 2 Dec. 1741.
270. ——, Anne Mackay, w.—Scotch.
271. ——, Angus, son—Age 7; Scotch.
272. ——, Christiana, d.—Age 16; Scotch.
273. ——, Isabel, d. Age 13; Scotch.
274. ——, William, son—Age 11; Scotch.
275. Cole, Ja.—Apprentice to Jo. Robinson; embark'd 14 Oct. 1735; arrived Feb. 1735-6.
276. Coles, Joseph—Age 28; Miller & baker; embark'd 6 Nov. 1732; arrived 1 Feb. 1732-3; lot 27 in Savannah; dead 4 Mar. 1734-5.
277. ——, Anne, w.—Age 32. Re-marry'd to Tho. Salter 9 Sept. 1736 & lives with him on his lot 68.
278. ——, Anne, d.—Age 13.
279. Collins, Deborah—Servt. to Tho. Proctor; embark'd 14 Oct. 1735; arrived Feb. 1735-6.
280. Colthred, Will.—Servant; embark'd 17 May 1737; arrived 20 Nov. 1737.
281. Comberger, Jo.—Saltsburger. Settled at Ebenezar. Living 13 March 1738/9.
282. Cooper, Joseph—Age 37; writer; embark'd 6 Nov. 1732; arrived 1 Feb. 1732-3; lot 20 in Savannah; dead 29 Mar. 1735.
283. Cooper, Ri.—Millwright; embark'd 18 June 1736.
*284. Cornock, Mary—Age 11; servt. to Noble Jones, embark'd 6 Nov. 1732; arrived 1 Feb. 1732-3.
285. Cotton, Anne—Age 23; single woman; Scotch; embark'd 21 Sept. 1741; arrived 2 Dec. 1741.
286. Coulton, Jennet—Servt. to Ja. Willoughby; embark'd 11 Sept. 1733; arrived 16 Dec. 1733. Marry'd to Will. Grickson 9 Mar. 1734-5.
287. Cousins, Jo.—Tr. servt.; embark'd 14 Oct. 1735; arrived Feb. 1735-6.
288. Cox, Will.—Age 41; surgeon; embark'd 6 Nov. 1732; arrived 1 Feb. 1732-3; lot 6 in Savannah; dead 6 April 1733.
289. ——, Fra., w.—Age 35. Re-marry'd to Ja. Watts Lieut. 1 June 1734 who died the same month. She afterwd. went to England with her two children. Quitted 1734.
290. ——, Eunice, d.—Age 3; quitted 1734.
291. ——, Will., son—Age 12; quitted 1734.
292. Crader, Abrm.—Palatin; Tr. servt.; embark'd Oct. 1737; arrived 20 Dec. 1737.
293. Craus, Lemand—Age 35; labourer; embark'd 20 Oct. 1735; arrived Feb. 1735-6. Saltsburger settled at Ebenezar, living 13 March 1738/9.
294. ——, Barbara, w.—Age 33. Saltsburger settled at Ebenezar, living 13 March 1738/9.
295. Croft, Peter—Age 40; Palatin; Tr. servt.; embark'd Oct. 1737; arrived 20 Dec. 1737.
296. ——, Maria, w.—Age 40.
297. ——, Cath., d.—Age 13.
298. ——, Jo. Selden, son—Age 8.
299. Cundall, Eliz.—w. of Jo. Cundall; embark'd 31 Oct. 1734; arrived 28 Dec. 1734; lot 52 in Savannah. Prosecuted for keeping a bawdy house 6 Dec. 1736; and fyn'd for the same 17 April 1737.
300. ——, John, son.
301. ——, Tho., son.
302. ——, Will., son.
303. Cunningham, Sam.—Coal seller; embark'd 15 June 1733; arrived 29 Aug. 1733.
304. Curles, Jo. Jacob—Age 27; Palatin; Tr. servt.; embark'd Oct. 1737; arrived 20 Dec. 1737.
305. Curtis, Will.—Leather dresser; embark'd 11 Sept. 1733; arrived 16 Dec.

* Same as Charnock, p. 67, no. 203.

1733. Settled at Abercorn. Dead 26 May 1734.

306. Custabader, Cath.—Age 50; German; embark'd July 1738; arrived 7 Oct. 1738. Given to the orphan house at Ebenezar. Her passage paid for to Capt. Thompson by the Trustees, to be repaid, but the Trustees gave the repayment to the Saltsburgers. A Palatine.

307. Dalmass, Will.—Soldier; embark'd 28 Sept. 1733; arrived 14 Jan. 1733-4. Tything man and settled at Skidaway 1734. Dead July 1735.

308. Danner, Barbara—Age 25; Germ. Swiss; w. of Jacob; embark'd 21 Sept. 1741; arrived 4 Dec. 1742 [intended for 1741]. Settled with her husband Jacob on a grant S. E. of Hampstead.

309. Darber, Mary—Servt. to Will. Bradley; embark'd 20 Oct. 1735; arrived Feb. 1735-6.

310. Davant, John—Cabinet maker; embark'd 15 June 1733; arrived 29 Aug. 1733. Settled at Tybee. Dead Sept. 1733.

311. ——, Hester, w.—Dead 26 Feb. 1733-4.

312. ——, John, son—The grant at Abercorn which John his father did not live to take out was made to this youth his son 2 April 1734.

313. Davant, Lewis—Shoemaker; embark'd 15 June 1733; arrived 29 Aug. 1733; dead 19 Sept. 1733.

314. ——, Eliz., w.—Dead 11 Jan. 1734-5.

315. Davis, Jo.—Glazier; embark'd 11 Sept. 1733; arrived 16 Dec. 1733. Convicted of assault & bound in recognisance 5 Aug. 1734. Settled at Abercorn. He surrendered his grant to Isaac Gibbs, and became an inmate at Savannah. Dead 1740.

316. ——, Fra., w.—Convicted of the same.

317. ——, Eliz., d.

318. Davis, Will.—Tanner; embark'd 14 Oct. 1735; arrived Feb. 1735-6; lot 46N. in Frederica; quitted 8 Oct. 1738, ret. and was at Savannah Oct. 1741.

319. Davison, Edwd.—Age 16; Tr. servt. for 5 yrs.; embark'd 19 Nov. 1737; arrived 14 Jan. 1737-8. He was hired and carry'd over at Capt. Thompson the owners risk, but the Planters not being able to pay for him, the charge fell upon the Trustees, by Mr. Causton receiving him & certifying the same wch. made us lyable.

320. Davison, Saml.—Chairman; embark'd 14 Oct. 1735; arrived Feb. 1735-6; lot 2S. in Frederica; said to be at Charlestown Oct. 1741. Made 2d. Constable at Frederica & appointed a Bailif in case others die. In 1739 appointed overseer of the Trust Servants at Frederica. I know not yet his lot.

321. ——, Susannah, w.

322. ——, Susannah, d.

323. Dean, Ja., Senr. — Carpenter; embark'd 11 Sept. 1733; arrived 16 Dec. 1733; lot 140 in Savannah; dead 1738.

324. ——, Lydia, w.

325. ——, Hen., son.

326. ——, James, junr., son—Lot 139 in Savannah. Fyn'd for defamation 0.6.8. 28 July 1735, and cast in a debt to Ri. Lobb 9 July 1737. Went to Carolina 1739.

327. ——, Lydia, d.—Embark'd 11 Sept. 1733; arrived 16 Dec. 1733.

328. Dean, Saml.—Apprent. to James Dean Senr.; embark'd 11 Sept. 1733; arrived 16 Dec. 1733.

329. Deigler, Danl.—Age 45; Farmer; Palatin Tr servt.; arrived 20 Dec. 1737.

330. ——, Maria, w.—Age 48.

331. ——, Cath., d.—Age 13.

332. ——, Maria, d.—Age 11.
333. Deikin, Benj.—Embark'd 18 June 1736.
334. ——, Eliz., w.
335. Dela-Fons, Geo.—Saw mill wright; embark'd 15 June 1733; arrived 29 Aug. 1733. Marry'd Susanna Rivett. Quitted; dead in Charlestown.
336. Delamot, Cha.—Schoolmaster; embark'd 14 Oct. 1735; arrived Feb. 1735-6; ret. to Engl. 2 June 1738.
337. Delgrass, Fran.—Shoemaker; embark'd 15 June 1733; arrived 29 Aug. 1733; lot 117 in Savannah. Fyn'd for scandal 2.2.0. 30 Aug. 1734 and convicted of selling flesh meat that had been buried 16 April 1737; he died in Charlestown Sept. 1739. Quitted; 1737 in Carolina.
338. ——, Martha, w.—Arrived 16 Dec. 1733. She came for England, but on the 14 Oct. 1735 return'd. She was the widow of Peter Fage of Highgate.
339. ——, Lewis, son—embark'd 14 Oct. 1735; arrived Feb. 1735-6.
340. ——, Solomon, son—Embark'd 14 Oct. 1735; arrived Feb. 1735-6.
341. Delieg, Lewis—Servt.; embark'd 14 Oct. 1735; arrived Feb. 1735-6.
342. Demight, Gotlieb—Carpenter; embark'd 14 Oct. 1735; arrived Feb. 1735-6. Moravian.
343. Demitifin, Regina—Embark'd 14 Oct. 1735; arrived Feb. 1735-6. Moravian.
344. Denune, Jo.—Age 26; Tr. servt.; embark'd 20 Oct. 1735; arrived 10 Jan. 1735-6.
345. Denzler [?], Conrad—Age 34; farmr. Palatin Tr. servt.; arrived 20 Dec. 1737.
346. ——, Hanah Wichine, w.—Age 35; I suppose dead before Oct. 1739.
347. ——, Anna, d.—Age 11.
348. ——, Caspar, son—Age 3; I suppose dead before Oct. 1739.
349. ——, Hans Jacob, son—Age 1; I suppose dead before Oct. 1739.
350. ——, Henry, son—Age 9.
351. ——, Regula, d.—Age 7.
352. Derrick, [?] widow—Age 26; Palatine; embark'd July 1738; arrived 7 Aug. 1738. Widow Derick & family, settled at Village Bluff on St. Simons. Gave Bond to repay the Trustees their passage.
353. ——, Eliz., d.—Age 8.
354. ——, Jacob, son—Age 5.
355. ——, Margart., d.—Age 1.
356. ——, Melchior, son—Age 7.
357. Desborough, Jo. — Carpenter; embark'd 15 June 1733; arrived 29 Aug. 1733; lot 86 in Savannah; quitted to Carolina 1739; dead Sept. 1739.
358. ——, Eliz., w.—Dead 1740.
359. ——, Dedson, son—Quitted to Carolina 1739; dead Sept. 1739.
360. ——, Edwd., son—Quitted to Carolina 1739; dead Sept. 1739.
361. ——, Jo., son—Lot No. 87 in Savannah. Quitted to Carolina; dead Sept. 1739.
362. Dice, Jacob—Age 28; weaver; Palatin Tr. servt.; arrived 20 Dec. 1737.
363. ——, Maria Margt., w.—Age 26.
364. Dober, Jo. Andr.—Potter; embark'd 14 Oct. 1735; arrived Feb. 1735-6. Moravian School Master at Highgate in Savannah Province. Quitted 1740.
365. ——, Ann Cath., w.—Do. [Moravian School Mistress at Highgate?] Quitted 1740.
366. Doble, Jo.—Servt. to Cha. Wesley; embark'd 6 Jan. 1737/8; arrived 7 May 1738; ret. to Engld. 2 Jan. 1740/1 & went back 1741.
367. Dobson, Nathl.—Woolcomber; embark'd 11 Sept. 1733; arrived 16 Dec. 1733; dead 15 Feb. 1733-4.
368. ——, Hester, w.—Dead 7 Feb. 1733-4.
369. ——, Hannah, d.—

370. ——, James, son—Dead 10 Feb. 1733-4.
371. ——, John, son—Dead.
372. ——, Saml., son—Dead 4 Mar. 1733-4.
373. ——, Tho., son—Dead 8 Feb. 1733-4.
374. Dollas, Duncan—Age 21; Tr. servt.; embark'd 24 June 1737; arrived 20 Nov. 1737. He was School Master at Highgate & ret. to Engld. with Mr. Whitfeild 2 Jan. 1740/1. He returned School Master and Register of Savannah 1741.
375. Domuth, Gothard—Watchmaker; embark'd 23 Jan. 1733-4.
376. Douglass, Geo.—Age 28; labourer; Scotch; embark'd 21 Sept. 1741; arrived 4 Dec. 1741.
377. ——, Marg. Monro, w.—Age 29.
378. ——, Isabel, d.—Age 2.
379. Dowl, Hans Adam—Age 53; Farmr.; Palatin Tr. servt.; arrived 20 Dec. 1737; dead abt. June 1738.
380. ——, Anne, w.—Age 50.
381. ——, Anna Margt., d.—Age 26.
382. ——, Feogolt, son—Age 4; I suppose dead before Oct. 1739.
383. ——, Maria Cath., d.—Age 24.
384. ——, Paulzer, son—Age 22; I suppose dead before Oct. 1739.
385. ——, Peter, son—Age 20.
386. Dudley, Saml.—Upholster; embark'd 15 June 1733; arrived 29 Aug. 1733; dead 3 Dec. 1733.
387. Du-Ferron, Joseph—Half pay Officer; embark'd 11 Sept. 1733; arrived 16 Dec. 1733. Settled at Highgate. Dead 27 Feb. 1733-4.
388. ——, Eliz., w.—Quitted 20 April 1734; in England.
389. ——, Eliz., d.—Quitted 20 April 1734; in England.
390. ——, Joseph, son—Quitted 20 April 1734; in Charlestown.
391. Duncan, Geo.—Age 38; servt. for 4 yrs.; embark'd 19 Nov. 1737; arrived 14 Jan. 1737-8. Hired & carr'd over at Capt. Thompson the owners risk: but the Planters not being able to pay for them the charge fell on the Trustees by Mr. Caustons receiving him and certifying the same which made us lyable.
392. Ecles, Ri.—Tallow chandler; embark'd 15 June 1733; arrived 29 Aug. 1733; dead 28 Dec. 1733.
393. Edgcomb, Arthr.—Wyre drawer; embark'd 11 Sept. 1733; arrived 16 Dec. 1733. He settled at Fort Arguile.
394. ——, Mary, w.—Quitted 20 Jan. 1734-5; in Engld.
395. Egerton, Thos. — Gr. son to Tho. Young; embark'd 31 Oct. 1734; arrived 28 Dec. 1734; lot 85 in Savannah; a minor.
396. Egger, Margt.—Spinster; embark'd 29 Mar. 1738/9. A Saltsburger. Settled at Ebenezar. Marry'd to ——.
397. Eincherrin, Gertr.—Embark'd 20 Oct. 1735; arrived Feb. 1735-6. A Saltsburger. Settled at Ebenezar.
398. Eisperger, Ruprech—Husbandman; embark'd 31 Oct. 1734; arrived 28 Dec. 1734. A Saltsburger. Settled at Ebenezar; living 13 March 1738/9.
399. ——, Maria, w.
400. Elliot, [?]—Went companion to Mr. Walton; embark'd 20 Feb. 1740/1; arrived May 1741; drowned June 1742.
401. Ellis, Tho.—Age 17; servt. to Noble Jones; embark'd 6 Nov. 1732; arrived 1 Feb. 1732-3; lot 55 in Savannah. He had first lot 5A, but exchanged it with Will. Mackay for this; afterwards deserted the Colony. As late as 14 June 1737 he was a servant and consequently had then no lot. Quitted Dec. 1738; ret.
402. Elphingston, Will—Apothecary; embark'd 28 Sept. 1733; arrived 14 Jan. 1733-4; dead 27 Jan. 1733-4.

403. ——, Anne, w.
404. Engely, Hans Jacob—Age 32; farmer; Swiss; embark'd 29 Sept. 1741; arrived 4 Dec. 1741. Settled on a grant S.E. of Hampstead with his family.
405. ——, Anna, w.—Age 34.
406. ——, Jacob, son—Age 7.
407. Erinxman, Barinker—Age 28; farmer; Palatin Tr. servt.; arrived 20 Dec. 1737.
408. ——, Rebecca, w.—Age 22.
409. Ernst, Joseph—Brazier; embark'd 20 Oct. 1735; arrived Feb. 1735-6; Saltsburger. Settled at Ebenezar; living 13 March 1938/9.
410. ——, Anna Maria, w.—Saltsburger. Settled at Ebenezar; living 13 March 1738/9.
411. ——, Susannah, d.—Saltsburger. Settled at Ebenezar; living 13 March 1738/9.
412. Evans, Danl.—Servt. to Isaac K. Clark; embark'd 11 Sept. 1733; arrived 16 Dec. 1733.
413. Evans, Jo.—Trust servant; embark'd Oct. 1737; arrived 16 Jany. 1737/8.
*414. Eversen, Martin — Embark'd Feb. 1734-5; lot 225 in Savannah; in Engl. June 1736 but keeps his Lott.
415. Ewen, Will—Basket maker & servt. to Tho. Causton at the stores; embark'd 31 Oct. 1734; arrived 28 Dec. 1734. Quits his settlement at Skidaway through loss by cultivation & retired to Savannah Dec. 1740, where John Bromfeild employ'd him to look after his private store. In the Colony the end of the year 1746.
416. Ewin, Jo.—Servt. to Will Stephens, Esq.; embark'd 16 Aug. 1737; arrived 31 Oct. 1737; dead 1738.
417. Eysperger, David—Age 25; Saltsburger; miller & baker; embark'd 21 Sept. 1741; arrived 2 Dec. 1741.
418. ——, Anna Maria, w.—Age 23.

419. Fage, Peter—Carpenter; embark'd 11 Sept. 1733; arrived 16 Dec. 1733. Settled at Highgate. Dead.
420. ——, Martha, w.—Quitted. See Delgrass.
421. ——, Ant., son—Dead 8 July 1734.
422. ——, Mary, d.
423. Farrel, Jo.—Servt. to Will Bradley; embark'd 20 Oct. 1735; arrived Feb. 1735-6.
424. Faulcon, Jacob—Age 51; milwright; embark'd 2 Dec. 1735; arrived 2 Feb. 1735-6. Lot 35N. in Frederica. He held two lots in Frederica & expected leave to settle on a creek in the South part of the Island to erect a corn mill. But on news of the Trustees shutting their stores quitted the Colony. He afterwards return'd, but went again to Carolina Dec. 1740. Quitted Nov. 1738.
425. ——, Jeremy, son—Age 17. He went to Carolina Dec. 1740. Quitted Nov. 1738 [sic.].
426. Felser, Geo.—Husbandman; embark'd 31 Oct. 1734; arrived 28 Dec. 1734. Saltsburger. Settled at Ebenezar.
427. Ferguson, Geo.—Age 17; Tr. servt.; embark'd 24 June 1737; arrived 20 Nov. 1737.
428. Fierer, Conrad—Age 28; carpenter; Palatin Tr. servt.; arrived 20 Dec. 1737.
429. ——, Christiana, w.—Age 26; Palatin Tr. servt.
430. ——, Hans Yerick, son—Age 2.
431. ——, Yerick Levalt, son—10 days old.
432. Finlay, John—Servt. to Will Bradley; embark'd 20 Oct. 1735; arrived Feb. 1735-6.
433. Finlay, Will. Atchinson—Writer; embark'd 11 Sept. 1733; arrived 16 Dec. 1733. Settled at Fort Arguile.
434. Fitzpatrick, Cath.—Tr. servt. Con-

---

* Same as Aversen, p. 62, no. 42.

victed of having a bastard child 26 May 1735.

435. Fitzwalter, Joseph—Age 31; gardiner; embark'd 6 Nov. 1732; arrived 1 Feb. 1732-3; Lot 8 in Savannah. He marry'd Molly an Indian girl d. of Capt. Tuscanee 8 April 1735 who ran from him. A Rambler. He went over 1. Constable of Savannah. He was Publick gardiner till 1736 Mr. Oglethorpe removed him for insufficiency 21 Oct. 1738.

436. Fleiss, Balthasar—Miner & husbman.; embark'd 14 Dec. 1733; arrived 12 Mar. 1733-4. Saltsburger. Settled at Ebenezar. Dead 28 May 1734.

437. Fletcher, Hen.—Salter; embark'd 4 April 1733; arrived 21 July 1733. He had a grant made him of 500 acres 28 March 1733. Supposed dead.

438. ——, Mary, w.
439. ——, Ellen, d.
440. ——, Hen., son.
441. ——, Mary, d.

442. Floerl, Carolus—Labourer; embark'd 20 Oct. 1735; arrived Feb. 1735-6. Saltsburger. Settled at Ebenezar. Living 13 March 1738/9.

443. Floerl, Jo.—Labourer; embark'd 20 Oct. 1735; arrived Feb. 1735-6. Saltsburger. Settled at Ebenezar. Living 13 March 1738/9.

444. ——, Anna Maria, w.—Saltsburger. Settled at Ebenezar. Living 13 March 1738/9.

445. Flower, Jo.—Grocer; embark'd 20 Oct. 1735; arrived Feb. 1735-6.

446. Foley, Waltr.—Servt. to Tho. Hawkins; embark'd 14 Oct. 1735; arrived Feb. 1735-6.

*447. Folly, [?]—Schoolmaster; embark'd 6 Jan. 1737-8; arrived 7 May 1738.

448. Forster, Will.—Servt. to Will Heddon; embark'd 14 Oct. 1735; arrived Feb. 1735-6; lot 21 N. in Frederica. Lot granted him 11 May 1737.

449. Forsyth, Cath.—Age 19; servt. for 4 years; embark'd 19 Nov. 1737; arrived 14 Jan. 1737-8. Hired & carry'd at Capt. Thompson the owners risk 19 Nov. 1737, but the Planters not being able to pay for her, Mr. Causton without order took her as ship'd on the Trustees acct. & so certifying, the Trustees were made lyable. Dead.

450. Forsyth, Margaret—Age 20; servt. for 4 years; embark'd 19 Nov. 1737; arrived 14 Jan. 1737-8. Hers was the same case.

451. Foster, Tho.—Apprentice to Jo. Ambrose; embark'd 21 Sept. 1733; arrived 12 Jan. 1733-4. Apprentice first to Jo. Ambrose; afterwards Servt. to Jos. Wardrope.

452. Foulds, Jo.—Servt. to Will. Bradley; embark'd 20 Oct. 1735; arrived Feb. 1735-6.

453. Fox, Robert—Servt. to Will Stephens, Esq.; embark'd 16 Aug. 1737; arrived 31 Oct. 1737.

454. Fox, Walter—Age 35; Turner; embark'd 6 Nov. 1732; arrived 1 Feb. 1732-3; lot 2 in Savannah. Made Tything Man 23 Nov. 1736. In all his time he only fell'd 1 acre of ground.

455. Franks, Jacob—Vintager; embark'd 14 Oct. 1735; arrived Feb. 1735-6. Moravian.

456. Frazer, Anne—Age 35; servt. for 4 years; embark'd 19 Nov. 1737; arrived 14 Jan. 1737-8. Hired & carry'd at Captn. Thompson the owners risk, but the Planters not able to pay for them, Mr. Causton without order paid the acct. and by certificate charged the Trustees therewith.

457. ——, Cath.—Age 16; servt. for 4 years; embark'd 19 Nov. 1737; ar-

---

* Same as Tolly, p. 53, no. 1516.

rived 14 Jan. 1737-8. The same case hers.

458. ——, Henrietta—Age 16; servt. for 5 years; embark'd 19 Nov. 1737; arrived 14 Jan. 1737-8. The same case hers.

459. ——, Hugh—Taylor; embark'd 15 June 1733; arrived 29 Aug. 1733; lot 97 in Savannah. Fyn'd 20 shill. for retailing strong liquors without lycense 16 Sept. 1734. Lot I suppose vact. Dead Jan. 1738-9.

460. ——, Hugh—Age 19; servt. for 5 years; embark'd 19 Nov. 1737; arrived 14 Jan. 1737-8. Hired & carry'd at Captn. Thompson the owners risk, but the Planters not able to pay for them, Mr. Causton without order paid the acct. and by certificate charged the Trustees therewith.

461. ——, Jannett—Age 18; servt. for 4 years; embarked 19 Nov. 1737; arrived 14 Jan. 1737-8. The same case hers. Alive at Darien 6 May 1741.

462. ——, John—Age 21; Tr. servt.; embark'd 24 June 1737; arrived 20 Nov. 1737. Living at Darien still a servant 6 May 1741.

463. ——, John—Age 28; Tr. servt.; embark'd 24 June 1737; arrived 20 Nov. 1737; out of his time.

464. ——, Margaret—Alive at Darien 6 May 1741.

465. Fritz, Henry—Age 50; carpenter; Palatin Tr. servt.; arrived 20 Dec. 1737; dead 18 July 1740.

466. ——, Maria Margt., w.—Age 48; I suppose dead before Oct. 1739.

467. ——, Anabel, d.—Age 6; I suppose dead before Oct. 1739.

468. ——, Johan, son—Age 4.

469. ——, Jo. Hieri, son—Age 15.

470. ——, Jo. Michl., son—Age 13; run away to Carolina Dec. 1740.

471. ——, Susana Cath., d.—Age 18; I suppose dead before Oct. 1739.

472. Furcerd, Chetwynd—Age 16; apprentice to Saml. Grey; embark'd Nov. 1732; arrived 1 Feb. 1732-3; Lot 152 in Savannah. After discharge from his service he took this lot, but went to serve in the Scout boat 1736. Abst. Feb. 1736-7.

473. Fuzler, Sabina—Servt. to Hen. Fletcher; embark'd 4 April 1733; arrived 21 July 1733.

474. Gaddis, Ja.—Age 21; servt. for 4 yrs.; embark'd 19 Nov. 1737; arrived 14 Jan. 1737-8. Hired & carry'd at Capt. Thompson the owners risk but the Planters not being able to pay for him, Mr. Causton without orders took him, and so certified, which made the Trustees lyable to the charge.

475. ——, John—Age 20; servt. for 4 yrs.; embark'd 19 Nov. 1737; arrived 14 Jan. 1737-8. His was the same case.

476. Gallier, Cha.—Weaver; embark'd 28 Sept. 1733; arrived 14 Jan. 1733-4. Settled at Highgate. Quitted & ret. to England.

477. ——, Cath., w.—Dead 23 Mar. 1733-4.

478. ——, Mary, d.

479. Gapan, Tho.—Farmer; embark'd 15 June 1733; arrived 29 Aug. 1733; Lot 116 in Savannah. Fyn'd thirteen pence half peny for assault 16 Mar. 1733-4. Also fyn'd for letting a prisoner out of custody 23 May 1735. He practiced the butchers trade but finally ran away for debt. Run away 6 Feb. 1736-7.

480. Garden, Pet. de—Cooper; embark'd 11 Sept. 1733; arrived 16 Dec. 1733; Lot 129 in Savannah. Fyn'd 13 shilling currency for assault 24 April 1734. Lot vacant Feb. 1738-9. Dead 15 May 1735.

481. ——, Mary Anne, w.—Dead 7 June 1735.

482. ——, James, son—Dead.
483. Gardiner, Head—Weaver; embark'd 28 Sept. 1733; arrived 14 Jan. 1733-4. Settled at Skideway, but left it in 1737, & let himself out for hire in Savannah. Slayn in felling a tree. Killed accidently 18 Dec. 1739.
484. ——, Mary, w.
485. ——, Mary Anne, d.
486. Gebhard, Hans Henry—Age 45; cooper & millwright; Swiss; embark'd 29 Sept. 1741, arrived 4 Dec. 1741.
487. ——, Cath., w.—Age 30.
488. ——, Anna, d.—Age 6; dead soon after landing.
489. ——, Anna Maria, d.—Age 6 months; dead in the passage.
490. ——, Magdalene, d.—Age 10.
491. ——, Saml., son—Age 22.
492. ——, Susanna, d.—Age 20.
493. Gephart, Eliz.—Age 14; Palatine; servt.; embark'd July 1738; arrived 7 Oct. 1738.
494. ——, Eva—Age 10; Palatine; servt.; embark'd July 1738; arrived 7 Oct. 1738.
495. ——, Magdalene—Age 19; Palatine; servt.; embark'd July 1738; arrived 7 Oct. 1738. Magdalene Gephart & her family. Given to the Saltsburgers, to whom also the Trustees gave the repaymt. of their passage.
496. Gephart, Philip—Age 45; Farmer; Palatine; servt.; embark'd July 1738; arrived 7 Oct. 1738. Philip Gephart & his family. Given to the Saltsburgers to whom also the Trustees gave the repaymt. of their passage.
497. ——, Martha, w.—Age 43.
498. ——, Hans George, son—Age 2.
499. ——, Maria Catha., d.—Age 17.
500. ——, Philip, son—Age 6.
501. Germain, Anne—W. of Pet. Germain; embark'd 11 Sept. 1733; arrived 16 Dec. 1733. Re-marry'd to Peter Emery 12 Jan. 1734-5. In 1739 she came to England and obtained promise of a lycence to keep an ale house at Tybee. Her husband is Pylot there. She return'd with her daughter & a maid servt. to Georgia with Capt. Thompson July 1738 & arrived there the 7 Oct. following.
502. ——, Mary Margt., d.—Carry'd to Georgia by her mother; embarked July 1738; arrived 7 Oct. 1738.
503. ——, Michl., son—Lot 78 in Savannah.
504. Gibbons, Loyd—Apothecary; embark'd 17 Dec. 1733; arrived 12 Mar. 1733-4; Lot 109 in Savannah; dead 27 Sept. 1734.
505. ——, Fra., w.—Re-marry'd to Hen. Molton 7 Sept. 1736.
506. ——, Christr., son—Dead 30 May 1735.
507. ——, Mary, d.
508. Gilbert, Eliz.—Servt. to Will Stephens, Esq.; embark'd 16 Aug. 1737; arrived 31 Oct. 1737.
509. Giovannoli, Jo.—Tr. servt. for 5 years; embark'd 1 Aug. 1735; in the Colony the end of the year 1746.
510. ——, Maria, w.—Tr. servt. for 5 years; in the Colony the end of the year 1746.
511. ——, John, son—In the Colony the end of the year 1746.
512. ——, Seger, son—In the Colony the end of the year 1746.
513. Glantz, Sebastian — Husbandman; embark'd 31 Oct. 1734; arrived 28 Dec. 1734. Saltsburger. Settled at Ebenezar.
514. Goddard, Ja.—Age 38; carpenter; embark'd 6 Nov. 1732; arrived 1 Feb. 1732-3; Lot 1 in Savannah; dead 1 July 1733.
515. ——, Eliz., w.—Age 42; dead 28 July 1733.
516. ——, Eliz., d.—Age 5; servt. to Tho. Christie.

517. ——, John, son—Age 9; servt. to Tho. Christie.
518. Goldwyre, Benj.—Servt. to Jos. Wardrope; embark'd 14 Oct. 1735; arrived Feb. 1735-6; run away to Carolina Aug. 1742.
519. ——, Jo.—Brother of Benj.; age 19; son in law to Robt. Potter; embark'd 15 June 1733; arrived 29 Aug. 1733; lot 153 in Savannah; run away to Carolina Aug. 1742.
520. Gordon, Donald—Age 16; Tr. servt.; embark'd 24 June 1737; arrived 20 Nov. 1737.
521. ——, James—Age 23; Tr. servt.; embark'd 20 Oct. 1735; arrived 10 Jan. 1735-6.
522. Gordon, Pet.—Age 35; upholster; embark'd 6 Nov. 1732; arrived 1 Feb. 1732-3; lot 23 in Savannah. 1 Bailif of Savannah, but removed 1738. He thereupon return'd & remain'd with his wife in England, & by leave parted with his lot to the daughters of Major Will. Cook, 12 April 1738. Dead 1740. Quitted 12 April 1738.
523. ——, Catherine, w.—Age 28; quitted, both ret. to England.
524. Goy, Jacob—Weaver; embark'd 11 Sept. 1733; arrived 16 Dec. 1733. Settled at Highgate. Dead 29 Mar. 1734.
525. Graham, Cath.—Age 24; servt. for 5 years; embark'd 19 Nov. 1737; arrived 14 Jan. 1737-8. Hired & carry'd at Capt. Thompson the owners risk but the Planters not being able to pay for her Mr. Causton without orders took her, and so certified, which made the Trustees lyable to the charge.
526. Graham, Jo.—Tanner & farmer; embark'd 15 June 1733; arrived 29 Aug. 1733; lot 98 in Savannah. He quitted after the 9 Dec. 1738 & went to Carolina, a riotous fellow & fyned for keeping on his hat in Court 16 Sept. 1734. Quitted Dec. 1739.
527. ——, Mary, w.
528. ——, John, son—Dead 22 Nov. 1733.
529. ——, Mary, d.
530. ——, Will., son—Dead 28 Nov. 1733.
531. Grananch, Caspar—Age 36; brewer; Saltsburger; embark'd 21 Sept. 1741; arrived 2 Dec. 1741.
532. ——, Anne Cath., w.—Age 23.
533. Grant, Christian—Age 16; servt. for 5 years; embark'd 19 Nov. 1737; arrived 14 Jan. 1737-8. Hired & carry'd at Capt. Thompson the owners risk but the Planters not being able to pay for him, Mr. Causton without orders took him, and so certified, which made the Trustees lyable to the charge.
534. ——, Gilbert—Age 9; servt. 10 yrs. & ½; embark'd 19 Nov. 1737; arrived 14 Jan. 1737-8. His was the same case. Return'd by Col. Oglethorpe to be a soldier in the Highland Independt. Compy. 6 May 1741.
535. ——, Jo.—Age 19; Tr. servt.; embark'd 24 June 1737; arrived 20 Nov. 1737.
536. ——, Jo.—Age 15; servt. 9 yrs.; embark'd 19 Nov. 1737; arrived 14 Jan. 1737-8. Hired & carry'd at Capt. Thompson the owners risk but the Planters not being able to pay for him Mr. Causton without orders took him, and so certified, which made the Trustees lyable to the charge. Return'd by Col. Oglethorpe to be a soldier in the Highland Independt. Compy. 6 May 1741.
537. ——, Jo.—Age 22; labourer; Scotch; embark'd 21 Sept. 1741; arrived 4 Dec. 1741.
538. ——, Peter—Age 18; servt. 5 years; embark'd 19 Nov. 1737; arrived 14 Jan. 1737-8. Hired & carry'd at Capt. Thompson the owners risk but the

Planters not being able to pay for him Mr. Causton without orders took him, and so certified, which made the Trustees lyable to the charge.

539. ——, Will.—Age 14; servt. 10 yrs.; embark'd 19 Nov. 1737; arrived 14 Jan. 1737-8. His was the same case.

540. Gray, Margt.—Age 24; single woman; Scotch; embark'd 21 Sept. 1741; arrived 4 Dec. 1741.

541. Gready, Jo.—Age 22; farmer; embark'd 6 Nov. 1732; arrived 1 Feb. 1732-3; lot 3 in Savannah. Frequently in Carolina. Try'd & cast for breach of Covent. with Geo. Smith 9 July 1737.

542. Greenfeild, Cha.—Age 16; nephew of Will. Calvert; embark'd 6 Nov. 1732; arrived 1 Feb. 1732-3.

543. ——, Sarah—Age 16; niece of Will. Calvert and sister of Cha.; embark'd 6 Nov. 1732; arrived 1 Feb. 1732-3. Marry'd to Will. Elbert 22 June 1734 and lives mostly in Carolina. Quitted.

544. ——, Will.—Age 19; nephew of Will Calvert and brother of Cha.; embark'd 6 Nov. 1732; arrived 1 Feb. 1732-3. Settled at Fort Arguile. Out of his time.

545. Grey, Jo.—Age 50; servt. 3 yrs.; embark'd 19 Nov. 1737; arrived 14 Jan. 1937-8. Hired & carry'd at Capt. Thompson the owners risk but the Planters not being able to pay for him Mr. Causton without orders took him, and so certified, which made the Trustees lyable to the charge.

546. ——, Saml.—Age 30; silk throwster; embark'd Nov. 1732; arrived Feb. 1732-3. Expell'd the Province 17 June 1733. Expell'd 17 June 1733.

547. Grickson, Will.—Apprentice to Hugh Frazer; embark'd 15 June 1733; arrived 29 Aug. 1733; Lot 107 in Savannah. Sentenc'd 50 lashes for deserting and again attempting to run away 29 April 1734. After his discharge from service he marry'd Janet Colstong May 1734, took this lot, and was made hangman.

548. Griffin, Jo.—Weaver; embark'd 28 Sept. 1733; arrived 14 Jan. 1733-4. Settled at Skidaway.

549. ——, Sarah, w.—Dead in the passage.

550. ——, Sarah, d.—Servt. to Saml. Parker.

551. Griffith, Danl.—Cord wainer; embarke'd 20 Oct. 1735; arrived Feb. 1735-6; lot 10S. in Frederica; quitted 1736-7.

552. Grill, Waldeburga—Age 18; single woman; Saltsburger; embark'd 21 Sept. 1741; arrived 2 Dec. 1741.

553. Griminger, Andrew—Labourer; embark'd 20 Oct. 1735; arrived Feb. 1735-6. Saltsburger settled at Ebenezar, living 13 March 1738/9.

554. ——, Sabina, w.—Saltsburger settled at Ebenezar, living 13 March 1738/9.

555. ——, Cath., d.—Saltsburger settled at Ebenezar, living 13 March 1738/9.

556. Gronau, Israel—Cathecist & minister; embark'd 14 Dec. 1733; arrived 12 Mar. 1733-4. Saltsburger. Settled at Ebenezar. He marry'd Cath. Rhomorisine 1 Oct. 1734.

557. Grueber, Hans—Husbandman; embark'd 14 Dec. 1733; arrived 12 Mar. 1733-4; dead 3 Nov. 1734. Saltsburger. Settled at Ebenezar.

558. ——, Peter—Husbandman; embark'd 14 Dec. 1733; arrived 12 Mar 1733-4. Saltzburger. Settled at Ebenezar; living 13 March 1738/9.

559. Gruning, Abrm.—Labourer; embark'd 20 Oct. 1735; arrived Feb. 1735-6. Saltsburger. Settled at Ebenezar. Living 13 March 1738/9.

560. Gun. Geo.—Age 18; servt. 6 yrs.; embark'd 19 Nov. 1737; arrived 14

Jan. 1737-8. Hired & carry'd at Capt. Thompson the owners risk but the Planters not being able to pay for him, Mr. Causton without orders took him, and so certified, which made the Trustees lyable to the charge.

561. Guring, Simon—Age 32; farmer; Palatine servt.; embark'd July 1738; arrived 7 Oct. 1738. Simon Guring & wife: Delivered to Jo. Fallowfeild 2nd to be accounted as pt. paymt. of his present sallary.
562. ——, Maria, w.—Age 30.
563. Haberechten, Godfrit — Weaver & dyer; embark'd 23 Jan. 1734-5. Moravian.
564. ——, Rosine, w.—Embark'd 14 Oct. 1735, arrived Feb. 1735-6. Moravian.
565. Haberer, Michl.—Age 27; tanner & bricklayer; Saltsburger; embark'd 21 Sept. 1741; arrived 2 Dec. 1741.
566. ——, Ana Barbara, w.—Age 40.
567. Haberland, Geo.—Mason; embark'd 23 Jan. 1734-5. Moravian.
568. ——, Michl.—Carpenter; embark'd 23 Jan. 1734-5. Moravian.
569. Habersham, [?] — Habersham [?] bro. of James Habersham, died at Frederica. Dead Jan. 1738-9.
570. ——, Ja.—Schoolmaster at Savannah; embark'd 3 Jan. 1737/8; arrived 7 May 1738. A Methodist, and taken great care of the children. Quitted Jan. 1740-1 but ret.
571. Hadley, Will.—Embark'd Aug. 1734; arrived 21 Oct. 1734. Bound to good behaviour for defamation & ordered to recant 22 Nov. 1735.
572. Hag, Hans Ulric—Age 33; carpenter; Swiss; embark'd 29 Sept. 1741; arrived 4 Dec. 1741.
573. ——, Maria, w.—Age 33.
574. ——, Catharina, d.—Age 9.
575. ——, Hans Jacob, son—Age 5.
576. Hag, Maria Anna—Age 46; w. of Jo. Ulric Hag; Swiss; embark'd 29 Sept. 1741; arrived 4 Dec. 1741.
577. ——, Barbara, d.—Age 18.
578. ——, Ferena, d.—Age 6.
579. ——, Hans Jacob, son—Age 13.
580. ——, Hans Michl., son—Age 9.
581. ——, Hans Ulric, son—Age 11.
582. ——, Joannes, son—Age 20.
583. ——, Maria, d.—Age 16.
584. Haines, Edwd.—Servt. to Will. Stephens, Esq.; arrived 16 Jan. 1737-8. A sad rogue 15 Feb. 1738-9. **Bound to the Trust but made over to Mr.** Stephens to fill up the number of servants promised him.
585. Hainks, Robt.—Mercer; embark'd 15 June 1733; arrived 29 Aug. 1733; lot 84 in Savannah; quitted Jan. 1738-9; returned.
586. ——, Anne, w.—Embark'd 11 Sept. 1733; arrived 16 Dec. 1733; dead 26 Oct. 1738.
587. ——, Anne, d.
588, ——, Frances, d.
589. ——, Josua, son.
590. ——, Robt., s.—Dead in the passage.
591. ——, Susanna, d.
592. Haismere, Martin—Age 44: miller, Palatin Tr. Servt.; embark'd Oct. 1737; arrived 20 Dec. 1737.
593. ——, Cath., w.—Age 35.
594. ——, Clement, son—Age 4.
595. Halter, Hans Kunroth—Age 38; locksmith; Swiss; embark'd 29 Sept. 1741; arrived 4 Dec. 1741; dead soon after landing.
596. ——, Eliz., w.—Age 42.
597. ——, Barbara, d.—Age 6.
598. ——, Catherina, d.—Age 3.
599. ——, David, son—Age 8.
600. ——, Martha, d.—Age 11; dead soon after landing.
601. ——, Ulrick, son—Age 10.
602. Halter, Hans Kunroth—Age 44;

bricklayer; Swiss; embark'd 29 Sept. 1741; arrived 4 Dec. 1741.
603. ——, Barbara, w.—Age 31.
604. ——, Anna, d.—Age 2.
605. ——, Barbara, d.—Age 4.
606. Haner, Nics.—Age 36; shoemaker; Swiss; embark'd 29 Sept. 1741; arrived 4 Dec. 1741. Nics. Haner & family settled on a grant S. E. of Hampstead.
607. ——, Eliz., w.—Age 38.
608. ——, Eliz., d.—Age 7.
609. ——, Ferena, d.—Age 1; dead soon after landing.
610. ——, Jo, son—Age 11; in the Colony the end of the year 1746.
611. ——, Joseph, son—Age 4; dead soon after landing.
612. ——, Margt., d.—Age 9.
613. ——, Nics., son—Age 15.
614. Hanouren, M. Louis—Age 16; spinster; Palatin; Tr. Servt.; arrived 20 Dec. 1737; free Oct. 1740 or perhaps in June.
615. Harbach, Caspar—Palatin Tr. servt.; arrived 20 Dec. 1737.
616. Hardman, Tho.—Servt. to Will Bradley; embark'd 20 Oct. 1735; arrived Feb. 1735-6.
617. Harling, Cath.—Servt. to Tho. Hawkins; embark'd 14 Oct. 1735; arrived Feb. 1735-6.
618. Harrison, Anne;—Servt. to Will Moore; embark'd 14 Oct. 1735; arrived Feb. 1735-6.
619. Hart, Ri.—Servt. to Will Abbot; embark'd 20 Oct. 1735; arrived Feb. 1735-6; lot 40N. in Frederica.
620. Hasler, Christian—Husband man; embark'd 31 Oct. 1734; arrived 28 Dec. 1734. Saltsburger; settled at Ebenezar, living 13 March 1738/9.
621. Hassel, Will.—Son of Martha Tucker; embark'd 14 Oct. 1735; arrived Feb. 1735-6; lot 37N. in Frederica.

A new Freeholder 29 Sept. 1738. Quitted before Aug. 1741.
622. ——, Eliz., d.—Quitted before Aug. 1741.
623. Havener, Paul—Age 30; farmer; Palatin; Tr. servt.; arrived 20 Dec. 1737.
624. ——, Piatta Clara, w.—Age 26.
625. ——, Jo. Yerick, son—Age 2.
626. ——, Maria Dorothy, d.—Age 9. I suppose dead before Oct. 1739.
627. Haverfahner, Fra.—Labourer; embark'd 20 Oct. 1735; arrived Feb. 1735-6. Saltsburger settled at Ebenezar.
628. ——, Maria, w.—Saltsburger settled at Ebenezar.
629. ——, Magdalene, d.—Saltsburger settled at Ebenezar.
630. ——, Susanna, d.—Saltsburger settled at Ebenezar.
631. Hawkins, Tho.—Surgeon; embark'd 14 Oct. 1735; arrived Feb. 1735-6; lot 2S. in Frederica. 1st Bailif at Frederica.
632. ——, Beata, w.
633. Heale, Tho.
634. Heddon, Will.—Farmer; embark'd 14 Oct. 1735; arrived Feb. 1735-6.
635. Heldt, Conrad—Age 52; weaver; German Tr. servt.; embark'd July 1738; arrived 7 Oct. 1738. Heldt: this family employ'd in the Publick Garden under Jos. Fitzwalter Jany. 1738-9. Palatines.
636. ——, Eliz., w.—German Tr. Servt. Age 53.
637. ——, Eliz., d.—German; Tr. Servt. Age 17.
638. ——, Hans Michael, son—Age 23; German; Tr. Servt.
639. Helfenstein, Jo. Jacob—Tanner; embark'd 20 Oct. 1735; arrived Feb. 1735-6. Saltsburger. Settled at Ebenezar living 13 March 1738/9.
640. ——, Anne Dorothy, w.—Saltsburger.

Settled at Ebenezar living 13 March 1738/9.
641. ——, Frederick, son—Saltsburger. Settled at Ebenezar living 13 March 1738/9.
642. ——, Jeremias, son — Saltsburger. Settled at Ebenezar living 13 March 1738/9.
643. ——, Joannes, son—Saltsburger. Settled at Ebenezar living 13 March 1738/9.
644. ——, Jo. Jacob, son—Saltsburger. Settled at Ebenezar living 13 March 1738/9.
645. ——, Maria Christina, d.—Saltsburger. Settled at Ebenezar living 13 March 1738/9.
646. ——, Maria Fred., d.—Saltsburger. Settled at Ebenezar living 13 March 1738/9.
647. Henrich, Cath.—Age 20; Palatine; embark'd July 1738; arrived 7 Oct. 1738. Given to the Saltsburgers, as also the repayment of their passage.
648. ——, Margareta—Age 15; Palatine; embark'd July 1738; arrived 7 Oct. 1738. Given to the Saltsburgers, as also the repayment of their passage.
649. Henrich, Peter—Age 48; Palatine; embark'd July 1738; arrived 7 Oct. 1738. Peter Henrich & his family: Given to the Saltsburgers; and also the repayment of their passage.
650. ——, Juliana, w.—Age 54; dead 1738.
651. ——, Eve Barbara, d.—Age 22.
652. Herba, Jacob—Age 30; farmer; Palatin Tr. servt.; arrived 20 Dec. 1737.
653. ——, Maria Eva, w.—Age 25; Palatin Tr. servt; arriv'd 20 Dec. 1737.
654. Herbert, Hen.—Minister at Savannah; embark'd Nov. 1732; arrived 1 Feb. 1732-3. This clergyman was bastard son to the E. of Torrington. He was obliged to leave the Colony on acct. of sickness, and died at sea in his return 15 June 1733. Dead 15 June 1733.
655. Herbzog, Martin—Miller; embark'd 14 Dec. 1733; arrived 12 Mar. 1733-4, Saltsburger. Settled at Ebenezar living 13 March 1738/9.
656. Herrenberger, Hans—Taylor; embark'd 20 Oct. 1735; arrived Feb. 1735-6. Saltsburger settled at Ebenezar; living 13 March 1738/9.
657. Hersterin, Christina—Age 20; single woman; Saltsburger; embark'd 21 Sept. 1741; arrived 2 Dec. 1741.
658. Hert, Michl.—Age 45; farmer; Palatin Tr. servt.; arrived 20 Dec. 1737; dead about May 1738.
659. ——, Susanna, w.—Arriv'd 20 Dec. 1737.
660. Hewet, Ja.—Servt. to Hen. Fletcher; embark'd 4 April 1733; arrived 21 July 1733.
661. Hewet, James, senr.—Peruke maker; embark'd 15 June 1733; arrived 29 Aug. 1733; dead 28 Sept. 1734. Settled at Tybee 2 April 1734.
662. ——, James, s.—Settled at Tybee 2 April 1734.
663. Hicks, Mary—Servt. to Ri. Canon; embark'd 6 Nov. 1732; arrived 1 Feb. 1732-3. Discharged by consent and marry'd Fra. Wicks 17 April 1733.
664. Hird, Tho.—Dyer; embark'd 14 Oct. 1735; arrived Feb. 1735-6; Lot 12N. in Frederica. Constable at Frederica on 1 Feb. 1738-9. Col. Oglethorp sent him on the Trustees Acct. 68.0.9 to set up a Brewhouse.
665. ——, Grace, w.
666. ——, Frances, d.
667. ——, John, son.
668. ——, Mark, son—Lot 11N. in Frederica.
669. ——, Phoebe, d.
670. Hodges, Ri.—Age 50; basket maker; embark'd 6 Nov. 1732; arrived 1 Feb.

1732-3; Lot 17 in Savannah. He was 2d Bailif of Savannah, and succeeded by Tho. Causton 16 Oct. 1734. Dead 20 July 1733 [sic.].

671. ——, Mary, w.—Age 42. In possession of the lot design'd her husband. She marry'd Edwd. Townsend 22 Feb. 1734-5. She was fyned 20 shil. for retailing liquours without lycence 2 Oct. 1734. A vile foul mouthed Male-content, & fled the Colony 21 July 1740 with her young daughter. Run away 29 July 1740 to Carolina & there died.

672. ——, Eliz., d.—Age 16. She marry'd Ri. Lobb 8 May 1734. Dead 4 Aug. 1735.

673. ——, Mary, d.—Age 18.

674. ——, Sarah, d.—Age 5; run away 29 July 1740.

675. Hodgkinson, Saml.—Flax dresser; embark'd 14 Oct. 1735; arrived Feb. 1735-6.

676. Hofferin, Anne—Spinster; embark'd 14 Dec. 1733; arrived 12 Mar. 1733-4. Saltsburger. Settled at Ebenezar.

677. Hoffman, Adail Hait—Tr. servt. for 10 years; embark'd 14 May 1735. A German.

678. Holemark, Tho.—Servt. to Hen. Fletcher; embark'd 4 April 1733; arrived 21 July 1733.

679. Holland, Jo. George—Age 22; taylor; Palatin Tr. servt.; embark'd July 1738; arrived 7 Oct. 1738. Holland: Delivered Mr. Christie Recorder of Savanah, in discharge of one of the 2. assign'd him 11 Aug. 1738.

680. Holt, Ezekiel—Age 30; Smith Swiss; embark'd 29 Sept. 1741; arrived 4 Dec. 1741.

681. ——, Magdalene, w.—Age 28.

682. ——, Jacob, son—A month old.

683. Holterin, Susanna—Widow; embark'd 20 Oct. 1735; arrived Feb. 1735-6. Saltsburger settled at Ebenezar.

684. ——, Cath., d.

685. Hopkey, Sophia—Niece to Martha Causton; embark'd 25 May 1733; arrived 23 Sept. 1733.

686. Hosker, Thurston—Servt. to Jo. Brownfeild; embark'd 14 Oct. 1735; arrived Feb. 1735-6.

687. Hover, Plessi—Tr. Servt.

688. Hows, Geo.—Br. of Robert a boy; embark'd 31 Oct. 1734; arrived 28 Dec. 1734.

689. Hows, Henry—Sawyer; embark'd 24 Jan. 1732-3; arrived 16 May 1733; Lot 67 in Savannah. Took possession of his Lot 21 Dec. 1733. Dead 16 Sept. 1733 [sic.].

690. ——, Anne, d.

691. Hows, Robt.—Sawyer; embark'd 24 Jan. 1732-3; arrived 16 May 1733; Lot 66 in Savannah. He went to England, & surrender'd his grant, to be apply'd to the use of an orphan house; but return'd to Georgia with Mr. Whitfeild. Quitted by leave Feb. 1738-9 but returned.

692. ——, Anne, w.—Dead 3 Oct. 1733.

693. ——, Anne.

694. ——, Mary, d.—Age 8; dead 1738.

695. Huber, Andr. Blaize—Age 28; carpenter; Germ. Tr. servt.; embark'd July 1738; arrived 7 Oct. 1738. Huber: employ'd in the Publick garden under Jos. Fitzwalter Jan. 1738-9. Palatine.

696. Hueber, Lorent—Husbandman; embark'd 14 Dec. 1733; arrived 12 Mar. 1733-4; Saltsburger settled at Ebenezar. Dead 2 June 1734.

697. ——, Maria, w.—Saltsburger settled at Ebenezar. Dead 5 July 1734.

698. ——, John, son—Saltsburger settled at Ebenezar. Dead 11 Jan. 1734-5.

699. ——, Magdalene, d.—Saltsburger settled at Ebenezar. Dead 21 Sept. 1734.

700. ——, Margt., d.—Saltsburger settled at Ebenezar. Dead 13 Feb. 1734-5.
701. ——, Mary, d.—Saltsburger settled at Ebenezar. Dead 5 April 1735.
702. Hughes, Jo. Servt. to Fra. Moore; embark'd 14 Oct. 1735; arrived Feb. 1735-6. Lot in Savannah No. 155 was granted him, but he refused afterwards to accept it. A tallow chandler by trade.
703. Hughes, Joseph—Age 28; cyder mercht.; embark'd 6 Nov. 1732; arrived 1 Feb. 1732-3; Lot 16 in Savannah. Storekeeper to the Trust while he lived. Dead 30 Sept. 1733.
704. ——, Eliz., w.—Age 22. Re-marry'd to Jo. West, and at both their desires this lot was granted to Danl. Prevost 31 May 1738. She marry'd John West 20 April 1734 who dying 1739 she lived with Will. Killeway as wife with the character of a lewd woman. Dead 5 June 1740.
705. Hughes, Richd.—Saw maker & blacksmith; embark'd 11 Sept. 1733; arrived 16 Dec. 1733. Settled at Abercorn, but deserted with his family Feb. 1737-8. Dead 1738.
706. ——, Eliz., w.
707. ——, Edmond, son.
708. ——, Humphrey, son.
709. ——, James, son.
710. ——, Job, son.
711. ——, Joseph, son.
712. Hughs, John—Age 22; Nephew to Will. Bradley; embark'd 2 Dec. 1735; arrived 2 Feb. 1735-6.
713. Humble, John—Labourer; embark'd 20 Oct. 1735; arrived Feb. 1735-6; Lot 7S. in Frederica. He turn'd himself to the sea, and is Pylot at Frederica.
714. ——, Joanna, w.—Age 60; embark'd 20 Oct. 1735; arriv'd Feb., 1735-6. Dead, 1735-6.
715. Hurst, Saml.—Clerk of the stores to Mr. Causton; embark'd 17 May 1737; arrived 20 Nov. 1737.
716. Husbands, Jos.—Servt. to Mr. Whitfeild; embark'd 6 Jan. 1737-8; arrived 7 May 1738.
717. Hyland, Dominick—Age 15; servt. 5 years; embark'd 19 Nov. 1737; arrived 14 Jan. 1737-8. Hired & carried at Capt. Thompson the owners risk but the Planters not being able to pay for him, Mr. Causton without order took him & certified the same which made the Trustees lyable.
718. Ichinger [or Jchinger] Jacob—Age 48; farmer; Palatines; embark'd July 1738; arrived 7 Oct. 1738. Ichinger [or Jchinger] & family: Settled upon Village Bluff in St. Simons. Gave bond for repayment of their passage.
719. ——, Cath., w.—Age 52.
720. ——, Annah, d.—Age 9.
721. ——, Hans Michl., son—Age 14.
722. ——, Jacob, son—Age 5.
723. ——, Sophia, d.—Age 18.
724. Ingham, Ben.—A.M. Missioner to the Indians; embark'd 14 Oct. 1735; arrived Feb. 1735-6. He return'd to England to bring over more missioners, but never went back. A Methodist. Quitted 26 Feb. 1736/7.
725. Jackson, Abel—Servt. to Will. Bradley; embark'd 20 Oct. 1735; arrived Feb. 1735-6.
726. Jagg, David—Husbandman; embark'd 14 Oct. 1735; arrived Feb. 1735-6. Moravian.
727. Jaskin, Juliana—Spinster; embark'd 14 Oct. 1735; arrived Feb. 1735-6. Moravian.
728. Johnson, Alexander—Taylor; embark'd 15 June 1733; arrived 29 Aug. 1733. Settled at Tybee; comitted prisoner at Fort Arguile for desertion.
729. ——, Edward—Carpenter & sawyer; embark'd 24 Jan. 1732-3; arrived 16

May 1733; Lot 46 in Savannah; dead.

730. ——, Robt.—Age 17; servt. to Tho. Christie; 6 Nov. 1732; arrived 1 Feb. 1732-3; Lot 13 in Savannah. He marry'd Anne d. of Geo. Syms. His lot was granted him 21 Dec. 1733, and is supposed vacant. Dead 23 July 1734.

731. Jolliffe, Mary—Age 22; single woman; Scotch; embark'd 21 Sept. 1741; arrived 4 Dec. 1741.

732. Jones, Cornelius—Apprentice to Saml. Grey; embark'd Nov. 1732; arrived 1 Feb. 1732-3. Discharged by his master.

733. ——, John—Servt. to Josephy Smith; embark'd 29 Oct. 1734; arrived 28 Dec. 1734. He past from the service of Jos. Smith to that of Ja. Calloway.

734. ——, Mary—Age 17; Servt. for 4 yrs. to Wid. Vandeplank; embarked 19 Nov. 1737; arrived 14 Jan. 1737-8. Hired & carry'd at Capt. Thompson the owners risk, but the Planters not being able to pay such servants, Mr. Causton without order took them and certifyed the same which made the Trustees lyable to pay.

735. Jones, Noble—Age 32; carpenter; embark'd 6 Nov. 1732; arrived 1 Feb. 1732-3; lot 41 in Savannah. Employ'd to survey the peoples lots, but removed for negligence. He took posession of this lot 21 Dec. 1733 and afterwards improved land at some distance from the town. He was I think a constable also, and officer for executing the Rum Act. He now resides mostly at his new plantation abt. 10 miles from Savannah. On 21 Oct. 1738 Mr. Oglethorp removed him from being surveyor and first Constable, but afterwards gave him the comand of the Narrows. In the Colony the end of the year 1746.

736. ——, Sarah, w.—Age 32; in the Colony the end of the year 1746.

737. ——, Mary, d.—Age 3; in the Colony the end of the year 1746.

738. ——, Noble, son—Age 10; lot 46 in Savannah; in the Colony the end of the year 1746.

739. Jones, Thomas — Embark'd May 1738. Formerly High Constable of St. Gyles. Appointed storekeeper in Mr. Caustons place, & gave 1000£ Security.

740. Joubert, Pet.—Broker; embark'd 6 Aug. 1735; arrived 27 Nov. 1735; lot 231 in Savannah. An idle fellow, & on shutting up the Publick stores deserted the Colony none knows where. On 16 Jan. 1735-6 he had leave to dispose of his Townlot, and take a country one of 150 acres, but I can't find when a grant was made him. In July 1738 he was an inmate in Savannah on lot 232. Quitted Jan. 1738-9; returned.

741. ——, Mary, w.

742. Joyce, Paul—Dyer; embark'd 28 Sept. 1733; arrived 14 Jan. 1733-4. Settled at Skidaway. Dead 12 Feb. 1733-4.

743. Juker [or Iuker] Hans Adam—Age 45; farmer; Swiss; embark'd 21 Sept. 1741; arrived 4 Dec. 1741; dead soon after landing.

744. ——, Barbara, w.

745. Kalcher, Ruprecht — Husbandman; embark'd 31 Oct. 1734; arrived 28 Dec. 1734; Saltsburger, settled at Ebenezar; living 13 March 1738-9.

746. ——, Margt., w. Saltsburger, settled at Ebenezar; living 13 March 1738-9.

747. Kaudnoor, Lawrence—Age 58; weaver; Palatin Tr. servt.; arrived 20 Dec. 1737.

748. ——, Barbara, w.—Age 57.

749. ——, Maria Barbara, d.—Age 26.

750. ——, Nicolas, son—Age 21.

751. ——, Woohee, son—Age 13.
752. Keiffer, Theobald—Age 45; butcher; Palatin Tr. servt.; arrived 20 Dec. 1737.
753. ——, Maria Cath., w.—Age 45.
754. ——, Cath., d.—Age 5.
755. ——, Hier Frederick, son—Age 7.
756. ——, Hier Henry, d.—Age 3.
757. ——, Hierick Tavit, son—Age 18.
758. ——, Margt., d.—Age 20. I suppose dead before Oct. 1739.
759. ——, Mariabel, d.—Age 13.
760. Keller, Jo. Hierick—Age 45; schoolmaster; Palatin Tr. servt.; arrived 20 Dec. 1737; dead 1739.
761. ——, Anna Eliz, w.—Age 38.
762. ——, Anna Eliz., d.—Age 12.
763. ——, Heir Jacob, son—Age 2.
764. ——, Maria Barbara, d.—Age 14.
765. ——, Mariacker, d.—Age 16.
766. ——, Maria Cath., d.—Age 7; I suppose dead before Oct. 1739.
767. ——, Maria Dorothea, d.—Age 4; I suppose dead before Oct. 1739.
768. ——, Maria Sophia, d.—Age 9.
769. Kelly, John—Stocking weaver; embark'd 15 June 1733; arrived 29 Aug. 1733; lot 88 in Savannah. He deserted the Colony & shutting up the Publick Stores. His lot was swamp overflow'd, and succeeded thereto by the death of Jo. Lawrence without heirs male. He lived some time an inmate on lot 123 before he went off. Quitted Jan. 1738-9; returned.
770. Kemp, John—Age 30; servt. to Hen. Parker 4 years; embark'd 19 Nov. 1737; arrived 14 Jan. 1737-8. Hired & carry'd over at Capt. Thompson the owners risk, but the Planters not being able to pay such, Mr. Causton took them and certifyed the same which threw that expence upon the Trust.
771. ——, Jannet, w.—Age 30; Servt. for 4 years to Hen. Parker. Her case was the same.
772. Kensler, Christr.—Age 43; farmer; Palatin; embark'd July 1738; arrived 7 Oct. 1738. Kensler & his family, carry'd by Capt. Thompson at his own risk to dispose of to the Inhabitants, but they having no money to pay their passage, Col. Oglethorpe took & paid for them at the Trustees charge, and they gave bond to repay it: But the Trustees disapproved the taking them. Settled at Vilage Bluff on St. Simons.
773. ——, Christiana, w.—Age 39.
774. ——, Bashar, son—Age 3.
775. ——, Margareta, d.—Age 12.
776. Khredelin, Apolonia—Age 32; single woman; Saltsburger; embark'd 21 Sept. 1741; arrived 2 Dec. 1741.
777. Kimlin, Conrad—Age 42; vinedresser; Saltsburger; embark'd 21 Sept. 1741; arrived 2 Dec. 1741.
778. ——, Maria, w.—Age 34.
779. ——, Jo., a child—Age 2.
780. Kirby, Geo.—Servt. to Jo. Ambrose; embark'd 21 Sept. 1733; arrived 12 Jan. 1733-4; dead.
781. Klamer, Geo.—Age 37; farmer; Saltsburger. Embark'd 21 Sept. 1741; arriv'd 2 Dec. 1741.
782. ——, Gertrude, w.—Age 38.
783. Klocher, Bernard—Age 38; husbandman; Saltsburger; embark'd 21 Sept. 1741; arrived 2 Dec. 1741.
784. ——, Eliz., w.—Age 44.
785. ——, Eva, d.—Age 7.
786. ——, Gertrude, d.—Age 9.
787. ——, Paulus, son—Age ½.
788. ——, Sebastian, son—Age 4¼.
789. Knowart, Cunegunda, wid.—Age 54; given the Saltsburgers; embark'd July 1738; arrived 7 Oct. 1738. Widow Knowart carry'd by Capt. Thompson at his own risk: but Col. Oglethorpe

took her which the Trustees disapproved.

790. Kocher, Jo. Geo.—Age 40: gardiner; Saltsburger; embark'd 21 Sept. 1741; arrived 2 Dec. 1741.
791. ——, Apolonia, w.—Age 44.
792. ——, Geo., son—Age 9.
793. Kochleissen, Peter—Age 40; shomaker; Saltsburger; embark'd 21 Sept. 1741; arrived 2 Dec. 1741.
794. ——, Maria, w.—Age 49.
*795. Koglar, Geo.—Carpenter; embark'd 31 Oct. 1734; arrived 28 Dec. 1734. Saltsburger settled at Ebenezar; living 13 March 1738/9.
796. Kornberger, Jo. — Labourer; embark'd 20 Oct. 1735; arrived Feb. 1735-6. Saltsburger settled at Ebenezar; living 13 March 1738/9.
797. Kraierin, Cath.—D. of Barbara Rhosmarine; embark'd 14 Dec. 1733; arrived 12 Mar. 1733-4. Saltsburger settled at Ebenezar; living 13 March 1738/9. Marry'd to the Rev. Mr. Gronau one of the Saltsburg Ministers 1 Oct. 1734.
798. ——, Gertrude—D. of Barbara Rhosmarine. Saltsburger settled at Ebenezar; living 13 March 1738/9. Marry'd to the Rev. Mr. Boltzius the other Saltsburg minister 5 Aug. 1735.
799. Kreamer, Christian—Age 49; farmer; Tr. servt.; embark'd July 1738; arrived 7 Oct. 1738. Kreamer & his family, delivered to Mr. Habersham to be employ'd on the lands for Religious uses at Savannah.
800. ——, Clara, w.—Age 43; Tr. servt.; supposed dead Oct. 1739.
801. ——, Anna Maria, d.—Age 14.
802. ——, Christopher, son.—Age 12.
803. Kreamp, Jo.—Age 35; fisherman & Palatin; Tr. servt.; embark'd July 1738; arrived 7 Oct. 1738. Kreamp & his family delivered to Mr. Tho. Christie Recorder. Capt. Thompson carryed them at his own risk, but Col. Oglethorpe charged the Trust with them which they disapproved. They were delivered to Mr. Tho. Christie the Recorder, but he return'd them on the Trustees hands: about Michs. 1739 he petitioned Col Oglethorpe to buy out his time, and maintain his family by his own Labour, wch. was granted: he makes canoes, nets, etc. and in 1741 paid to the Trust 17.0.0 for the passage of himself and family, being 3 heads and half. Bought his & his family's freedom Michs. 1739.
804. ——, Sophia, w.—Age 40.
805. ——, A. Margareta, d.—Age 2.
806. ——, Catherina, d.—Age 10.
807. ——, Jo. Ulric, son—Age 4.
808. ——, M. Magdalene, d.—Age 7.
809. Kreu, Hans Cunroth—Age 45; labourer; Swiss; embark'd 21 Sept. 1741; arrived 4 Dec. 1741; dead soon after landing.
810. ——, Eliz., w.—Age 40; dead soon after landing.
811. ——, Eliz., d.—Age 20; dead soon after landing.
812. ——, Ferena, d.—Age 22.
813. ——, Frederick, son—Age 7; dead soon after landing.
814. ——, Henrich, son—Age 12; dead soon after landing.
815. Kuntz, Hans Jacob—Age 40; schoolmaster; Swiss; embark'd 21 Sept. 1741; dead in the passage.
816. ——, Maria, w.—Age 40; dead in the passage.
817. ——, Erhar, son—Age 8; dead in the passage.
818. ——, Hans Henry, son—Age 3; arrived 4 Dec. 1741; dead soon after landing.
819. ——, Hans Jacob, son—Age 11; dead in the passage.
820. ——, Margareta, d.—Age 12; ar-

---

* Same as Coglar, p. 10, no. 268.

rived 4 Dec. 1741; dead soon after landing.

821. Kuradi, Hans Kunroth—Age 42; farmer; Swiss; embark'd 21 Sept. 1741; arrived 4 Dec. 1741; dead soon after landing.
822. ——, Anna Barbara, w.—Age 40. Widow Kuradi and her sons Adam & Hans Kunroth settled on a grant S. E. of Hampstead.
823. ——, Adams, son—Age 14. Settled with his mother on a grant S. E. of Hampstead.
824. ——, Hans Kunroth, son—Age 3. Settled with his mother on a grant S. E. of Hampstead.
825. ——, Henrich, son—Age 20.
826. Lachner, Martin—Labourer; embark'd 20 Oct. 1735; arrived Feb. 1735-6. Saltsburger settled at Ebenezar; living 13 March 1738/9.
827. Lachner, Martin—Age 29; Husbandman; Salts., embark'd 21 Sept. 1741; arrived 2 Dec. 1741.
828. ——, Cath. Barbara, w.—Age 22.
829. Lachner, Vite—Age 28; locksmith; Salts.; embark'd 21 Sept. 1741; arrived 2 Dec. 1741.
830. ——, Magdalene, w.—Age 48.
831. Lachnere, Gertrude—Spinster. Saltsburger settled at Ebenezar.
832. Lambert, Ri.—Servt. to Will. Watkins; embark'd 11 Sept. 1733; arrived 16 Dec. 1733.
833. Lander, Saml.—Tr. Servt.; embark'd 10 Aug. 1737; arrived 31 Oct. 1737. Sent to be under Cooper the millright.
834. Landfelder, Veit. — Husbandman; embark'd 31 Oct. 1734; arrived 28 Dec. 1734. Saltsburger settled at Ebenezar; living 13 March 1738/9.
835. Landry, Ja.—Gardiner; embark'd 28 Sept. 1733; arrived 14 Jan. 1733-4; settled at Highgate and remarkably industrious.
836. ——, Marian, w.

837. ——, Eliz., d.
838. ——, Ja., son—Dead 21 Feb. 1733-4.
839. ——, Jeanne, d.
840. ——, Jo., son.
841. ——, [?]—Wife.
842. ——, Simon, son—Dead 23 Dec. 1735.
843. Lang, Barbara—Age 34; w. of Abrahm. Lang; Swiss; embark'd 29 Sept. 1741; arrived 4 Dec. 1741.
844. ——, Anne, d.—Age 11.
845. ——, Hans Kunroth, son—Age 7.
846. Larkner, Tobias—Husbandman; embark'd 14 Dec. 1733; arrived 12 Mar. 1733-4; dead 13 April 1734. Saltsburger settled at Ebenezar.
847. Lascelles, Hen.—Surgeon; embark'd 20 Oct. 1735; arrived Feb. 1735-6.
848. ——, Hen., son—Dead 1738. Dyed at Frederica.
849. Lauchenauwen, Geo.—Age 21; millwright; Swiss; embark'd 29 Sept. 1741; arrived 4 Dec. 1741.
850. Lauder, Samuel—Servant; embark'd 16 Aug. 1737.
851. Lawrence, Jo.—Bookbinder; embark'd 15 June 1733; arrived 29 Aug. 1733; Lot 88 in Savannah; dead 10 Jan. 1733-4.
852. Leak, Jane—Widow; schoolmistress & midwife; embark'd 31 Oct. 1734; arrived 28 Dec. 1734.
853. ——, Cath., d.—Marry'd to John Dun 20 Feb. 1734-5.
854. LeBlon, Pet.—Apprentice to Danl. Revett; embark'd 11 Sept. 1733; arrived 16 Dec. 1733.
855. Lee, Samuel—Servt. to Levi Bennet; embark'd 20 Oct. 1735; arrived Feb. 1735-6; lot 14 N. in Frederica. A new Freeholder, and hard at work on his 5 acre lot; he succeeded Levi Bennet (who deserted before April 1740 in lot 9. N.
856. ——, Tho.—Tr. Servt. 10 years; embark'd 14 May 1735.

857. Leidner, Martin—Labourer; embark'd 20 Oct. 1735; arrived Feb. 1735-6. Saltsburger; settled at Ebenezar.
858. Leimberger, Christr.—Husbandman; embark'd 14 Dec. 1733; arrived 12 Mar. 1733-4. Saltsburger; settled at Ebenezar; living 13 March 1738/9.
859. Leitner, Joseph—Saltsburger. Settled at Ebenezar; living 13 March 1738/9.
860. Lemenhoffer, Paul—Blacksmith; embark'd 31 Oct. 1734; arrived 28 Dec. 1734. Saltsburger; settled at Ebenezar.
861. Lemenhoffer, Veit—Age 29; arrived 28 Dec. 1734. Saltsburger settled at Ebenezar; living 13 March 1738/9.
862. ——, [?], w.—Saltsburger settled at Ebenezar; living 13 March 1738/9.
863. Leonard, Jo.—Age 19; German; weaver; Tr. servt.; embark'd July 1738; arrived 7 Oct. 1738. Maintain'd by the Trust for the Revd. Mr. Norris's use. Palatine.
864. Leshofferin, Anna;—Embark'd 20 Oct. 1735; arrived Feb. 1735-6. Saltsburger; settled at Ebenezar.
865. Levally, Jo., junr.—Shoemaker; embark'd 20 Oct. 1735; arrived Feb. 1735-6; Lot 9S. in Frederica. Levally, Jo., junr. went to settle in Carolina Dec. 1740 with Sarah his wife John & Mary his daughters. Quitted Dec. 1740.
866. Lewenberger, Christr.—Age 32; German weaver; servant; embark'd July 1738; arrived 7 Oct. 1738. Maintained by the Saltsburgers for the use of the Schoolmaster at Ebenezar. Passage pd. for by the Trustees, to Capt. Thompson, to be repaid, but the Trustees gave the repayment to the Saltsburgers. Palatine.
867. ——, Margt., w.—Age 35; Palatin Servt. Maintained by the Saltsburgers for the use of the Schoolmaster at Ebenezar. Passage pd. for by the Trustees, to Capt. Thompson, to be repaid, but the Trustees gave the repayment to the Saltsburgers. Palatine.
868. Lichliege, Anne, w.—Age 34; wife of Hans Henrich; Swiss; embark'd 29 Sept. 1741; arrived 4 Dec. 1741.
869. ——, Anne, d.—Age 11.
870. ——, Barbara, d.—Age 2.
871. Littel, Will.—Age 31; flax dresser; embark'd 6 Nov. 1732; arrived 1 Feb. 1732-3; lot 37 in Savannah; dead 12 July 1733.
872. ——, Eliz., w.—Age 31. Re-marry'd to John West 28 Aug. 1733, and had possession of the lot intended her husband Will. Littel 31 Dec. 1733. Dead 26 Sept. 1733.
873. ——, Mary, d.—Age 5; dead 12 July 1733.
874. ——, Will, son—Age 2; born in Georgia.
875. Long, Will.—Taylor; embark'd 15 June 1733; arrived 29 Aug. 1733. Settled at Tybee where he took up his grant 2 April 1734. Dead 2 Dec. 1734.
876. ——, Mary, d.
877. Loope, Tho.—Wheelright; embark'd 20 Oct. 1735; arrived Feb. 1735-6; Lot 18N. in Frederica. Tything man at Frederica.
878. ——, Agnese, w.
879. Lossley, Christian—Age 30; widow; Highlander; embark'd 21 Sept. 1741; arrived 4 Dec. 1741.
880. Louch, Tho.—Embark'd 21 Sept. 1741; arrived 4 Dec. 1741. He went to Settle at Frederica.
881. Loyd, Hen.—Age 21; Servt. to Will. Cox; embark'd 6 Nov. 1732; arrived 1 Feb. 1732-3; lot 171 in Savannah. He bought out his time, & had lycense to keep a publick house 2 Dec. 1736. He marry'd Phobe . . . . He

went to Carolina to get work. His wife return'd to England with Capt. Thompson & arrived 2 May 1740. Abst. 6 Feb. 1738-9 but returned.

882. ——, Phoebe, w.—Embark'd 31 Oct. 1734; arrived 28 Dec. 1734. She returned to Georgia with her child and a maid servant in October 1740. Quitted 1739-40 but ret. Oct. 1740.

883. Loyer, Adrian—Bookkeeper; embark'd 14 Dec. 1733; arrived 12 Mar. 1733-4; lot 149 in Savannah. An industrious man, and thoroughly cultivated his 5 acre lot 1738-9. He had the chief direction of the Accts. of the stores under Mr. Causton, and not being able to justify several alterations by endorsements went away to Port Royal about Sept. 1739. Quitted Sept. 1739.

884. ——, Adrian, son.

885. ——, Peter, son—Dead 9 June 1734.

886. Lucas, Tho.—Servt. to Will. Stephens, Esq.; embark'd 16 Aug. 1737; arrived 31 Oct. 1737.

887. Maack, Martin—Weaver; embark'd 14 Oct. 1735; arrived Feb. 1735-6. Moravian.

888. Macannon, Margt.—Age 21; servt. for 4 yrs.; embark'd 19 Nov. 1737; arrived 14 Jan. 1737-8. Hired & carry'd at Capt. Thompson the owners risk, but taken by Mr. Causton as on the Trustees Acct. & by him so certifyed, tho without order, which made us lyable.

889. Macbean, Archibald—Indian trader; arrived 16 Jan. 1737-8. He came to Engl. to carry over Servt. and therefore the Trustees paid his passage back.

890. ——, Elizabeth—Age 40; servt. 4 years; embark'd 19 Nov. 1737; arrived 14 Jan. 1737-8. Hired & carry'd at Capt. Thompson the owners risk, but recd. by Mr. Causton as on the Tr. Acct. which made us lyable.

891. ——, Margaret—Age 13; servt. for 7 years; embark'd 19 Nov. 1737; arrived 14 Jan. 1737-8. In the same case.

892. Macbean, Will.—Age 27; Tr. servt.; embark'd 20 Oct. 1735; arrived 10 Jan. 1735-6. Living at Darien, still a servt. 6 May 1741.

893. ——, Will—Age 17; Tr. servt.; embark'd 24 June 1737; arrived 20 Nov. 1737. Living at Darien still a Tr. Servant 6 May 1741.

894. ——, Will—Age 21; Tr. servt.; embark'd 24 June 1737; arrived 20 Nov. 1737.

895. Macdonald, Alexr.—Alive at Darien 6 May 1741 but an invalid.

896. ——, Archibald—Age 22; Tr. servt.; embark'd 24 June 1737; arrived 20 Nov. 1737.

897. ——, Christian—Age 21; servt. for 4 years; embark'd 19 Nov. 1737; arrived 14 Jan. 1737-8. Hired & carry'd at Capt. Thompson the owners risk, but recd. by Mr. Causton as on the Tr. Acct. which made us lyable.

898. ——, Donald—Age 16; Tr. servt.; embark'd 24 June 1737; arrived 20 Nov. 1737.

899. ——, Dugald—Age 40; Tr. servt.; embark'd 24 June 1737; arrived 20 Nov. 1737.

900. ——, Eliz.—Age 19; servt. for 4 yrs.; embark'd 19 Nov. 1737; arrived 14 Jan. 1737-8. Hired & carry'd at Capt. Thompson the owners risk, but recd. by Mr. Causton as on the Tr. Acct. which made us lyable; alive at Darien 6 May 1741 but named Hellen.

901. ——, Florenica—Age 20; servt. for 1 yr.; embark'd 19 Nov. 1737; arrived 14 Jan. 1737-8. In the same case; alive at Darien 6 May 1741.

902. ——, Geo.—Age 19; of Tar. labour.

Tr. servt; embark'd 20 Oct. 1735; arrived 10 Jan. 1735-6.
903. Macdonald, Geo.—Age 21; labourer; highlander; embark'd 21 Sept. 1741; arriv'd 2 Dec. 1741.
904. ——, Hugh—Age 37; of Tar. labour.; Tr. servt.; embark'd 20 Oct. 1735; arrived 10 Jan. 1735-6.
905. Macdonald, Jo.—Age 32; hunter; highlander; a late freeholder of Savannah; embark'd 21 Sept. 1741; arrived 2 Dec. 1741.
906. ——, Marian Cadach, w.—Age 29; dead 5 Aug. 1742.
907. ——, Donald, son—Age 2.
908. ——, Elizabeth, d.—Age 6.
909. ——, William, son—Age 4.
910. Macdonald, Norman—Age 32; labourer; Highlander; embark'd 21 Sept. 1741; arrived 2 Dec. 1741.
911. ——, Eliz. Mackay, w.—Age 29.
912. ——, Catherine, d.—Age 9.
913. ——, John, son—Age 6.
914. Macdonald, Rachel—Age 19; servt. for 4 yrs.; embark'd 19 Nov. 1737; arrived 14 Jan. 1737-8. Hired & carry'd at Capt Thompson the owners risk, but recd, by Mr. Causton as on the Tr. Acct, which made us lyable.
915. MacEever, Evander—Age 22; Tr. servt.; embark'd 24 June 1737; arrived 20 Nov. 1737.
916. ——, Rodorick—Age 22; servt. for 4 yrs.; embark'd 19 Nov. 1737; arrived 14 Jan. 1737-8. Hired and carry'd at Capt. Thompson the owners risk, but Mr. Causton recd. such servants on the Trustees acct. and certifyed the same which made us lyable.
917. Macgilivray, Duncan—Age 24; Tr. servt.; embark'd 24 June 1737; arrived 20 Nov. 1737.
918. Macgregor, Gregy.—Age 18; servt. for 5 yrs.; embark'd 19 Nov. 1737; arrived 14 Jan. 1737-8. Hired and carry'd at Capt. Thompson the owners risk, but Mr. Causton recd. such servants on the Trustees acct. and certifyed the same which mad us lyable.
919. Macgruer, Alex.—Age 30; Tr. servt.; embark'd 24 June 1737; arrived 20 Nov. 1737.
920. ——, Anne—Age 4; servt. for 20 yrs.; embark'd 19 Nov. 1737; arrived 14 Jan. 1737-8. Hired and carry'd at Capt. Thompson the owners risk, but Mr. Causton recd. such servants on the Trustees acct. and certifyed the same which made us lyable.
921. ——, als. Frazer, Jo.—Age 24; Tr. servt.; embark'd 24 June 1737; arrived 20 Nov. 1737.
922. Mackany, Rodorick—Age 20; Tr. servt.; embark'd 24 June 1737; arrived 20 Nov. 1737.
923. Mackay, Alexr.—Age 26; of Lange; labourr.; Tr. servt.; 20 Oct. 1735; arrived 10 Jan. 1735-6.
924. ——, Angus—Age 19; of Tonge; Labourr.; Tr. servt.; embark'd 20 Oct. 1735; arrived 10 Jan. 1735-6.
925. ——, Angus—Age 28; of Andratichlis; Tr. servt.; embark'd 20 Oct. 1735; arrived 10 Jan. 1735-6.
926. ——, Angus—Age 21; taylor; Highlander; embark'd 21 Sept. 1741; arrived 2 Dec. 1741.
*927. ——, Bain Donald—Age 39; of Tar.; labourr.; Tr. servt.; embark'd 20 Oct. 1735; arrived 10 Jan. 1735-6.
928. ——, Catherine.
929. ——, Catherine—Daughter to widow Christian Lossley; embark'd 21 Sept. 1741; arrived 2 Dec. 1741.
930. ——, Donald—Age 39; of Tar.; Tr. servt.; embark'd 20 Oct. 1735; arrived 10 Jan. 1735-6.
931. Mackay, Donald—Age 32; labourer; Highlander; embark'd 21 Sept. 1741; arrived 2 Dec. 1741.
932. ——, James, son—Age 8.
933. ——, Margaret, d.—Age 12.

* Same as no. 930.

934. Mackay, Donald—Age 21; labourer; Highlander; embark'd 21 Sept. 1741; arrived 2 Dec. 1741.
935. ——, Elizabeth—Age 20; single woman; Highlander; embark'd 21 Sept. 1741; arrived 2 Dec. 1741.
936. ——, George—Age 20; of Tar.; labourr.; Tr. servt.; embark'd 20 Oct. 1735; arrived 10 Jan. 1735-6.
937. ——, Geo.—Age 20; cow heardr.; Highlander; embark'd 21 Sept. 1741; arrived 2 Dec. 1741.
938. ——, Isabel—Age 18; single woman; Highlander; embark'd 21 Sept. 1741; arrived 2 Dec. 1741.
939. ——, John—Age 22; of Tonge; labourr.; Tr. servt.; embark'd 20 Oct. 1735; arrived 10 Jan. 1735-6. Out of his time.
940. ——, Jo.—Age 25; servt. to Joseph Stanley; embark'd 6 Nov. 1732; arrived 1 Feb. 1732-3. He left neither wife nor child. Dead 25 July 1733.
941. ——, Marian—Age 16; single woman; Highlander; embark'd 21 Sept. 1741; arrived 2 Dec. 1741.
942. ——, als. Morison, Robt.—Age 23; Tr. servt.; embark'd 24 June 1737; arrived 20 Nov. 1737.
943. ——, Niel—Age 40; of Tar.; Tr. servt.; embark'd 20 Oct. 1735; arrived 10 Jan. 1735-6. Living at Darien still a servt. 6 May 1741 but said to be then but 23 years old.
944. ——, Will.—Age 24; of Tar.; Tr. servt.; embark'd 20 Oct. 1735; arrived 10 Jan. 1735-6.
945. ——, Will.—Age 18; of Tar.; cooper; Tr. servt.; embark'd 20 Oct. 1735; arrived 10 Jan. 1735-6.
946. ——, Will.—Age 19; Tr. servt.; embark'd 24 June 1737; arrived 20 Nov. 1737. Liv.
947. ——, Will.—Age 21; cow heard; Highlander; embark'd 21 Sept. 1741; arrived 2 Dec. 1741.
948. Mackensie, Alexr.—Age 24; Tr. servt.; embark'd 24 June 1737; arrived 20 Nov. 1737.
949. ——, Andrew;—Age 24; servt. for 5 yrs.; embark'd 19 Nov. 1737; arrived 14 Jan. 1737-8. Hired & carry'd at Capt. Thompson the owners risk, but taken by Mr. Causton as on the Trustees Acct. & by him so certifyed, tho without order, which made us lyable. Dead about June 1738.
950. ——, Donald—Age 22; Tr. servt.; embark'd 24 June 1737; arrived 20 Nov. 1737.
951. ——, Jo.—Age 29; Tr. servt.; embark'd 24 June 1737; arrived 20 Nov. 1737.
952. ——, Tho.—Age 23; Tr. servt.; embark'd 24 June 1737; arrived 20 Nov. 1737. Living at Darien still a servt. 6 May 1741.
953. ——, Will.—Age 17; Tr. servt.; embark'd 24 June 1737; arrived 20 Nov. 1737. Living at Darien still a servt. 6 May 1741.
954. Mackintosh, Adam—Age 22; of Lange; labourr.; Tr. servt.; embark'd 20 Oct. 1735; arrived 10 Jan. 1735-6.
955. ——, Cath. Monro, w.—Age 25; embark'd 20 Oct. 1734; arrived 10 Jan. 1735-6.
956. ——, Donald—Age 22; servt. for 5 yrs.; embark'd 19 Nov. 1737; arrived 14 Jan. 1737-8. Hired & carry'd at Capt Thompson the owners risk, but taken by Mr. Causton as on the Trustees Acct. & by him so certifyed, tho without order, which made us lyable.
957. ——, Isabel—Age 18; servt. for 4 yrs.; embark'd 19 Nov. 1737; arrived 14 Jan. 1737-8. In the same case; alive at Darien 6 May 1741.
958. ——, Jo.—Age 21; of Inverness; labourr.; Tr. servt.; embark'd 20 Oct. 1734; arrived 10 Jan. 1735-6. Kill'd or taken prisoner; I believe at Moosa

June 1741, leaving a widow and 3 children.

959. ——, Mary—Age 20; servt. 4 yrs.; embark'd 19 Nov. 1737; arrived 14 Jan. 1737-8. Hired & carry'd at Capt. Thompson the owners risk, but taken by Mr. Causton as on the Trustees Acct. & by him so certifyed, tho without order, which made us lyable.

960. Mackintyre, Hugh—Age 18; servt. for 7 yrs.; embark'd 19 Nov. 1737; arrived 14 Jan. 1737-8. In the same case.

961. Maclain, Alexr.—Age 36; Tr. servt.; embark'd 24 June 1737; arrived 20 Nov. 1737.

962. Maclean, Jo.—Age 30; servt. 4 years; embark'd 19 Nov. 1737; arrived 14 Jan. 1737-8. Hired & carry'd at Capt. Thompson the owners risk, but taken by Mr. Causton as on the Trustees Acct. & by him so certifyed, tho without order, which made us lyable.

963. Macleod, Alexr.—Age 19; Tr. servt.; embark'd 24 June 1737; arrived 20 Nov. 1737.

964. ——, Angus—Age 17; of Apint.; labourr.; Tr. servt.; embark'd 20 Oct. 1735; arrived 10 Jan. 1735-6. Of the Highland Independt. Company & so return'd by Col. Oglethorpe 6 May 1741.

965. ——, Cath.—Age 19; servt. for 4 years; embark'd 19 Nov. 1737; arrived 14 Jan. 1737-8. Hired & carry'd at the owner Capt. Thompson's risk, but taken by Mr. Causton as on the Trustees acct. without order, and so certified, which made us lyable.

966. ——, Evan—Age 16; Tr. servt.; embark'd 24 June 1737; arrived 20 Nov. 1737.

967. ——, Jo.—Age 35; fisherman; Highlander; embark'd 21 Sept. 1741; arrived 2 Dec. 1741.

968. ——, Roderick—Age 24; Tr. servt.; embark'd 24 June 1737; arrived 20 Nov. 1737. Of the Highland Independt. Company, & so return'd by Col. Oglethorpe 6 May 1741.

969. ——, Rodorick—Age 26; Tr. servt.; embark'd 24 June 1737; arrived 20 Nov. 1737.

970. Macpherson, Jo.—Age 20; Tr. servt.; embark'd 24 June 1737; arrived 20 Nov. 1737.

971. ——, Jo.—Age 20; Tr. servt.; embark'd 24 June 1737; arrived 20 Nov. 1737.

972. Madreuter, Hans—Husbandman; embark'd 31 Oct. 1734; arrived 28 Dec. 1734. Saltsburger settled at Ebenezar. Dead 30 April 1735.

973. Magan, Marie—Age 19; Spinster; Palatin Tr. servt.; arrived 20 Dec. 1737.

974. Marcer, Tho.—Son to Martha Causton; embark'd 25 May 1733; arrived 23 Sept. 1733.

975. Marold, Peter—Age 30; Farmer; Palatin Tr. servt.; arrived 20 Dec. 1737.

976. ——, Maria Barbel, w.—Age 24.

977. ——, Jacob, son—Age 6.

978. ——, Susanna, d.—Age 2.

979. Martin, John—Age 21; servt. for 4 yrs.; embark'd 19 Nov. 1737; arrived 14 Jan. 1737-8. Hired & carry'd at the owner Capt. Thompson's risk, but taken by Mr. Causton as on the Trustee acct. without order, and so certified, which made us lyable.

980. Maurer, Gabriel—Mason; embark'd 31 Oct. 1734; arrived 28 Dec. 1734. Saltsburger settled at Ebenezar; living 13 March 1738/9.

981. ——, Hans—Carpenter; embark'd 31 Oct. 1734; arrived 28 Dec. 1734. Saltsburger settled at Ebenezar; living 13 March 1738/9.

982. Maurer, Jo—Age 26; carpenter & brewer; embark'd 21 Sept. 1741; arrived 2 Dec. 1741. Saltsburger.

983. ——, Maria, w.—Age 26.
984. Maurin, Barbara—Embark'd 20 Oct. 1735; arrived Feb. 1735-6. Saltsburger; settled at Ebenezar.
985. Mayer [or Meyer] Tho.—Tr. Servt. 5 yrs.; embark'd 31 Oct. 1734; arrived 28 Dec. 1734. German. Dead 1739.
986. ——, Ursula, w.—Tr. Servt. 5 yrs. German. Dead I suppose.
987. ——, Danl., son. German. Dead.
988. ——, Geo., son. German. Dead.
989. ——, Hen., son.—Tr. servt. 10 yrs. German; lame and assists at the jail in Savanah.
990. ——, Ursula, d. German. Dead I suppose.
991. Mercer, Jane Parker—W. of Saml. [Tho.] Mercer; embark'd 6 Nov. 1732; arrived 1 Feb. 1732-3. Widow of Saml. Parker who died 20 July 1733 & 2d wife Tho. Mercer.*
992. Mercer, Saml.—Tanner; embark'd 15 June 1733; arrived 29 Aug. 1733; Lot 99 in Savannah. His 1. wife dying, he marry'd Jane the widow of Samuel Parker 6 May 1734, and lives on her lot when in town, but he took land up in the country tho he has no grant of it. In 1736 he cultivated 5 acres, from 2 of which he had 25 bushells of Indian corn, the other 3 being under pease were destroyed by deer; he also split 6000 pine trees on this lot. Made 2 constable 24 Oct. 1738.
993. ——, Anne, w.—Dead 29 Sept. 1733.
994. Meyer, Hen.—Embark'd 1 Aug. 1735; lot 22S. in Frederica. German; a most contented industrious planter; keeping a wife and 8 children entirely thereby.
995. ——, Cath., w.
996. ——, Anne, d.—Marry'd to John Henney settled at Frederica.
997. ——, Cath., d. Dead May, 1741.
998. ——, Danl., son.
999. ——, Jo., son.
1000. ——, Margt., d.
1001. ——, Peter, son.
1002. Meyer, Jo. Lodowich—Age 30; surgeon; Saltsburger; embark'd 21 Sept. 1741; arrived 2 Dec. 1741.
1003. ——, Eliz. Mulocin, w.—Age 38.
1004. Meyer, Jo. Geo.—Brother of Jo. Lodowich; glover; Saltsburger; embark'd 21 Sept. 1741; arrived 2 Dec. 1741.
1005. Meyer, Michl.—Taylor; embark'd 14 Oct. 1735; arrived Feb. 1735-6. Moravian.
1006. Meyerin, Maria—Age 23; Widow of Mathias Backer; Saltsburger; embark'd 21 Sept. 1741; arrived 2 Dec. 1741.
1007. Michel, Andrew—Tr. Servt. 5 years; embark'd 14 May 1735; lot 13S. in Frederica. German. Quitted to Carolina Dec. 1740.
1008. ——, Margt., w.—Tr. servt. 5 years. German. Quitted same time.
1009. ——, Ursula, d.—Quitted same time.
1010. Middleton, Ja.—Servt. to Mr. Quincy; embark'd 4 April 1733; arrived 21 July 1733; dead 23 Oct. 1733.
1011. Miettensteiner, Math.—Husbandman; embark'd 14 Dec. 1733; arrived 12 Mar. 1733-4. Saltsburger, settled at Ebenezar. Lost in the woods 1734.
1012. Miller, Jo. Adam—Age 48; Taylor; German; Tr. servt.; embark'd July 1738; arrived 7 Oct. 1738. Miller, & his family employ'd 1739 in cultivating land for religious uses under Mr. Habersham. Dead 1739.
1013. ——, Christina, w.—Age 30; Tr. servt. At Savannah. Palatines.
1014. ——, Jo. Nicolas, son—Age 12. Tr. Servt. In the Colony the end of the year 1746.
1015. ——, M. Cath., d.—Age 10; Tr. servt.
1016. ——, Philip, son—Age 14; Tr. servt. Remainder of his service given by Col. Oglethorpe to the widow Harris

---

* Samuel, see: no. 992, and no. 1121.

1 April 1740. Given away 1 April 1740 to wid. Harris.

1017. ——, Veronica, d.—Age 16; Tr. servt.
1018. Millidge, Tho.—Age 42; carpenter; embark'd 6 Nov. 1732; arrived 1 Feb. 1732-3; lot 36 in Savannah; dead 29 July 1733.
1019. ——, Eliz., w.—Age 40; dead 2 June 1734.
1020. ——, Fra., d.—Age 5.
1021. ——, Ja., son—Age 2; dead 4 Nov. 1734.
1022. ——, Jo., son—Age 12; lot 91 in Savannah; quitted, ret. Engl.
1023. ——, Ri., son—Age 8.
1024. ——, Sarah, d.—Age 9.
1025. Mitchel, Steven—Servt. to Jos. Ferron; embark'd 11 Sept. 1733; arrived 16 Dec. 1733. He was assign'd to Mr. Tho. Causton, but ran from the Colony 1734. Run away 1734.
1026. Monro, Donald—Age 16; servt. 7 yrs.; embark'd 19 Nov. 1737; arrived 14 Jan. 1737-8. Hired & carry'd at the owner Capt. Thompson's risk, but taken by Mr. Causton as on the Trustees acct. without order, and so certified, which made us lyable. Dead about June 1738.
1027. ——, Hector—Age 19; of Tonge.; labourr.; Tr. servt.; embark'd 20 Oct. 1735; arrived 10 Jan. 1735-6.
1028. ——, John—Age 15; servt. 7 yrs.; embark'd 19 Nov. 1737; arrived 14 Jan. 1737-8. Hired & carry'd at the owner Capt. Thompson's risk, but taken by Mr. Causton as on the Trustees acct. without order, and so certified, which made us lyable.
1029. Moore, Fra.—Storekeeper; embark'd 14 Oct. 1735; arrived Feb. 1735-6; Lot 20N. in Frederica. Appointed Recorder of Frederica 26 Sept. 1735, resigned the office Aug. 1740.
1030. ——, Mary, w.
1031. Moore, Robt.—Cabinet maker; embark'd 15 June 1733; arrived 29 Aug. 1733; lot 82 in Savannah; dead.
1032. ——, Eliz., w.—Dead.
1033. ——, Eliz., d.—Marry'd to —— Sicem of Carolina & there settled with him 24 Aug. 1734. Quitted.
1034. ——, Mildred, d.—Marry'd to Ja. Wilson 1 Feb. 1734-5.
1035. Moore, Will.—Tanner; embark'd 14 Oct. 1735; arrived Feb. 1735-6; Lot 37N. in Frederica. Follows his trade industriously, built a large house, & set up a good mill for grinding bark.
1036. Morchison, Jo.—Age 30; of Kildruth; labourr.; Tr. servt.; embark'd 20 Oct. 1735; arrived 10 Jan. 1735-6.
1037. Morel, Pet. Rodolf—Weaver; embark'd 28 Sept. 1733; arrived 14 Jan. 1733-4. Settled at Highgate.
1038. ——, Martine, w.—Settled at Highgate. Dead 5 Feb. 1733-4.
1039. ——, Jo. Ant., son—Settled at Highgate.
1040. ——, Mariane, d.—Settled at Highgate.
1041. Morrison, Hugh—Age 22; of Tonge.; labourr.; Tr. servt.; embark'd 20 Oct. 1735; arrived 10 Jan. 1735-6. Of the highland independt. company, & so return'd by Col. Oglethorpe 6 May 1741.
1042. Moshamer, Jo.—Husbandman; embark'd 14 Dec. 1733; arrived 12 Mar. 1733-4. Saltsburger settled at Ebenezar.
1043. ——, Maria, w.—Saltsburger settled at Ebenezar.
1044. Mostoud, Hierom—Age 59; farmer; Palat. Tr. servt.; arrived 20 Dec. 1737.
1045. ——, Susana Margt., w.—Age 50.
1046. ——, Jo. Stout, son—Age 22.
1047. ——, Maria Margt., d.—Age 19.
1048. Mouse, Tho.—Clogmaker; embark'd 28 Sept. 1733; arrived 14 Jan. 1733-4.

Settled at Skidaway where the lands were run out 17 Dec. 1734. Dead.

1049. ——, Lucy, w.—Inmate at Savannah on lot 174.

1050. ——, Anne, d.—Mar. to Fra. Brooks. Inmate at Savannah on lot 174. Marry'd to Fr. Brooks Freeholder of Savannah, who being kill'd by the Spaniards in Feb 1739/40 was left a widow with 2 small children.

1051. ——, Cath., d.

1052. ——, Eliz., d.

1053. ——, Lucy, d.

1054. ——, Mary, d.

1055. Muggiser, Hans—Miller; embark'd 31 Oct. 1734; arrived 28 Dec. 1734. Saltsburger settled at Ebenezar.

1056. Mugridge, Fra.—Age 39; sawyer; embark'd 8 Nov. 1732; arrived 1 Feb. 1732-3; lot 12 in Savannah. Possest of his lot 21 Dec. 1733. Doubted if he left not a minor in England. Dead 1 July 1735.

1057. Muir, Ja.—Age 38; peruke maker; embark'd 8 Nov. 1732; arrived 1 Feb. 1732-3; lot 18 in Savannah. Possest of his lot 21 Dec. 1733. Re-marry'd to Mary Woodman 29 Dec. 1734. No cultivater of land. Ran to Carolina in 1739 and died there Sept. 1739. Quitted to Carolina 1739; dead Sept. 1739.

1058. ——, Ellen, w.—Age 38; dead 10 July 1733.

1059. ——, Geo., son—Embark'd 14 May 1735.

1060. ——, Jo., son—Age 2. Went away to Charlestown. Quitted Mar. 1732-3.

1061. Muller, Christr. Hervack—Servt. to Ern: Von Reck; embark'd 20 Oct. 1735; arrived Feb. 1735-6. Saltsburger settled at Ebenezar; living 13 March 1738/9.

1062. Muller, Fred. Will.—Watch maker; embark'd 20 Oct. 1735; arrived Feb. 1735-6. Saltsburger settled at Ebenezar; living 13 March 1738/9.

1063. ——, Anne Christ., w.—Saltsburger settled at Ebenezar; living 13 March 1738/9.

1064. ——, Frederica, d.—Saltsburger settled at Ebenezar; living 13 March 1738/9.

1065. ——, Joana Agnese, d.—Saltsburger settled at Ebenezar; living 13 March 1738/9.

1066. ——, Joanna Margt., d.—Saltsburger settled at Ebenezar; living 13 March 1738/9.

1067. ——, Jo. Paul, son—Saltsburger settled at Ebenezar; living 13 March 1738/9.

1068. ——, Jo. Simon, son—Saltsburger settled at Ebenezar; living 13 March 1738/9.

1069. Muller, Leonard—Age 41; farmer; Palatin servt.; embark'd July 1738; arrived 7 Oct. 1738. Muller & his family: Delivered Noble Jones, on his bond to repay the Trustees their passage.

1070. ——, Eve, w.—Age 40.

1071. ——, Hans Bernard, son—Age 6.

1072. ——, Hans Michl., son—Age 13.

1073. Munro, Ja.—Age 33; cow heard; Highlander; embark'd 21 Sept. 1741; arrived 2 Dec. 1741.

1074. ——, Janet Macleod, w.—Age 26.

1075. Murray, Alexr.—Age 26; of Rogart; labourr.; Tr. servt.; embark'd 20 Oct. 1735; arrived 10 Jan. 1735-6.

1076. ——, Anne—Age 18; single woman; Highlander; embark'd 21 Sept. 1741; arrived 2 Dec. 1741.

1077. ——, Christian—Age 18; servt. for 4 yrs.; embark'd 19 Oct. 1737; arrived 14 Jan. 1737-8. Hired and carry'd at Capt. Thompson the owners risk, but taken by Mr. Causton as on the Trustees acct. and so certified, tho without orders, which made us

lyable. Alive at Darien 6 May 1741.
1078. Neizar, Austen—Smith; embark'd 14 Oct., 1735; arrived Feb. 1735-6.
1079. ——, Jurgan—Clerk; embark'd 14 Oct. 1735; arrived Feb. 1735-6.
1080. Nelt, Frederick—Age 31; weaver; German servt.; embark'd July 1738; arrived 7 Oct. 1738. He and his wife given to the Saltsburgers. Their passage pd. for by the Trustees which they were to repay, but the Trustees gave that repayment when made or work'd out to the Saltsburgers. Palatines.
1081. ——, Eliz., w.—Age 36; Palatin also.
1082. Nichols, Eliz.—Servt. to Edw. Seymour; embark'd 1 Aug. 1735.
1083. Nitchman, David—Moravian minister; embark'd 14 Oct. 1735; arrived Feb. 1735-6; lot 219 in Savannah. Tho in Germany, his agent Jo. Teltchig cultivates his lot. In 1737 he desired leave to make his lot over in comon to the Moravians. In 1740 they all abandon'd the Colony. In Germany.
1084. Nongazer, Philip—Age 55; farmer; Palatin Tr. servt.; arrived 20 Dec. 1737; I suppose dead before Oct. 1739.
1085. ——, Annapel, w.—Age 43.
1086. ——, Anna Cath., d.—Age 14.
1087. ——, Annaliz, d.—Age 17; I suppose dead before Oct. 1739.
1088. ——, Jo. Hanna, son—Age 21; weaver.
1089. ——, Jo. Jacob, son—Age 26; taylor.
1090. ——, Jo. Martin, son—Age 3.
1091. ——, Jo. Philip, son—Age 5.
1092. Noris, Will., A.M.—Minister in Georgia; embark'd 24 June 1738; arrived 15 Oct. 1738. He did not answer what was expected of him, he quarreld with Col. Oglethorpe & the officers, and behaved very malapertly, he also neglected his duty. A German wench his servant laid a child to him, but cleared him on oath before a magistrate; afterwards she again swore it to him. Quitted for England 26 June 1741.
1093. Oakes, Tho.—Tr. Servt. 6 yrs.—embark'd 1 Aug. 1735. Made over by the Trustees to Tho. Young. Idle and orderd home to his father in England Dec. 1740.
1094. Ordner, Jerick Adam—Age 29; farmer; Palatin Tr. servt.; arrived 20 Dec. 1737.
1095. ——, Maria Christina, w.—Age 28.
1096. ——, Jo. Hier Frederick, son—Age 1.
1097. ——, Maria Eliz., d.—Age 4; I suppose dead before Oct. 1739.
1098. Ortman, Christr.—Schoolmaster; embark'd 14 Dec. 1733; arrived 12 Mar. 1733-4. Saltsburger settled at Ebenezar. Complaint was made 1739 that he is not fit for his business of teaching the Saltsburg children to speak English; living 13 March 1738/9. In the Colony the end of the year 1746.
1099. ——, Juliana, w.—In the Colony the end of the year 1746.
1100. Orton, [?]—New minister of Savanah; embark'd 21 Sept. 1741; arrived 2 Dec. 1741; dead 1742 12 Aug.
1101. Ossencker, Tho.—Labourer; embark'd 20 Oct. 1735; arrived Feb. 1735-6. Saltsburger, settled at Ebenezar.
1102. ——, Anne Cath., w.—Saltsburger, settled at Ebenezar.
1103. Ott, Carl Sigismond—Husbandman; embark'd 31 Oct. 1734; arrived 28 Dec. 1734. Saltsburger, settled at Ebenezar; living 13 March 1738/9.
1104. Overend, Josua—Age 40; Mercer; embark'd 6 Nov. 1732; arrived 1 Feb. 1732-3; lot 11 in Savannah. The lot supposed vacant Feb. 1738-9. Dead 23 June 1733.

1105. ——, Mary, w—Quitted not known where.
1106. Papot, James—Carpenter; embark'd June 15, 1733; arrived 29 Aug. 1733; lot 120 in Savannah. He took to his 2d wife Jane Robe 10 Jan. 1734-5. In 1736 he only fell'd & clear'd 1 acre, since neglected.
1107. ——, Mary, w.—Dead 14 Oct. 1733.
1108. Papot, Jeremy—Vine dresser; embark'd 15 June 1733; arrived 29 Aug. 1733; dead 23 Oct. 1733.
1109. ——, Magdalene, w.—Embark'd 11 Sept. 1733; arrived 16 Dec. 1733. Re-marry'd to Jo. Fontain 31 Jan. 1734-5. Run away 1737.
1110. ——, Jane, d.
1111. ——, Susan, d.
1112. Parker, Edwd.—Brother of Robt.; embark'd 11 Sept. 1733; arrived 16 Dec. 1733.
1113. Parker, Hen.—Linnen draper; embark'd 15 June 1733; arrived 29 Aug. 1733; lot 111 in Savannah. Made 3d. Bailif 1734, and 2d Bailif 1736. Lastly appointed 1st Bailif in Mr. Caustons room June 1738, but removed 20 June 1739, for drunkenness, debasing the character of a magistrate, and countenancing the insolent application made to the Trustees for introducing Negroes & changing the Tenure of lands. He took land some miles up in the country, but has yet no grant of it. He lives inmate on the Wid. Coopers lot No. 20. But she complains he pays her no rent. 25 March 1740 he was restored to his office of 1. Bailif, having left of drinking.
1114. ——, Anne, w.
1115. ——, Hen., son—Dead 20 Sept. 1733.
1116. ——, Jo. Savile, son—Dead 4 Sept. 1733.
1117. Parker, Robt.—Ald. of Lyn; embark'd 28 Sept. 1733; arrived 14 Jan. 1733-4. Lot 133 in Savannah. Quitted July 1736.
1118. ——, Eliz., d.—Arrived 28 Dec. 1734; quitted July 1737.
1119. Parker, Robt., junr.—Brother of Edwd.; embark'd 11 Sept. 1733; arrived 16 Dec. 1733; lot 20N. in Frederica. In 1734 he was concern'd in the design'd insurrection. In Nov. 27, 1736 convicted of beating his servant to make her give a false certificate of her demand of wages. Marry'd the widow Sale 30 Sept. 1734. Run away.
1120. Parker, Saml.—Age 33; heel maker; embark'd 6 Nov. 1732; arrived 1 Feb. 1732-3; lot 38 in Savannah. He lived not to take up his lot, which was possest by his widow. He went over 2. Constable of Savannah. Dead 20 July 1733.
1121. ——, Jane, w.—Age 36. She took possession of the lot intended her husband 21 Dec. 1733. Re-marry'd to Saml. Mercer 6 May 1734. Dead 9 Aug. 1742.
1122. ——, Saml., s.—Age 16; smith; lot 93 in Savannah. He went to Carolina to seek for work, but return'd, and in July 1740 work'd at the orphan house. Dead 1741.
1123. ——, [?], wife—Dead Aug. 1742.
1124. Parker, Tho.—Brother; age 9.
1125. Parker, Will.—Silversmith; embark'd 15 June 1733; arrived 29 Aug. 1733; lot 114 in Savannah. Brother of Henry, reported to be a Papist. He neglects his own lot and rents his br. Henry's.
1126. Parnel, Danl.—Brazier; embark'd 20 Oct. 1735; arrived Feb. 1735-6; lot 20N. in Frederica. Quitted Jan. 1738-9.
1127. Pater, Anne Maria—Servt. to Pet. Morell; embark'd 28 Sept. 1733; arrived 14 Jan. 1733-4.

1128. Patterson, Robt.—Accompt.; embark'd 14 Oct. 1735; arrived Feb. 1735-6; lot 21 S. in Frederica.
1129. ——, Mary, w.—Supposed dead before Aug. 1741.
1130. Pelekew, John—Age 28; weaver; Palatin Tr. servt.; arrived 20 Dec. 1737.
1131. ——, Eliz. Barbara, w.—Age 36.
1132. ——, Conra, son—Age 4.
1133. ——, Susana, d.—Age 5.
1134. Pember, Mary—Widow; embark'd 1 Aug. 1735. A grant of 50 acres was past to her 13 Aug. 1735. She was 2d w. to Sr. Fra. Bathurst. This lot was purchas'd by her of a person who left the Colony, —— was a town lot in Savannah but I can't find the number. Dead Oct. 1736.
1135. Penket, Sarah—Age 38; servt. to Tho. Christie; embark'd 2 Dec. 1735; arrived 2 Feb. 1735-6.
1136. Penner, Christr.—Taylor; Tr. servt. Left to work for himself. Infirm and unable to labour, but maintains himself.
1137. ——, Eliz., w.—Was servt. to Col. Stephens till Feb. 1739/40, when not behaving well, she was sent to Col. Oglethorpe at Frederica, where being in the service of the Revd. Mr. Norris, she returnd with him to Savannah and Jany. 1740/1 was delivered of a bastard which she lay to him.
1138. Penrose, Jo.—Age 35; husbandman; embark'd 6 Nov. 1732; arrived 1 Feb. 1732-3; Lot 15 in Savannah. Fyn'd thrice for retayling spirituous liquors without lycense. And twice for assault and defamation. His lot swamp overflow'd. He went over 2d. Tything man of Savannah. Run away to Carolina Aug. 1742.
1139. ——, Eliz., w.—Age 46. Found guilty of the same things, and also of keeping a bawdy house 26 May 1736. Went to Carolina for fear of the Spaniards. Quitted Sept. 1740.
1140. Pensyre, Saml.—Surgeon; embark'd 15 June 1733; arrived 29 Aug. 1733. Settled at Tybee, and had possession of his lot 2 April 1734. Dead 12 June 1735.
1141. ——, Tamar, w.
1142. ——, John, son.
1143. Perkins, Saml.—Coachmaker; embark'd 14 Oct. 1735; arrived Feb. 1735-6; lot 2N. in Frederica. 2d. Bailif of Frederica. Quitted his office and afterwds. went to Charlestown May 1741. Quitted 4 May 1741.
1144. ——, Cath., w.—Quitted May 1741.
1145. Peters, David—Shipwright; embark'd 14 Dec. 1733; arrived 12 Mar. 1733-4; Lot 148 in Savannah. Dead 1737.
1146. ——, Elenor, w.—Re-mar. to Geo. Garland. She marry'd again to John Garlant 3 Dec. 1738 and deserted the Colony with him 1738-9; returned. Dead 1740. Quitted 1738/9; dead 1739 [sic.].
1147. ——, David, son.
1148. ——, Elenor, d. — Return'd dead 1740. Quitted; dead 1739 [sic.].
1149. ——, Geo., son.
1150. ——, Priscilla, d.
1151. Phizzel, Mary—Wife of Peter; Tr. servt. 5 years; embark'd 14 May 1735. German. Allow'd to work for herself March 1739. She promising to keep her son Christian.
1152. ——, Barbara, d.—Tr. servt. 6 years. German. Michl. Miller bought the remainder of her time of John Clark, in April 1739.
1153. ——, Cath., d. — Tr. servt. 11 years; taken by Robt. Gilbert. German. Robert Gilbert promised to pay her passage when demanded.
1154. ——, Christn., son—German; deaf and dumb.

1155. ——, Dorothy, d.—German. Q. if dead.
1156. ——, Margt., d.—Tr. servt. 2 years. German. She marry'd Jo. Cameron of Darien, & if living resides there with him. Dead as supposed.
1157. Pichler, Tho.—Husbandman; embark'd 31 Oct. 1734; arrived 28 Dec. 1734. A Saltsburger, settled at Ebenezar, living 13 March 1738/9.
1158. ——, Maria, w.—Saltsburger, settled at Ebenezar.
1159. Picklie, Hans Geo.—Age 43; shoemaker; Palatin Tr. servt.; embark'd July 1738; arrived 7 Oct. 1738. Picklie & his family deliver'd for cultivating lands for Religs. uses at Frederica: otherwise to cultivate Tr. lands there.
1160. ——, Agnes, w.—Age 40.
1161. ——, Hans, son—Age 17.
1162. ——, Jacob, son—Age 8.
1163. ——, Thomas, son—Age 13.
1164. Piercy, Fra.—Gardiner; embark'd 31 Oct. 1734; arrived 28 Dec. 1734; Lot 208 in Savannah. A gardiner. He marry'd Mary, d. of Sr. Fra. Bathurst Feb. 9, 1734-5, and ran away to England in 1738 to avoid being questioned for secreting his brother in laws goods who was indebted to the Trust. In 1736 he succeed of Publick gardiner to Jos. Fitzwalter. Run away 1737.
1165. Piltz, Andreas—Age 38; carpenter; Saltsburger; embark'd 21 Sept. 1741; arrived 2 Dec. 1741.
1166. ——, Sybilla, w.—Age 27.
1167. Pitcher, Will.—Carpenter; embark'd 14 May 1735; lot 223 in Savannah. A German. Lot supposed vacant Feb. 1738/9. Dead 14 Oct. 1735.
1168. Platrier, Jo.—See Rigby.
1169. Plessi, Jo. Jacob—Age 50; saltpeter man. Palat. Tr. Servt.; arrived 20 Dec. 1737.

1170. ——, Anna Cath., w.—Age 51.
1171. ——, Anna Ulric, d.—Age 19; dead or marry'd before Oct. 1739 but I think dead May 1738.
1172. ——, Maria Eliz., d.—Age 21; dead or marry'd before Oct. 1739.
1173. Pletter, Jo.—Labourer; embark'd 20 Oct. 1735; arrived Feb. 1735-6. Saltsburger settled at Ebenezar. Living 13 March 1738/9.
1174. Potter, Robt.—Alehouse keeper; embark'd 15 June 1733; arrived 29 Aug. 1733; lot 83 in Savannah. An industrious man till taken off from cultivating by some petty employmt. given him, he made one year 5£ sterl. of his mulberry leaves. In 1736 he had fell'd and cleared 5 acres which produced 70 bushells of Indian corn. Dead March 1739-40.
1175. ——, Cath., d.
1176. ——, Deborah, d.
1177. ——, Mary, d.
1178. Pratt, Tho.—Age 21; embark'd 6 Nov. 1732; arrived 1 Feb. 1732-3; lot 33 in Savannah. Possest of his lot 21 Dec. 1733. His lot was given to Mr. Bovey, he forfeiting it by re-returning to England without leave 23 April 1735 contrary to covenant. Forfeited 23 April 1735.
1179. Preston, Danl.—Carver; embark'd 15 June 1733; arrived 29 Aug. 1733; dead in the passage.
1180. ——, Mary, w.—Re-marry'd to Ri. Cannon 14 Oct. 1733.
1181. ——, Danl., son—Dead 3 Nov. 1733.
1182. ——, Jane, d.—Dead 19 Sept. 1733.
1183. Privet, Anne—Servt. to Will. Bradley; embark'd 20 Oct. 1735; arrived Feb. 1735-6.
1184. Proctor, Tho.—Carpenter; embark'd 14 Oct. 1735; arrived Feb. 1735-6; lot 17N. in Frederica; quitted; dead before April 1740.
1185. ——, Eliz., w.

1186. ——, James, son—Quitted; dead 1740.
1187. ——, John, son—Quitted; dead 1740.
1188. ——, Susanna, d.—Dead.
1189. ——, Tho., son—Lot 34N. in Frederica. A new freeholder 1738 but I know not his lot. Quitted.
1190. ——, Will., son.
1191. Putwellee, Abrm.—Servt. to Will. Bradley; embark'd 20 Oct. 1735; arrived Feb. 1735-6.
1192. Pye, John—Clerk to the stores; embark'd 22 March 1736/7; arrived 4 June 1737. In Oct. 1739 Col. Oglethorpe recomended him to be Recorder of Savannah, and on March 25, 1740 he was appointed to act as such till Tho. Christie should make up his acct. with the Trustees store. Turn'd a busie malcontent 1740. Sworn Recorder Aug. 1740.
1193. Quincy, Saml., M.A.—Minister at Savannah; embark'd 4 April 1733; arrived 21 July 1733. He was of New England, and at first a Presbiterian Minister: afterwds. conform'd to the Church established, and on good recommendation appointed Minister at Savannah: but he absented himself so long at New York without taking care to see his duty discharged by others, and was so busy in encouraging a Party that flew in the face of the Magistracy, that the Trustees resolved to displace him, which he suspecting, to save appearances desired to be recall'd on pretence he could not remain longer absent from his wife. Quitted.
1194. Radick, John—Palatin Tr. servt.; arrived 20 Dec. 1737.
1195. ——, Maria Barbara, w.
1196. ——, Ann Apolonia, d.
1197. ——, Hans Michl., son.
1198. ——, John, son.
1199. ——, Jo. Peter, son.

1200. Ragnous, Jo.—Age 34; carpenter; Palat. Tr. servt.; embark'd July 1738; arrived 7 Oct. 1738. Ragnous & his family: delivered to cultivate lands for Religious uses at Frederica: otherwise Tr. lands there.
1201. ——, Margaretta, w.—Age 36.
1202. ——, Anna Maria, d.—Age 8.
1203. ——, John, son—Age 12.
1204. Randolf, Tim.—Servt. to Will Stephens, Esq.; embark'd 16 Aug. 1737; arrived 31 Oct. 1737.
1205. Rasch, Andreas—Husbandman; embark'd 31 Oct. 1734; arrived 28 Dec. 1734. Saltsburger, settled at Ebenezar.
1206. Rauner, Leonard—Husbandman; embark'd 14 Dec. 1733; arrived 12 Mar. 1733-4. Saltsburger, settled at Ebenezar; living 13 March 1738/9.
1207. Reifer, Simon — Husbandman; embark'd 14 Dec. 1733; arrived 12 Mar. 1733-4. Saltsburger, settled at Ebenezar; living 13 March 1738/9.
1208. Reitterin, Maria—Spinster; embark'd 14 Dec. 1733; arrived 12 Mar. 1733-4. Saltsburger, settled at Ebenezar. Dead 5 July 1734.
1209. Resmonsperger, Hans Jacob—Age 42; rope maker; Swiss; embark'd 29 Sept. 1741; arrived 4 Dec. 1741.
1210. Reuschgot, Simon — Husbandman; embark'd 14 Dec. 1733; arrived 12 Mar. 1733-4. Saltsburger, settled at Ebenezar.
1211. Reuter, Peter—Labourer; embark'd 20 Oct. 1735; arrived Feb. 1735-6. Saltsburger, settled at Ebenezar; living 13 March 1738/9.
1212. Rheinstetler, Anna Dorothea — Age 16; d. of Eliz. Pellekew; arrived 20 Dec. 1737. Palatin; Tr. servt.
1213. ——, Hans—Age 18; son of Eliz. Pellegew; Palat. Tr. Servt.; arrived 20 Dec. 1737. One of the conductors.
1214. ——, Matica—Age 14; d. of Eliz.

Pellekew; arrived 20 Dec. 1737. Palatin Tr. servt.

1215. Rheitter, Paul—Age 30; stocking weaver; Palat. Tr. servt. Arriv'd 20 Dec. 1737.
1216. ——, Maria Eliz., w.—Age 29; Palatin Tr. servt.
1217. ——, Jo. Michl., son—Age 4; Palatin Tr. servt. I suppose dead before Oct. 1739.
1218. ——, Jo. Philip, son—Age 5. Palatin Tr. servt.
1219. ——, Mariagot, d.—Age 3. Palatin Tr. Servt. I suppose dead before Oct. 1739.
1220. Rhode, Hans Jacob—Age 30; weaver; Palatin Tr. servt.; arrived 20 Dec. 1737; dead abt. June 1738.
1221. ——, Susana, w.—Age 42. Palatin Tr. servt.
1222. Rhomorisine, Barbara—Embark'd 20 Oct. 1735; arrived Feb. 1735-6. Saltsburgher, settled at Ebenezar.
1223. Rhomorisine, Barbara—Dead 1737.
1224. ——, Catherine, d.—See Kraierin. Child of Barbara Rhomorisine by a former husband.
1225. ——, Gertrude, d.—See Kraierin. Child of Barbara Rhomorisine by a former husband.
1226. ——, Mary, d.—Arrived 12 Mar. 1733-4. Saltsburger. Settled at Ebenezar. Marry'd to Jo. Moshammer.
1227. Ridley, Jo.—Tr. Servant; embark'd 14 Oct. 1735; arrived Feb. 1735-6. A boy—indented Tr. servt. Sept. 24, 1735.
1228. Riedelin, Fred.—Shoe maker & mason; embark'd 23 Jan. 1734-5. Moravian.
1229. ——, Cath., w.—Embark'd 14 Oct. 1735; arrived Feb. 1735-6. Moravian.
1230. Riedelsperger, Adam—Husbandman; embark'd 31 Oct. 1734; arrived 28 Dec. 1734. Saltsburger settled at Ebenezar.
1231. ——, Barbara, w.—Saltsburger settled at Ebenezar.
1232. Riedelsperger, Christr. — Arrived 28 Dec. 1734. Saltsburger. Settled at Ebenezar.
1233. Riedelsperger, Nicolas — Husbandman; embark'd 31 Oct. 1734; arrived 28 Dec. 1734. Saltsburger settled at Ebenezar.
1234. Riedelsperger, Steven—Husbandman; embark'd 14 Dec. 1733; arrived 12 Mar. 1733-4. Saltsburger settled at Ebenezar, living 13 March 1738/9.
1235. Rieser, Jo. Michl.—Dyer; embark'd 20 Oct. 1735; arrived Feb. 1735-6. Saltsburger settled at Ebenezar, living 13 March 1738/9.
1236. ——, Anna Maria, w—Saltsburger settled at Ebenezar.
1237. ——, Gotlieb, son—Saltsburger settled at Ebenezar.
1238. Rigby, als. Platrier, Jo.—Servt. to Will Stephens, Esq.; embark'd 18 Oct. 1737; arrived Dec. 1737. He took the name of Platrier to prevent being stopt from going by his creditors.
1239. Rigden, Will.—Carpenter; embark'd 14 Dec. 1733; arrived 12 Mar. 1733-4; lot 146 in Savannah. Deserted to Carolina. Quitted 1738.
1240. ——, Jane, w.
1241. ——, Joseph, son—Dead 19 July 1734.
1242. ——, Mary, d.
1243. ——, Will., son.
1244. Rigler, Leonard—Age 25; butcher; Swiss; embark'd 29 Sept. 1741; arrived 4 Dec. 1741.
1245. ——, Catherina, w.—Age 19.
1246. Riser, Bart. — Miner & husbman.; embark'd 31 Oct. 1734; arrived 28 Dec. 1734. Saltsburger settled at Ebenezar living 13 March 1738/9.

1247. ——, Maria, w.—Saltsburger settled at Ebenezar.
1248. ——, Balthasar, son—Saltsburger settled at Ebenezar.
1249. ——, Jo. George, son—Saltsburger settled at Ebenezar.
1250. ——, Michl., son—Saltsburger settled at Ebenezar.
1251. Risera, Simon—Age 55; husbandman; Saltsburger; embark'd 21 Sept. 1741; arrived 2 Dec. 1741.
1252. ——, Magdalena, w.—Age 37.
1253. Rivett, Danl.—Weaver; embark'd 11 Sept. 1733; arrived 16 Dec. 1733; Lot 209 in Savannah; dead 22 Mar. 1733-4.
1254. ——, Barbara, w. Re-marry'd to Jo. Ashfield 17 July 1735 and went to England. Quitted in Engl.
1255. ——, Eliz., d.
1256. ——, Susana, d.—Marry'd to George de la Fons. Dead.
1257. Roberson, Jo.—Bricklayer; embark'd 20 Oct. 1735; arrived Feb. 1735-6; Lot 11S. in Frederica. Built a good house in 1740.
1258. ——, Hanah, w.—Dead.
1259. ——, Will., son.
1260. Roberts, Thomas—Servt. to Will. Stephens, Esq.
1261. Robertson, Willm.—Age 21; cowheard; Highlander; embark'd 21 Sept. 1741; arrived 2 Dec. 1741.
1262. Robinson, Jo.—Tr. Servant 9 years; embark'd 14 May 1735. In Mr. Caustons service Feb. 1738-9 afterwds. given to Mr. Bolzius, who return'd him to the Trust for misbehavior Aug. 1740. In Sept. following he ran to Carolina. Run away to Carolina Aug. 1740.
1263. ——, Jo.—Accompt.; embark'd 20 Oct. 1735; arrived Feb. 1735-6.
1264. ——, John—Seaman; embark'd 14 Oct. 1735; arrived Feb. 1735-6.
1265. Rogers, Jane—Servt. to Will. Bradley; embark'd 20 Oct. 1735; arrived Feb. 1735-6.
1266. ——, [?], son—A child; embark'd 20 Oct. 1735; arrived 10 Jan. 1735-6.
1267. Ronerina, Magdalene—Age 29; single woman; Saltsburger; embark'd 21 Sept. 1741; arrived 2 Dec. 1741.
1268. Rooff, Jacob—Age 48; farmer; Palatin servt.; embark'd July 1738; arrived 7 Oct. 1738. Delivered to Mr. Perkins Bailif of Frederica, to be accompted as pt. paymt. of his present sallary.
1269. ——, Jacob, son—Age 21. Delivered to Mr. Perkins Bailif of Frederica, to be accompted as pt. paymt. of his present sallary.
1270. ——, Margareta, d.—Age 7. Delivered to Mr. Perkins Bailif of Frederica, to be accompted as pt. paymt. of his present sallary.
1271. Rose, Donald—Age 25; Tr. servt.; embark'd 24 June 1737; arrived 20 Nov. 1737. Of the Highland Independt. Company, & so return'd by Col. Oglethorpe 6 May 1741.
1272. Rose, Donald—Age 7; servt. for 17 years; embark'd 19 Nov. 1737; arrived 14 Jan. 1737-8. Hired & carry'd at Capt. Thompson the owners risk, but the Planters not being able to pay for such servt. Mr. Causton without orders took him as on the Trustees Acct. & so certified, which made us lyable.
1273. Rose, Pet. Rodolf—Huntsman; embark'd 23 Jan. 1734-5.
1274. Rose, Robt.—Servt. to Will. Bradley; embark'd 20 Oct. 1735; arrived Feb. 1735-6.
1275. Ross, Daniel—Age 16; servt. for 6 years; embark'd 19 Nov. 1737; arrived 14 Jan. 1737-8. Hired & carry'd at Capt. Thompson the owners risk, but the Planters not being able to pay for such servt. Mr. Causton with-

out orders took him as on the Trustees Acct. & so certified, which made us lyable. Dyed at Darien. Dead 1738.
1276. ——, Will.—Age 32; Tr. servt; embark'd 24 June 1737; arrived 20 Nov. 1737.
1277. ——, Will.—Age 25; Tr. servt.; embark'd 24 June 1737; arrived 20 Nov. 1737.
1278. Roth, Geo. Bartol.—Scrivener; embark'd 14 Dec. 1733; arrived 12 Mar. 1733-4. Saltsburger settled at Ebenezar. Misbehaved & sent with his family to Fort Arguile 22 Feb. 1734-5. Dead 15 Mar. 1735-6.
1279. ——, Mary Barbara, w.—Saltsburger; settled at Ebenezar.
1280. Rothenberger, Steven—Mason; embark'd 31 Oct. 1734; arrived 28 Dec. 1734. Saltsburger settled at Ebenezar. Living 13 March 1738/9.
1281. ——, Cath., w—Saltsburger settled at Ebenezar.
1282. Rouviere, Paul—Stocking weaver; embark'd 11 Sept. 1733; arrived 16 Dec. 1733. Settled at Highgate. Dead 2 Sept. 1734.
1283. ——, Anne Boifois, w.—Re-marry'd to Steven Mumford at Purysburg 8 Feb. 1734/5.
1284. ——, Anne Magdalene, d.—Marry'd to David Hender at Savannah 25 March 1737.
1285. ——, John, son.
1286. ——, Paulina, d.
1287. ——, Simon, son—A minor, and lives with his father in law.
1288. Ruscher, Godtfrid—Linnen weaver; embark'd 14 Oct. 1735; arrived Feb. 1735-6. Moravian.
1289. Rusminsha, Eliz.—Age 22; spinster; Palatin Tr. servt.; arrived 20 Dec. 1737.
1290. Russel, Will.—Servt. to Tho. Christie; embark'd 31 Oct. 1734; arrived 28 Dec. 1734; in the Colony the end of the year 1746.
1291. Ryley, Will—Merchant; embark'd 11 Sept. 1733; arrived 16 Dec. 1733; dead 20 Jany. 1733-4.
1292. ——, Dorothy, w.—Dead 5 Nov. 1734.
1293. ——, John, son—Servt. to Jo. Vandeplank. Servt. to Mr. Causton after his service with Mr. Vandeplank.
1294. ——, Will., son—Servt. to Jo. Fellowfeild. An orphan.
1295. Salice, Ant.—Tr. servt. 5 years; embark'd 1 Aug. 1735; arrived 27 Nov. 1735. German. He and his family Grisons. He latterly was employ'd in the publick garden and had the chief care of it. His time being expired he quitted the Colony with his family to return to his own country and arrived in London March 1739/40 but on the 5th Oct. 1741 was at his desire sent back with his son Anthony 9 years old & daughter Maria Catherine 11 years old. Quitted Dec. 1739 but ret. 2 Dec. 1741.
1296. ——, Cath., w.—Tr. servt. 5 years. German. Dead Dec. 1739.
1297. ——, Ant., son—German. Quitted Dec. 1739, ret. 1741.
1298. ——, Maria Cath., d.—German. Quitted Dec. 1739, ret. 1741.
1299. Samms, Jo.—Age 42; Cordwainer; embark'd 6 Nov. 1732; arrived 1 Feb. 1732-3; lot 9 in Savannah. Had possession of his lot 21 Dec. 1733. Dead 21 Au. 1733.
1300. Santfleben, Geo.—Carpenter; embark'd 31 Oct. 1734; arrived 28 Dec. 1734. Saltsburger. Settled at Ebenezar. Returned to England to carry over 6 more Saltsburgers; embark'd 29 Mar. 1739; arrived 27 June, 1739. Ret. to Engl. 2 Mar. 1737/8.
1301. ——, Anna Eliz.—Sister of Geo.; embark'd 29 Mar. 1739; arrived 27 June

1739. Saltsburger, settled at Ebenezar.
1302. Satchfeild, Eliz.—Age 25; servt. to Ja. Muir; embark'd 6 Nov. 1732; arrived 1 Feb. 1732-3.
1303. Savery, Will.—Blacksmith; embark'd 24 Jan. 1732-3; arrived 16 May 1733; Lot 76 in Savannah. He had possession of his lot 21 Dec. 1733. Dead Dec. 1733/4.
1304. Schad, Hans Joachim—Age 50; smith; Swiss; embark'd 29 Sept. 1741; arriv'd 4 Dec. 1741. Settled on a grant S. E. of Hampstead.
1305. ——, Eva, w.—Age 47.
1306. ——, Ana, d.—Age 24. Settled S. E. of Hampstead.
1307. ——, Hans Joachim, son—Age 16.
1308. ——, Margareta, d.—Age 12. Settled S. E. of Hampstead.
1309. ——, Solomon, son—Age 18. Settled on a grant S. E. of Hampstead.
1310. Schefler, Geo.—Age 27; stocking weaver; Saltsburger; embarked 21 Sept. 1741; arrived 2 Dec. 1741.
1311. ——, Catharina, w.—Age 26.
1312. Scheraus, Jo.—Age 35; linnen draper; Saltsburger; embark'd 21 Sept. 1741; arrived 2 Dec. 1741.
1313. ——, Maria Helena, w.—Age 44.
1314. ——, John, son—Age 6.
1315. Schmidt, Jo.—Labourer; embark'd 20 Oct. 1735; arrived Feb. 1735-6. Saltsburger settled at Ebenezar living 13 March, 1738/9.
1316. ——, Cath., w.
1317. ——, Jacob, son.
1318. Schopaker, Ruprecht—Husbandman; embark'd 31 Oct. 1734; arrived 28 Dec. 1734. Saltsburger settled at Ebenezar. Dead 16 April 1735.
1319. ——, Ursula, w.—Saltsburger settled at Ebenezar.
1320. ——, Agatha, d.—Saltsburger settled at Ebenezar.
1321. ——, Margt., d.—Saltsburger settled at Ebenezar. Dead 23 Jan. 1734/5.
1322. ——, Maria, d.—Saltsburger settled at Ebenezar. Dead 4 April 1735.
1323. Schortner, Jacob—Mason & husbman.; embark'd 31 Oct. 1734; arrived 28 Dec. 1734. Saltsburger settled at Ebenezar. Living 13 Mar. 1738/9.
1324. Schreyder, Adam—Age 22; drumer; Swiss; embark'd 29 Sept. 1741; arrived 4 Dec. 1741.
1325. Schreyder, Hen.—Age 30; labourer; Swiss; embark'd 29 Sept. 1741; arrived 4 Dec. 1741.
1326. ——, Elizabeth, w.—Age 30; dead soon after landing.
1327. ——, Anna Barbara—Sister of Hen.; Age 29.
1328. Schumaker, Caspar—Tr. servt. for 5 years; embark'd 14 May 1735. German. Their time of service being over, they quitted the Colony to return to their native country, the Grisons: and arrived in London May 1740. Quitted 1739-40.
1329. ——, Christian, w.—Tr. servt. 5 years; quitted 1739-40.
1330. Schwabb, J. Michl.—Moravian boy; embark'd 3 Nov. 1737.
1331. Schwabb, Sibilla — Spinster; embark'd 31 Oct. 1734; arrived 28 Dec. 1734. Saltsburger settled at Ebenezar.
1332. Schwaighoffer, Paul — Husbandman; embark'd 14 Dec. 1733; arrived 12 Mar. 1733-4. Saltsburger settled at Ebenezar.
1333. ——, Marg., w.—Saltsburger settled at Ebenezar.
1334. ——, Maria, d.—Saltsburger settled at Ebenezar.
1335. ——, Tho., son—Saltsburger settled at Ebenezar.
1336. ——, Ursula, d.—Saltsburger settled at Ebenezar.
1337. Schwandel, Tho.—Miner & husbman.;

embark'd 14 Dec. 1733; arrived 12 Mar. 1733-4. Saltsburger settled at Ebenezar, living 13 March 1738/9.

1338. ——, Margt., w.—Saltsburger, settled at Ebenezar.

1339. ——, Margt., d.—Saltsburger, settled at Ebenezar. Dead 2 April 1735.

1340. Schweiger, Geo.—Husbandman; embark'd 14 Dec. 1733; arrived 12 Mar. 1733-4. Saltsburger settled at Ebenezar, living 13 March 1738/9.

1341. Schwerchort, Christr.—Servt. to Phil. Von Reck; embark'd 14 Dec. 1733; arrived 12 Mar. 1733-4. Saltsburger settled at Ebenezar. Living 13 Mar. 1738/9.

1342. Scot, Fra.—Age 40; reduced officer; embark'd 6 Nov. 1732; arrived 1 Feb. 1732-3; dead 2 Jan. 1733-4.

1343. Scot, John—Gunsmith; embark'd 17 Dec. 1733; arrived 12 Mar. 1733/4; Lot 144 in Savannah. Convicted of selling rum agst. law 27 Nov. 1736; and again 24 Feb. 1737/8. He ran away to Carolina for debt. Run away Mar. 1738.

1344. ——, Henrietta, w.

1345. ——, James, son.

1346. ——, Sarah, d.

1347. Seabry, Mary—Servt. to Fr. Moore; embark'd 14 Oct. 1735; arrived Feb. 1735-6.

1348. Seidbolt, Mathias—Joyner; embark'd 14 Oct. 1735; arrived Feb. 1735-6. Moravian.

1349. Seiffart, Ant.—Weaver & musitian; embark'd 23 Jan. 1734-5. Moravian.

1350. Settler, Mathias—Labourer; embark'd 20 Oct. 1735; arrived Feb. 1735-6. Saltsburger settled at Ebenezar.

1351. Seymour, Edwd.—Embark'd 6 Aug. 1735; arrived 27 Nov. 1735; lot 232 in Savannah. He held this lot as heir to Mary Pember the 2d. w. of Sr. Fra. Bathurst. He went to live with Mr. Eveleigh in Carolina 1736 and is not return'd. Quitted 1736.

1352. Shanbacker, [?], widow—Age 36; Palatine; embark'd July 1738; arrived 7 Oct. 1738. Widow Shanbacker & children settled on Village Bluff on St. Simons, & gave bond to repay the Trustees their passage.

1353. ——, Hans George, son—Age 7.

1354. ——, Hans Michl., son—Age 8.

1355. ——, Magdalena, d.—Age 3.

1356. Shantz, Christr.—Age 21; Palatin servt.; embark'd July 1738; arrived 7 Oct. 1738. Deliver'd to Andrew Duché the Potter at Savannah who is to repay the Trustees their passage.

1357. ——, Willm.—Brother of Christr.; age 18; Palatin; servt.; embark'd July 1738; arrived 7 Oct. 1738. Deliver'd to Andrew Duché the Potter at Savannah who is to repay the Trustees their passage.

1358. Shantz, Jo. Peter—Age 42; gardiner; Palat. Tr. servt.; embark'd July 1738; arrived 7 Oct. 1738. Shantz: & his family: delivered to cultivate lands for Religious uses at Frederica: otherwise Trust lands there.

1359. ——, A. Maria, w.—Age 41.

1360. ——, A. Magdalena, d.—Age 18.

1361. ——, Andreas, son—Age 4.

1362. ——, Charles, son—Age 7.

1363. ——, Hans Adams, son—Age 12.

1364. ——, Philip, son—Age 2.

1365. Shearer, Donald—Age 16; of Tonge; labourr.; Tr. servt.; embark'd 20 Oct. 1735; arrived 10 Jan. 1735-6.

1366. Shears, Jo.—Servt. to Jo. Millidge; embark'd 31 Oct. 1734; arrived 28 Dec. 1734; drownd June 1735.

1367. Shefer, Jo. Christr.—Age 26; weaver; Palatin Tr. servt.; arrived 20 Dec. 1737; free, his time of service being expired 20 Oct. 1740.

1368. ——, Barbara, w.—Free, her time of service being expired 20 Oct. 1740.

1369. Shepherd, Ja.—Wheelwright; embark'd 20 Oct. 1735; arrived Feb. 1735-6; lot 10N. in Frederica. He went away on shutting up the stores having cultivated no land. Quitted Jan. 1738-9.
1370. Shrimp, Elizabeth—Age 10. Daughter in law to Veit Lacher.
1371. ——, Ruprecht—Age 19; locksmith; Saltsburger; embark'd 21 Sept. 1741; arrived 2 Dec. 1741. Son in law to Veit Lachner.
1372. Sigerist, Hans Martin—Age 35; farmer; Swiss; embark'd 29 Sept. 1741; arrived 4 Dec. 1741.
1373. ——, Anna, w.—Age 38.
1374. ——, Hans Jacob, son—Age 5; dead in the passage.
1375. ——, Hans Kunroth, son—Age 4; dead in the passage.
1376. ——, Hans Martin, son—Age 7.
1377. ——, Joannes, son—Age 12.
1378. Sigismond, Fra.—Arrived 28 Dec. 1734. Saltsburger. Settled at Ebenezar, living 13 March 1738/9.
1379. Simeon, Mary—Servt. to Magd. Papot; embark'd 11 Sept. 1733; arrived 16 Dec. 1733.
1380. Simons, John—Tr. Servt. for 10 years; embark'd 18 June 1736. Bound to the Trust for 10 years 2 June 1736 and employ'd under Ja. Smyther in erecting a saw mill.
1381. Slade, James—Shoemaker; embark'd 15 June 1733; arrived 29 Aug. 1733.
1382. Slechtermans, Jo.—Age 50; cooper; Palat. Tr. serv.; embark'd July 1738; arrived 7 Oct. 1738. Slechtermans & his family employ'd in cultivating Trust lands at Fort Arguile cleard by Capt. Macphersons R. Dead 1738-9 at Fort Arguile.
1383. ——, Anne Barbara, w. — Age 40; Dead 1738/9 at Fort Arguile.
1384. ——, Geo. Bartolmew, son—Age 10. Mr. Samuel Mercer has the use of his service. Given away to Saml. Mercer.
1385. ——, Geo. Maurice, son—Age 7; at the orphan house.
1386. ——, Jo. Lawrence, son—Age 8.
1387. ——, Jo. Peter, son—Age 16. Put apprentice to Tho. Young Wheelright to learn his trade. Given away to Tho. Young.
1388. ——, Jos. Michael, son—Age 18; dead 24 April 1741.
1389. ——, Juliana, d.—Age 11. Put servant to Tho. Young. Given away.
1390. ——, Margt. Barbara, d.—Age 19; serves Mr. Tho. Jones.
1391. ——, Margareta, d.—Age 4 months.
1392. Smalley, Jo.—Servt. to Fra. Brooks; embark'd 14 Oct. 1735; arrived Feb. 1735-6.
1393. Smallwood, Sam'l.—Clerk to the stores; embark'd 24 June 1737; arriv'd 20 Nov. 1737. Clerk of the Publick Stores on pay 1738/9 at Frederica, no lot.
1394. ——, Mary, w.—Embark'd 16 Aug. 1737; arriv'd 31 Oct. 1737.
1395. Smith, Elizabeth—Mother to Will. Parker; embark'd 15 June 1733; arrived 29 Aug. 1733; dead 7 Dec. 1733.
1396. Smith, John—Servt. to Sam Hodgkinson; embark'd 14 Oct. 1735; arrived Feb. 1735-6.
1397. Smith, Jo.—Apothecary & surgeon; embark'd 1 Aug. 1735; Lot 33N. in Frederica.
1398. ——, Mary, w.
1399. ——, Mary, d.
1400. ——, Will., son.
1401. Smith, Jo.—Age 44; baker; Palatin; servt.; embark'd July 1738; arrived 7 Oct. 1738. Smith: Delivered to Mr. Mouse at Skidaway to encourage his remaining there: repaymt. for passage not required. Mouse turnd him

back upon the Trust, and he was sent to Fort Arguile where a Spaniard murdered him Sept. 1740. Murdered Sept. 1740.

1402. Smith, Joseph—Grasier; embark'd 29 Oct. 1734; arrived 28 Dec. 1734; Lot 212 in Savannah. He quitted on shutting up the stores. In 1737 he fell'd & cleard 9½ acres, and of them fenced 4½ but planted none. Was in Carolina Feb. 1738/9. Quitted Jan. 1738-9.

1403. ——, Anne, w.—Return'd dead 1740. Dead.

1404. ——, Eliz., d.—Return'd dead 1740. Dead.

1405. Smith, Nevil—Servt. to Hen. Bishop; embark'd 31 Oct. 1734; arrived 28 Dec. 1734. He afterwds. became a Trust Servt. at Frederica.

1406. Smith, Thomas—Victualler; embark'd 28 Sept. 1733; arrived 14 Jan. 1733-4. Settled at Skidaway. Dead 16 May 1735.

1407. ——, Frances, w—Re-marry'd to Tho. Wattle 15 July 1735 and lives with him an inmate at Savannah on lot 78. Her husband a lot at Abercorn.

1408. Smith, Will.—Apprentice to Tho. Chewter; embark'd 15 June 1733; arrived 29 Aug. 1733. Devised to Tho. Barnes, and set free Oct. 5, 1734.

1409. Smyther, Ja.—Millwright; embark'd 18 June 1736. Sent over by the Trustees to erect a saw mill wch. in 1739 was finish'd.

1410. Sneider, Caspar—Age 35; farmer; Palat. Tr. servt.; arrived 20 Dec. 1737.

1411. ——, Cath., w.—Age 32; Palat. Tr. servt.

1412. Sneiden, Michael—Age 40; taylor; Palatine; servt.; embark'd July 1738; arrived 7 Oct. 1738. Sneiden & his family: delivered for cowheards to the Saltsburgers, & repaymt. of their passage not desired.

1413. ——, Anne, w.—Age 30.
1414. ——, Hans George, son—Age 12.
1415. ——, John, son—Age 6.
1416. Snook, David—Baker; embark'd 11 Sept. 1733; arrived 16 Dec. 1733; Lot 132 in Savannah. In 1736 he had leave to sell his lot, but qy. if he did.
1417. ——, Eliz., w.
1418. ——, Jo., son.
1419. Spangenberg, Aug.—Moravian Minister; embark'd 23 Jan. 1734-5; Lot 214 in Savannah. Moravian. In March 1735-6 he sent to Pensilvania to bring Germans from thence, & had 40£ given him for that purpose, but he did not return, but ranged the British Islands in America, & in Oct. 1739 came to England. Abst. at Purysburg Mar. 1735/6.
1420. Spencer, [?] & family—Bailif & assistant at Savannah; embark'd 20 Feb. 1741-2; arrived May 1742.
1421. Spencer, Geo.—Bricklayer; embark'd 20 Oct. 1735; arrived Feb. 1735-6; lot 5N. in Frederica. Employ'd in his business at the Darien Jany. 1738/9. Gone before April 1740.
1422. ——, Mary, w.—Gone before April 1740.
1423. ——, Mary, d.—Gone before April 1740.
1424. Spielbeglerin, Rosine—Widow; embark'd 20 Oct. 1735; arrived Feb. 1735-6. Saltsburger settled at Ebenezar. Living 13 March 1738/9.
1425. Spielberger, Jo.—Mason; embark'd 20 Oct. 1735; arrived Feb. 1735-6. Saltsburger settled at Ebenezar. Living 13 March 1738/9. Quitted 1740.
1426. Stabler, David—Husbandman; embark'd 20 Oct. 1735; arrived Feb. 1735-6; Lot 16N. in Frederica; quitted before Aug. 1741.
1427. ——, Frances, w.—embark'd 2 Dec.

1735; arrived 2 Feb. 1735-6; quitted before Aug. 1741.
1428. ——, Susanna, d.—3 weeks old 2 Dec. 1735.
1429. Stanley, Joseph—Age 45; stocking maker; embark'd 6 Nov. 1732; arrived 1 Feb. 1732-3; lot 21 in Savannah. Possest of his lot 21 Dec. 1733, and had fell'd fenc'd & cleared 4 acres, which by his sickness were neglected: he left the Colony 29 July 1740 being superannuated and past labour. Quitted 1740.
1430. ——, Eliz., w.—Age 35; Public midwife of Savannah. She return'd to England to ly in Octbr. 1736. Quitted Oct. 1736.
1431. Starfitchet, Will.—Had a bounty on corn 1740, and so is a freeholder, but I know not where.
1432. Steinbacher, Barbara—Age 22; single woman; Saltsbr.; embark'd 21 Sept. 1741; arrived 2 Dec. 1741.
1433. Steiner, Christian—Miner; embark'd 14 Dec. 1733; arrived 12 Mar. 1733-4. Saltsburger settled at Ebenezar. Dead 26 Jan. 1734-5.
1434. Steiner, Ruprecht — Husbandman; embark'd 31 Oct. 1734; arrived 28 Dec. 1734. Saltsburger settled at Ebenezar, living 13 March 1738/9.
1435. ——, Maria, w.—Saltsburger settled at Ebenezar.
1436. Steiner, Simon—Husbandman; embark'd 31 Oct. 1734; arrived 28 Dec. 1734. Saltsburger settled at Ebenezar living 13 March 1738/9.
1437. ——, Gertrude, w.—Saltsburger settled at Ebenezar.
1438. Steinheavel, Christian—Age 45; farmer; Palatin Tr. servt.; arrived 20 Dec. 1737.
1439. ——, Apolonia, w.—Age 45; Palatin Tr. servt.; dead before Oct. 1739.
1440. ——, Anne Dorothy, d.—Age 7; Palatin Tr. servt.
1441. ——, Anna Eliz., d.—Age 4; Palatin Tr. servt.
1442. ——, Anne Marbel, d.—Age 12; Palatin Tr. servt.
1443. ——, Jo. Hendrick, son—Age 18; Palatin Tr. servt.
1444. Stelli, Hans Geo.—Age 22; Son in law to Schad; Swiss; embark'd 29 Sept. 1741; arrived 4 Dec. 1741. Son in law to Hans Joachim Schad.
1445. Stephens, Will, Esq.—Secy, of the Province; embark'd 16 Aug. 1737; arrived 31 Oct. 1737. 27 April 1737 he had a grant of 500 acres. He went over Secrety. to the Province into which office he was sworn 27 April 1737, and the same day his grant of 500 acres were seald. In the Colony the end of the year 1746.
1446. ——, Thomas, son—Embark'd 18 Oct. 1737; arrived Dec. 1737; quitted 3 Aug. 1739.
1447. Stewart, Donald—Age 24; Tr. servt.; embark'd 24 June 1737; arrived 20 Nov. 1737; drownd 1741.
1448. ——, Donald—Age 30; servt. for 4 years; embark'd 19 Nov. 1737; arrived 14 Jan. 1737-8. Hired & carry'd at Capt. Thomas the owners risk; but the Planters not being able to pay for such servt. Mr. Causton took him as on acct. of the Trust without orders, & so certified, which made us lyable. Shot by accidt. 6 Aug. 1741.
1449. ——, James—Age 27; Tr. servt.; embark'd 24 June 1737; arrived 20 Nov. 1737. Of the Highland Company of Rangers, & so return'd by Col. Oglethorpe 6 May 1741. Out of his time.
1450. Stok (or Stoll), Anna Magdalen—Age 28. Wife of Ezekiel; Swiss; embark'd 29 Sept. 1741; arrived 4 Dec. 1741; dead soon after landing.
1451. ——, Jacob, son—1 month old; dead soon after landing.
1452. Stonehewer, Jo.—Peruke maker; em-

bark'd 28 Sept. 1733; arrived 14 Jan. 1733-4. He had leave to return to England, & part with his lot. He was settled at Skidaway. Quitted 1738.

1453. Stout, Jo.—Palatin Tr. servant. The remainder of his time given to Jo. Milege by Col. Oglethorpe 1 April 1740. Given away 1 April 1740.

1454. Stronach, John—Age 28; servt. for 3 yrs.; embark'd 19 Nov. 1737; arrived 24 Jan. 1737-8. Hired & carry'd at Capt. Thomas the owners risk: but the Planters not able to pay for such servt. Mr. Causton without orders did it for them and by certificate charged the Trustees with the expence. An invalid (at Darien May 6, 1741).

1455. ——, Cath., w.—Age 35; servt. for 3 yrs. Her case the same. Alive at Darien 6 May 1741.

1456. ——, Priscilla, d.—Born in Georgia. Alive at Darien 6 May 1741 & then 3 months old.

1457. ——, Will, son—Born in Georgia. Alive at Darien 6 May 1741 then about 4 years old.

1458. ——, Michl.—Age 16; Tr. servt.; embark'd 24 June 1737; arrived 20 Nov. 1737.

1459. Stroup, Adam—Age 37; weaver; Palatin Tr. servt.; embark'd July 1738; arrived 7 Oct. 1738. Stroup: he was one of the 2 Trust servants assign'd to Mr. Christie the Recorder 11 Aug. 1738 to be maintain'd at the Trustees charge.

1460. Strubler, Hans Jacob—Age 22; rope maker; Swiss; embark'd 29 Sept. 1741; arrived 4 Dec. 1741.

1461. ——, Elizabeth, w.—Age 26; dead soon after landing.

1462. Stutz, Hans—Age 40; vinedresser; Swiss; embark'd 29 Sept. 1741; arrived 4 Dec. 1741.

1463. ——, Barbara, w.—Age 40; dead soon after landing.

1464. ——, Hans Caspar, son—Age 7; dead soon after landing.

1465. ——, Hans Henrich, son—Age 6; dead soon after landing.

1466. ——, Hans Jacob, son—Age 3; dead in the passage.

1467. ——, Hans Ulrich, son—Age 1; dead in the passage.

1468. ——, Michael, son—Age 9.

1469. Sutherland, Robt.—Age 35; of Leath.; labourr.; Tr. servt.; embark'd 20 Oct. 1735; arrived 10 Jan. 1735-6.

1470. Sutherland, Robt.—Age 21; labourer; Highlander; embark'd 21 Sept. 1741; arrived 4 Dec. 1741.

1471. Swartsfelder, Jo.—Age 44; miller; palatin Tr. servt.; arrived 20 Dec. 1737. Employed with his family in planting and other services at the Couper at Ebenezar, & not paid in money but provided with cloaths & provisions as formerly.

1472. ——, Anna Neice, w.—Age 42.

1473. ——, Hans Michl., son—Age 2.

1474. ——, Margarita, d.—Age 11.

1475. ——, Mariana, d.—Age 5.

1476. Swinney, Jeremy—Age 18; servt. for 4 yrs.; embark'd 19 Nov. 1737; arrived 12 Jan. 1737-8. Hired & carry'd at Capt. Thomas the owners risk: but the Planters not able to pay for such servt. Mr. Causton without orders did it for them and by certificate charged the Trustees with the expence.

1477. Sykes, Fra.—Mother in law to Robt. Clarke; embark'd 11 Sept. 1733; arrived 16 Dec. 1733; dead 16 June 1734.

1478. Symes, Geo.—Age 55; apothecary; embark'd 6 Nov. 1732; arrived 1 Feb. 1732-3. Possest of his lot 21 Dec. 1733. Re-marry'd to Eliz. Gray 10 Mar 1734-5. His lot supposed vacant. Dead.

1479. ——, Sarah, l. w.—Age 52; dead 21 July 1733.
1480. ——, Anne als. Mary, d.—Age 21. Marry'd 1st to Robt. Johnston. 2dly. to Morgan Davis 26 Mar. 1735. Dead 1739.
1481. ——, Eliz. Gray, 2d. wife
1482. Taissoux, Danl.—Tr. servt. 5 years; embark'd 14 May 1735. German.
1483. Talbot, Hen.—Apprentice to Jo. Roberson; embark'd 20 Oct. 1735; arrived Feb. 1735-6.
1484. Tannerberger, David — Shoemaker; embark'd 14 Oct. 1735; arrived Feb. 1735-6. Moravian.
1485. ——, Jo., son—Moravian.
1486. Taverner, Will.—Age 15; servt. to Jo. Welch; embark'd 14 Oct. 1735; arrived Feb. 1735-6. He ran distracted on ship board.
1487. Taylor, Abraham—Age 20; a taylor; embark'd July 1738; arrived 7 Oct. 1738. Taylor: Deliver'd to Mr. Mathews who married Mr. Musgroves widow. Interpreter to the Indians as a recompence in lieu of her Indian servant killed in the disputes with Mr. Watson.
1488. Taylor, Joseph—Tallowchandler; embark'd 11 Sept. 1733; arrived 16 Dec. 1733; lot 137 in Savannah. His lot supposed vacant. In Aug. 1738 Patrick Graham rented it. Dead 16 Feb. 1733.
1489. ——, Eliz., w.—Re-marry'd to Tho. Antrobus 1 Dec. 1734. Dead 28 June 1737.
1490. ——, Eliz., d.—Dead 25 July 1734.
1491. ——, Mary, d.—Dead 26 June 1734.
1492. Taylor, Joseph—Age 25; servt. for 4 yrs.; embark'd 19 Nov. 1737; arrived 14 Jan. 1737-8. Hired at Capt. Thompson the owners risk & carry'd, but the Planters not being able to pay for such servants, Mr. Causton did it & so certified to the Trustees, which made them lyable.
1493. ——, Cath., w.—Age 23; servt. for 4 yrs. Her case the same.
1494. Taylor, Will.—Age 17; servt. for 4 yrs.; embark'd 19 Nov. 1737; arrived 14 Jan. 1737-8. His case the same.
1495. Teasdale, Jo.—Taylor; embark'd 11 Sept. 1733; arrived 16 Dec. 1733. Settled at Fort Arguile at first.
1496. Tebbut, Tho.—Sawyer; embark'd 24 Jan. 1732-3; arrived 16 May 1733; lot 28 in Savannah. Fyn'd for assaulting an officer on duty 1 June 1734. In possession of his lot 21 Dec. 1733. A roving fellow & generally absent in Carolina. He quitted on shutting up the stores 1739. Quitted Jan. 1738/9; returned 1741.
1497. ——, Anne, w.
1498. Telchigen, Judith—w. of ——; embark'd 14 Oct. 1735; arrived Feb. 1735-6. Moravian.
1499. ——, Isabel, w.—Lot 217 in Savannah. The widow of Willm. Cross who died 1738. She re-marry'd Jo. Teasdale who lives with her on this lot, wch. is swamp overflow'd.
1500. ——, Dinah, d.
1501. ——, John, son.
1502. ——, Saml., son.
1503. Theary or Tery—Recorder of Frederica; embark'd 21 Sept. 1741; arrived 2 Dec. 1741. Mr. Terry was appointed Recorder of Frederica.
1504. Thibaut, Danl.—Age 50; vintager; embark'd 6 Nov. 1732; arrived 1 Feb. 1732-3; lot 39 in Savannah; dead 24 Oct. 1733.
1505. ——, Mary, w.—Age 40. Put in possession of the lot design'd her husband 21 Dec. 1733. She re-marry'd Jo. Cellier of Purysburg 17 March 1734-5 who lives with her on this lot.
1506. ——, Diana, d.—Age 7; dead.

1507. ——, James, son—Age 12; afterwds. servt. to Will Bradley.
1508. Thilo, [?]—Surgn. to the Saltsburgers; embark'd Oct. 1737; arrived 16 Jan. 1737-8. Saltsburger settled at Ebenezar. It was agreed to give him his passage, 3 years allowance on the stores, and keep him a servant.
1509. Thompson, [?]—Maid Servt. to Mr. Terry; embark'd 21 Sept. 1741; arrived 2 Dec. 1741.
1510. Thompson, Jo. Senr.—Block maker; embark'd 11 Sept. 1733; arrived 16 Dec. 1733; lot 108 in Savannah. Settled at Abercorn, wch. he quitted & in 1736 this lot was granted him. It is swamp overflow'd. Dead 1738.
1511. ——, Rebecka, w.—Settled at Abercorn.
1512. ——, John, son. A riotous fellow & disobedient to the constable 15 June 1737. He quitted & went to Carolina on shutting up the stores Dec. 1738. Quitted Dec. 1738.
1513. ——, Jo., junr.—Settled at Abercorn, but quitted it for a lot at Augusta. Dead 1738.
1514. Thompson, Capt. Will—Lot 40 in Savannah. Thompson (Capt. Will.) purchased this lot of Ja. Smith for 20£ 1740.
1515. Thompson, Will. — Servt. to Benj. Deikin; embark'd 18 June 1736.
*1516. Tolly, [?]—Sent to be School master; embark'd 6 Jan. 1737/8; arrived 7 May 1738.
1517. Tolschig, Jo.—Gardiner; embark'd 23 Jan. 1734-5. Moravian.
1518. Torgler, Catherina—Age 33; W. of Joannes Torgler; Swiss; embark'd 29 Sept. 1741; arrived 4 Dec. 1741. Settled wth. Joannes her husband on a grant S. E. of Hampstead.
1519. ——, Anna, d.—9 months old. Settled on a grant S. E. of Hampstead.
1520. Tresler, Hans Joseph—Age 33; farmer; Palatin Tr. servt.; arriv'd 20 Dec. 1737.
1521. ——, Cath., w.—Age 27; Palatin Tr. Servt.
1522. Trip, Tho.—Carpenter; embark'd 28 Dec. 1733; arrived 1 Feb. 1733-4; Lot 156 in Savanah. He marry'd the widow Eliz. Herbert servt. to Tho. Fawsset 6 Oct. 1734 and lives with her, but cultivated nothing.
1523. Truby, Mary—Servt. to Jo. Roberson; embark'd 20 Oct. 1735; arrived Feb. 1735-6. She was l. servt. to Ja. Moore.
1524. Tuckner, Ambrose, als. Tatzer, al. Detzner—Locksmith; embark'd 14 Oct. 1735; arrived Feb. 1735-6; lot 17N. in Frederica. Als. Tatzner, als. Detzner.
1525. ——, Martha, w.—Dead before Aug. 1741.
1526. Turner, Ja.—Hosier; embark'd 15 June 1733; arrived 29 Aug. 1733; lot 95 in Savannah; quitted 1737.
1527. ——, Eliz., w.
1528. Turner, Richd.—Sawyer & carpenter; embark'd 11 Sept. 1733; arrived 16 Dec. 1733; lot 135 in Savannah. Fyn'd 3.10.0 for defraud in work 27 Sept. 1734. Also fyn'd 200.0.0 for unlawfull imprisonment & devising to get unlawfull possession of goods 14 July 1735. Kept to bail but ran away and cheated his creditors 29 Dec. 1737. On 11 Jan. he returnd and was imprisoned. In 1739 he shipt himself for the Islands: and his wife lives in open adultery with Mr. Christie Recorder of Savannah. Run away 29 Dec. 1737.
1529. ——, Sarah, w.—Quitted to Engld. 1740.
1530. ——, Tho., son—Dead 13 Feb. 1733-4.
1531. Upshaw, Joseph—Age 16; Palatine; servt.; embark'd July 1738; arrived 7 Oct. 1738. Upshaw: Deliver'd Mr.

* Same as Folly, p. 16, no. 447.

Mackintosh overseer of the Trust Servants at Darien in pt. paymt. of his present sallary.

1532. Valentine, Cath.—Cook; embark'd 20 Oct. 1735; arrived Feb. 1735-6. Saltsburger settled at Ebenezar.

1533. Vanderplank, Jo.—Age 48; seaman; embark'd Nov. 1732; arrived 1 Feb. 1732-3; lot 25 in Savannah. Made Naval Officer 7 Oct. 1735. Dead 1737.

1534. ——, Mary, w.; embark'd Aug. 1734; arrived 21 Oct. 1734. She has a Trust Servt. allow'd her in consideration of her husbands good service.

1535. Vansmaker, Jo. Jacob—Age 21; Palatin Tr. servt.; embark'd Oct. 1737; arrived 20 Dec. 1737. He marry'd Cath. Fritz at his embarkation Oct. 1738.

1536. ——, Cath. Fritz, w.—Age 18; Palatin Tr. servt. Daughter of Hen. Fritz.

1537. Vatt, Jo.—Conductor of the Saltsburgers; embark'd 31 Oct. 1734; arrived 28 Dec. 1734. German. He twice conducted the Saltsburgers, but afterwards proving troublesome to the ministers and people there, he was not sent back on his last return to England in 1737. Was not to fix, but ret.

1538. Vetterley, Henrich—Age 40; farmer; Swiss; embark'd 29 Sept. 1741; dead in the passage.

1539. ——, Catherina, w.—Age 40; w. of Henrich Vetterley; Swiss; embark'd 29 Sept. 1741; arrived 4 Dec. 1741; dead soon after landing.

1540. ——, Ann Magdalene, d.—Age 10.

1541. ——, Hans Jacob, son—Age 11; dead soon after landing.

1542. ——, Regula, d.—Age 6.

1543. Vicary, Ambrose—Seaman; embark'd 11 Sept. 1733; arrived 16 Dec. 1733; Lot 130 in Savannah; dead 3 April 1734.

1544. Victor, [?], widow—Age 36; Palatine; embark'd July 1738; arrived 7 Oct. 1738. Widow Victor & her family, settled on Village Bluff at St. Simons. Gave bond to repay their passage.

1545. ——, Anna, d.—Age 20.

1546. ——, Annalis, d.—Age 16.

1547. ——, Jacob, son—Age 10.

1548. ——, Peter, son—Age 17.

1549. ——, Sule, son—Age 7.

1550. Vigera, Jo. Fred.—Age 35; Saltsburger & Conductr. of them; embark'd 21 Sept. 1741; arrived 2 Dec. 1741.

1551. Viseren, Mar. Barbara—Spinster; Palat. Tr. servt.; arrived 20 Dec. 1737.

1552. Vogler, Hans Ulrich—Age 38; glasier; Swiss; embark'd 29 Sept. 1741.

1553. ——, Anna Maria—Age 39; Swiss; embark'd 29 Sept. 1741; arrived 4 Dec. 1741.

1554. ——, Ana Magdalene, d.—Age 11.

1555. ——, Hans Caspar, son—3 years & ½ old.

1556. ——, Hans Ulrich, son—Age 2.

1557. ——, Henrich, son—Age 9.

1558. Volmar, Michl.—Carpenter; embark'd 14 Oct. 1735; arrived Feb. 1735-6. Moravian.

1559. Volthoward, Andrew—Age 49; farmer; Palatine; embark'd July 1738; arrived 7 Oct. 1738. Andrew Volthoward & family; Settled on Village Bluff on St. Simons. Gave bond to repay their passage.

1560. ——, Anna, w.—Age 41.

1561. ——, Hans George, son—Age 9.

1562. ——, Tobias, son—Age 12.

1563. Volthoward, Barbara—Age 14; Palatine; embark'd July 1738; arrived 7 Oct. 1738. Barbara Volthoward: Given to the Saltsburgers, and also given them the repaymt. of her passage.

1564. Volthoward, Margart.—Age 19; Palatine servt.; embark'd July 1738; arrived 7 Oct. 1738. Margt. Volthoward: deliverd to Bailif Parker, to be accounted as part of his present sallary.

1565. Von Reck, Ernest Lewis—Br. to Philip; embark'd 20 Oct. 1735; arrived Feb. 1735-6. Saltsburger. I suppose he abandon'd the Colony with his brother. Quitted 15 Oct. 1736.

1566. ——, Phil. Geo.—Conductor of the Saltsburgers; embark'd 14 Dec. 1733; arrived 12 Mar. 1733-4. Saltsburger. He had a grant of 500 acres made him 7 Oct. 1735, but I know not if he took it up. He was twice over to conduct foreigners, but afterwards abandon'd the Colony. Quitted 15 Oct. 1736.

1567. Vonstermsdorf, Adolf — Gentleman; embark'd 14 Oct. 1735; arrived Feb. 1735-6. Moravian.

1568. Wachter, Joseph—Age 36; shoemaker; Swiss; embark'd 29 Sept. 1741; arrived 4 Dec. 1741. Settled with his family on a grant S. E. of Hampstead.

1569. ——, Susanna, w.—Age 32.

1570. ——, Elizabeth, d.—Age 6.

1571. ——, Susannah, d.—Age 3.

1572. Wagonerah, J. Clements — Age 48; Palatine; embark'd July 1738; arrived 7 Oct. 1738. Wagonerah: Delivered to the late Mr. Jo. West, whereof one was return'd to the Trustees, & the other is become an encrease to the Colony.

1573. ——, Catherina, w.—Age 23; Palatine.

1574. Walker, Andrew—Husbandman; embark'd 11 April 1734; arrived 21 Aug. 1734; lot 216 in Savannah. He quitted & went to Carolina abt. Jany. 1738-9. He had fell'd cleard & planted in 1737, 5 acres which produced 30 bushells of Indian corn, 10 of pease, & 10 of potatoes. Quitted Jan. 1738-9.

1575. Walker, John—Servt. to Will. Perkins; embark'd 14 Oct. 1735; arrived Feb. 1735-6.

1576. Walker, Thomas—Carpenter; embark'd 20 Oct. 1735; arrived Feb. 1735-6; lot 10N. in Frederica.

1577. ——, Mary, w.

1578. ——, Sarah, d.

1579. Wallace, Alexr.—Shopkeeper; embark'd 15 June 1733; arrived 29 Aug. 1733. Put in possess of a lot at Tybee 2 April 1734. Dead 18 July 1734.

1580. Wallis, Eliz.—Age 19; Servt. to Will. Calvert; embark'd 6 Nov. 1732; arrived 1 Feb. 1732-3. Became wife of Lawrence Cook. Dead.

1581. Ward, Barbara—Age 24; servt. for 4 yrs.; embark'd 19 Nov. 1737; arrived 14 Jan. 1737-8. Hired & carry'd by Capt. Thompson at his own risk, but the Planters being unable to pay for such servants, Mr. Causton did it and so certified which made the Trustees lyable for which he had no orders.

1582. Ward, Saml.—Rope maker; embark'd 28 Sept. 1733; arrived 14 Jan. 1733-4. Settled at Skidaway. Went for England 1739-40. Quitted 1739.

1583. Warren, Eliz.—Age 3; d. of John Warren Senr.; embark'd 16 Aug. 1737; arrived 31 Oct. 1737.

1584. ——, Geo.—Son of John Warren Senr; embark'd 16 Aug. 1737; arrived 31 Oct. 1737.

1585. Warrin, John—Age 34; flax dresser; embark'd 6 Nov. 1732; arrived 1 Feb. 1732-3; lot 10 in Savannah. He landed with a child born on shipboard whose name I know not. Dead 11 Aug. 1733.

1586. ——, Eliz., w.—Age 27; embark'd 16 Aug. 1737; arrived 31 Oct. 1737. She went to England on her husbands death in 1733-4 but marryed

again to Jonothan Hood and return'd. Quitted. [Originally came in 1733.]
1587. ——, John, son—Age 2; dead 12 June 1733.
1588. ——, Ri., son—Age 4. Went to England with his mother 1733 but his lot kept for him.
1589. ——, Will., son—Age 6; dead 5 Sept. 1733.
1590. Waschlin, Anne;—Widow; embark'd 14 Oct. 1735; arrived Feb. 1735-6. Moravian. Mother of George.
1591. ——, Geo.—Carpenter; embark'd 23 Jan. 1734-5; Moravian.
1592. Wasserman, Eliz.—Spinster; embark'd 29 Mar. 1739. Saltsburger settled at Ebenezar.
1593. Waterland, Will—Mercer; embark'd 6 Nov. 1732; arrived 1 Feb. 1732-3; Lot 34 in Savanah. 2d. Bailif of Savannah for a time but turnd out 2 Aug. 1733 for misbehaviour, and afterwds. went to Carolina & never returnd. Brother to Dr. Waterland the Kings chaplain, who for his drunkenness would take no notice of him. Quitted 4 Feb. 1734.
1594. Watkins, Will.—Age 44; Surgeon; embark'd 11 Sept. 1733; arrived 16 Dec. 1733. Sentenc'd 100 lashes for marrying a 2d. wife his first living and to give security to return to Abercorn his settlement 9 Oct. 1735. Also convicted of adultery & sentenc'd to imprisonment 3 Dec. 1736 where he lay 2 years & then ran away. Run away 1737.
1595. ——, [?], w.
1596. Watson, Charles—One of the Bailifs & assistants of Savannah; embark'd 20 Feb. 1741/2; arrived May 1742.
1597. Watts, Eliz.—Servt. to Will. Calvert; embark'd 6 Nov. 1732; arrived 1 Feb. 1732-3. She was in England 1737. Q. if return'd.
1598. Watts, Jacob—Sawyer & turner; embark'd 24 Jan. 1732-3; arrived 16 May 1733. Settled first at Fort Arguile, then Inmate at Savannah. Absent 24 Feb. 1736-7.
1599. Web, Tho., junr.—Servt. to Will. Stephens, Esq.; arrived 16 Jan. 1737-8. Bound servt. to the Trust, but made over to Mr. Stephens to make up the number of servants promised him. Quitted May 1742.
1600. Weddal, Austin—Farmer; embark'd 14 May 1735; Lot 230 in Savannah. Treasurer of the Indian Traders lycence money. In 1737 he belong'd to the Compy. settled at Fort Arguile. Dead Nov. 1738.
1601. ——, Margt., w.
1602. Weisseger, Danl.—Embark'd 31 Oct. 1734; arrived 28 Dec. 1734; —— in his way to Philadelphia.
1603. Welch, John—Carpenter; embark'd 14 Oct. 1735; arrived Feb. 1735-6; Lot 5S. in Frederica. On the 1. Feb. 1738-9 Col. Oglethorp advanc'd him on the Trustees Acct. 53.11.0 to set up a brew house. Quitted to Carolina 1740.
1604. ——, Anne, w.—Quitted to Carolina 1740.
1605. ——, James, son—Quitted to Carolina 1740.
1606. ——, John, son—Quitted to Carolina 1740.
1607. Wellen, Elias Anne—Age 18; servt. to Joseph Coles; embark'd 6 Nov. 1732; arrived 1 Feb. 1732-3; sent back to England.
1608. Wesley, Cha., A.B.—Embark'd 14 Oct. 1735; arrived Feb. 1735-6. Mr. Cha. Wesley took the oath of Secy. for the Indian trade 19 Feb. 1735-6 but quitted the Colony & ret. to England July 1736. Quitted July 1736.
1609. ——, Jn., A. M.—Brother of Cha.; Minister at Savannah; embark'd 14

1610. West, John—Age 33; Smith; embark'd 6 Nov. 1732; arrived 1 Feb. 1732-3; lot 31 in Savannah. Appointed 3d. Bailif 13 Oct. 1733, which he some years after resign'd. On 7 Oct. 1735 he had a grant of 500 acres, and 11 May 1737 was permitted to alienate this lot. He marry'd Eliz. Little his 2d. wife 28 Aug. 1733 and Eliz. Hughes his 3d. wife 24 April 1734. In June 1739 he had leave to sell his interest and quite the Colony by reason of ill health, but died of the consumption before he could set out. His wife remarry'd to Willm. Kelleway. Dead 1739.

1611. ——, w.—Age 33; dead 1 July 1733.

1612. ——, Ri., son—Age 5; dead 31 July 1733.

1613. Weston, Willes—Tanner; embark'd 14 Oct. 1735; arrived Feb. 1735-6; lot 43N. in Frederica. Return'd; dead 1740. Deserted before April 1740; dead.

1614. Wheeler, Cha.—Bookbinder; embark'd 28 Sept. 1733; arrived 14 Jan. 1733-4. Settled at Skidaway. Dead.

1615. ——, Eliz.—Servt. to Will. Bradley; embark'd 20 Oct. 1735; arrived Feb. 1735-6.

1616. White, Richd.—Hatter; embark'd 14 Oct. 1735; arrived Feb. 1735-6; lot 35S. in Frederica. Storekeeper at Frederica in Oct. 1738. He was on the 14 Oct. 1735 appointed to be a Bailif in case of vacancy. Dead Dec. 1740.

1617. Whitfeild, Geo.—A. B. minister at Savannah; embark'd 6 Jan 1737-8; arrived 7 May 1738. A grant of 300 acres was made him in Savannah District for supporting an Orphan house 1739. In 27 Aug. 1738 he left the Colony with purpose to return.

1618. Whiting, Leonard—Age 14; apprentice to Will. Brownjohn; embark'd 2 Dec. 1735; arrived 2 Feb. 1735-6; out of his time.

1619. Wick, Jo. Caspar—Shoemaker; embark'd 29 March 1739. Saltsburger settled at Ebenezar. Dead.

1620. Wierley, Margareta—Age 40; w. of Hans Caspar Wierley; Swiss; embark'd 29 Sept. 1741; arrived 4 Dec. 1741.

1621. ——, Elizabeth, d.—Age 20.

1622. ——, Hans Jacob, son—Age 15.

1623. ——, Margareta, d.—Age 6.

1624. Wiirth, Hans Jacob—Age 48; taylor; Swiss; embark'd 29 Sept. 1741; arrived 4 Dec. 1741; dead soon after landing.

1625. ——, Catharina, w.—Age 33.

1626. ——, Anna, d.—Age 11.

1627. ——, Catharina, d.—Age 9; dead in ye passage.

1628. ——, Elizabeth, d.—Age 6.

1629. ——, Salamena, d.—Age 12.

1630. ——, Sulama, d.—A year & half old.

1631. Willor, Maria Ewtch—Age 21; single woman; Swiss; embark'd 29 Sept. 1741; arrived 4 Dec. 1741.

1632. Willoughby, Ja.—Peruke maker; embark'd 15 June 1733; arrived 29 Aug. 1733; dead 17 Oct. 1734.

1633. ——, Hanah, w.—Embark'd 11 Sept. 1733; arrived 16 Dec. 1733. Imprison'd for marrying Ri. Mellichamp, Willm. Watkins her 1. husband being alive and she with child by him, and then leaving Mellichamp and by his consent bedding a third man who bought her for a shillin.

1634. ——, Alice, d.—Marry'd to George Stanton 3 Feb. 1734-5.

1635. ——, Hanah, d.—Marry'd to Alexr. Johnson.

1636. ——, James, son.
1637. ——, Richd., son—Dead 11 Mar. 1733-4.
1638. Wilson, Ja.—Age 21; sawyer; embark'd 6 Nov. 1732; arrived 1 Feb. 1732-3; Lot 32 in Savannah. Quitted, absent some years but ret. 1740. Bound in recognizance for assaulting the guard on duty 30 June 1734. Convicted of extorsion in selling flesh meet 14 July 1735. Fyn'd 5 shillings for wilfully destroying other mens hoggs 28 July 1735. M. Mildred d. of Robt. Moore 1 Feb. 1734-5. Quitted; absent some years but ret. 1740.
1639. Wilson, Michl.—Age 45; embark'd 2 Dec. 1735; arrived 2 Feb. 1735-6; Lot 6N. in Frederica. He paid 10£ towards his and his wifes passage.
1640. ——, Alkeu, w.—Age 45, embark'd 2 Dec. 1735; arrived 29 Aug. 1733 [sic.].
1641. Wise, Will.—Farmer; embark'd 11 Sept. 1733; arrived 16 Dec. 1733. Settled on Hutchinsons Island, and there murdered in his bed 1 March 1733-4. Dead 1 Mar. 1733-4.
1642. Woodman, Mary—Servt. to Anne Hainks; embark'd 11 Sept. 1733; arrived 16 Dec. 1733. Her master assign'd her to Ja. Muir who marry'd her 25 Dec. 1734.
1643. Wright, Jo.—Age 33; vintner; arrived 1 Feb. 1732-3; Lot 30 in Savannah. His lot swamp overflow'd. Dead Dec. 1737.
1644. ——, Penelope, w.—Age 33; remarry'd to Joseph Fitzwalter, and lives on his lot No. 8.
1645. ——, Eliz., d.—Age 11.
1646. ——, John, son—Age 13.
1647. Wright, Pet.—Servt. to Will. Bradley; embark'd 20 Oct. 1735; arrived Feb. 1735-6.
1648. Wrogeley, Hans Jacob—Age 40; cooper; Swiss; embark'd 29 Sept. 1741; arrived 4 Dec. 1741.
1649. ——, Rachel, w.—Age 40.
1650. ——, Anna Barbara, d.—Age 18.
1651. ——, Anna Maria, d.—Age 10.
1652. ——, Joannes, son—Age 11.
1653. Wuller, Hans Michl.—Age 36; Palatine servt.; embark'd July 1738; arrived 7 Oct. 1738. Wuller & his wife deliverd Mr. Fallowfeild 2d. Bailif of Savannah, to be accounted as pt. payment of his present sallary.
1654. ——, Maria, w.—Age 36.
1655. Young, Hier—Age 40; farmer; Palatin Tr. servt.; arrived 20 Dec. 1737.
1656. ——, Maria Barbel, w.—Age 34.
1657. ——, Jerrick Peter, son—Age 13.
1658. ——, Magdalena, d.—Age 9.
1659. ——, Mariagrote, d.—Age 8; I suppose dead before Oct. 1739.
1660. Young, John—Servt.; embark'd 27 May 1737; arrived 20 Nov. 1737.
1661. Young, Tho.—Age 45; wheelright; embark'd 6 Nov. 1732; arrived 1 Feb. 1732-3; lot 26 in Savannah. Possest of his lot 21 Dec. 1733. He marry'd the widow Box of Abercorn July 1734.
1662. ——, [?], w.—Quitted; dead 1740.
1663. ——, son—Quitted; dead 1740.
1664. ——, son—Quitted; dead 1740.
1665. Zand, Bartol—Dyer & husbman.; embark'd 31 Oct. 1734; arrived 28 Dec. 1734. Saltsburger. Settled at Ebenezar, living 1738/9.
1666. Zeisberger, David—Moravian boy; arrived 3 Nov. 1737.
1667. Zeizberger, David—Shoemaker; embark'd 14 Oct. 1735; arrived Feb. 1735-6; lot 214 in Savannah. Moravian; at work on Mr. Spangenbergs lot in Savannah No. 214.
1668. ——, Rosena, w.—Moravian; at work on Mr. Spangenbergs lot in Savannah No. 214.

1669. Zettler, Mathias—Saltsburger, living 13 March 1738/9.
1670. Zeitraur, Paul—Carpenter; embark'd 31 Oct. 1734; arrived 28 Dec. 1734. Saltsburger. Settled at Ebenezar living 13 March 1738/9.
1671. ——, Rupr.—Husbandman; embark'd 31 Oct. 1734; arrived 28 Dec. 1734. Saltsburger. Settled at Ebenezar, living 13 March 1738/9.
1672. Zimerman, Rupr.—Husbandman; embark'd 31 Oct. 1734; arrived 28 Dec. 1734. Saltsburger. Settled at Ebenezar, living 13 March 1738/9.
1673. Zuble, Jo. Jacob—Saltsburger, living 13 March 1738/9.
1674. ——, Ambrose—Saltsburger, living 13 March 1738/9.
1675. Zwiffler, J. Andrew—M. D.; embark'd 14 Dec. 1733; arrived 12 Mar. 1733-4. Saltsburger. Settled at Ebenezar, and constable there in 1736.

PART II

Persons Who Went from Europe to Georgia on Their Own Account

1. Aberdaun, Heyman—Jew inmate; arrived 10 July 1733. Fyn'd for scandal 0.13.4, 27 Sept. 1734. Inmate at Savannah. Fled the Colony with his wife & 2 small children for fear of the Spaniards 29 July 1740. Run away May 28, 1740 [*sic*].
2. ——, Abigail, w.—Jew. Run away 28 May 1740.
3. ——, Solomon, s.—Jew. Run away 28 May 1740.
4. Aberdaun, Simon, *als*., Bandenoon—Jew inmate; arrived 10 July 1733. Fyn'd for defamation £ 3.3.0, 27 Sept. 1734. Inmate at Savannah.
5. ——, Grace, w.—Jew.
6. Adams, Benj.—Lot 222 in Savannah. He became possest of this lot in April 1737, but neglects it & rents lot 78. A riotour in open court 20 Oct 1737. Run away.
7. Adams, Jo.
8. Addison, Eliz.—D. of Edward, Senr.; born in Georgia. Her father Edwd. Addison Senr. carry'd her to Carolina Dec. 1740. Quitted Dec. 1740.
9. Adriche, [?]—Servt. to Isaac Camuche. She was at first servt. to Ri. Warren.
10. Agerner, Hariet—Servt. to Ja. Baillou.
11. Aglionby, Will., Esq.—Attorney; lot 109 in Savannah. On 2d. June 1736 100 acres was granted him 2 June 1736 but he chose to dwell in Savanah and make mischief there. His lot in that town was order'd to be run out 4 May 1737. As he lived so he died a profest Deist. Lot vacant Feb. 1738-9. Dead 23 Aug. 1738.
12. Alban, Mary—Servt.; arrived 15 Mar. 1733-4.
13. Alfingston, Will.—Arrived 14 Jan. 1733-4. He was settled at Skidaway; dead 27 Jan. 1733-4.
14. ——, Anne, w.—Remarry'd to Ambrose Morrison, and remov'd from Skidaway to Savannah. She mar. Morrison 20 Mar. 1733-4. Dead 26 June 1737.
15. Alston, Joseph—Servt.; arrived 4 June 1737.
16. Amatis, Cath.—W. of Paul Amatis. Re-marry'd to Tho. Neale April 1737 and settled with him in Carolina. Quitted. Dead 1739.
17. Amory, John—Embark'd 19 Nov. 1737; arrived 14 Jan. 1737-8. He had a grant of 150 acres made him 5 Oct. 1737. He understands surveying. He went to Charlestown Nov. 1738 he had credit from the Trust for 50£,

and with his wife joyned in security for repayment wch. was an estate he had in England in possession. Quitted Nov. 1738.
18. ——, Sarah, w.
19. ——, John, son.
20. ——, Will., son.
21. Anderson, Hugh. Esq.—Arrived 27 June 1737; lot 178 in Savannah. This gentleman went over with a large family of servants as well as children, and was made Inspector Genl. of the Publick garden and mulberry plantations: but spending his substance in building, and falling dangerously ill by reason of the unhealthy situation where placed his dwelling, He in 1739 deserted the Colony and is settled in Carolina, where he teaches Philosophy. His Grant was of 50 acres & past 2 June 1736. It was in October 1738 that Mr. Oglethorp discharg'd him from the care of the garden to save expences. On 14 Dec. 1737 he was offered a grant of 500 acres in a younger sons name. Quitted 1739 and with his family went to Carolina.
22. ——, Eliz., w.
23. ——, Alexr., son.
24. ——, Cath., d.
25. ——, Moore, son.
26. Anderson, Ja.—Age 25; joyner; embark'd 20 Oct. 1735; arrived 10 Jan. 1735-6. Lot 235 in Savannah. He was possest of his lot 1 May 1737, but neglects it, & lives on his br. John's lot in Savannah No. 190, which John was not arrived in 1738.
27. ——, [?], w.
28. ——, James, son—Born in Georgia; dead 1740.
29. ——, John—Lot 190 in Savannah. Not arrived 1738. But James his brother improves on his lot, and built a good house.
30. Andrews, Benj., boy—Son of Willm. & Eliz.
31. Antonio, boy—Servt.
32. Antrobus, Eliz. Taylor—2d. w. of Thomas. Wid. of Joseph Taylor. Arriv'd 16 Dec. 1733. Lot 137 in Savannah. Her 1st. husband Jos. Taylor died 16 Feb. 1733-4, and on the l. Dec. 1734 she marry'd Tho. Antrobus. Lot supposed vact. Dead 30 June 1737.
33. Arlaix, Peter—Servt. to Elisha Dobree; arrived 30 June 1734. Indictment found against him for theft 2 Oct. 1734.
34. Armstrong, Andrew—Servt.; arrived 1 Aug. 1734.
35. Arnstein, Caspar—Age 28; German Swiss; taylor; embark'd 21 Nov. 1741; arrived Dec. 4, 1741; settled on a grant S. E. of Hampstead.
36. Arvic, Tho.—Servt. to Cha. Britain.
37. Attwell, Will.—A minor; lot 106 in Savannah. Lot vacant Feb. 1738-9. Dead 1738.
38. Attwell, Will. Hoyl—Son of Tho. Attwell, Senr.; born in Georgia, 26 Jan. 1733-4. Dead 1738.
39. Augustin, Walter—A grant of 500 acres was made him 24 Sept. 1735. He joyn'd the Colony from Cats Isld. in Carolina, and settled with 4 servants up the river 6 miles from Savannah. Quitted before Jan. 1738/9.
40. Ausperger, Saml.—Ingenier & Surveyr. of land. Ingenier of the Fort, and Land Surveyor till 7 Oct. 1738 when Mr. Oglethorp removed him, and then he retired to an island which he came to England to obtain Oct. 1739.
41. Austin, John—Servt.
*42. Aversen, Martin — Embark'd Feb. 1734-5; lot 225 in Savannah. He went to England in June 1736, but left

---
* Same as Everson, p. 15, no. 414.

the care of his lot to Jo. Burton. Quitted June 1736.
43. Avery, [?]—Embark'd 1737. He has 50£ advanc'd him by the Trust, for which he gave an English Estate Security Oct. 5, 1737.
44. Avery, Joseph.
45. ——, [?], w.
46. ——, [?], son.
47. ——, [?], d.
48. ——, [?], d.
49. Ayot, Tho.—Servt. to Tho. Hawkins.
50. Bailey, [?]—D. of Thomas Bailey, Smith; born in Georgia.
51. Baillie, James, servt. to Kenneth Baillie—Age 33; embark'd 20 Oct. 1735; arrived 10 Jan. 1735-6.
52. Baillie, John—Arrived 1 Aug. 1734. He had a grant of 400 acres 18 Oct. 1733.
53. Baillie, John of Fortrose—Farmer; embark'd 20 Oct. 1735; arrived 10 Jan. 1735-6. Dead April 1737.
54. Baillie, Kenneth—Age 20; farmer; embark'd 20 Oct. 1735; arrived 10 Jan. 1735-6. Ensign to the Darien Company, taken by the Spaniards at Moosa and made his escape from St. Sebastian to England Jany. 1741/2 and return'd to Georgia March 1741-2.
55. Baillie, Martha—D. of John Baillie, Smith; born in Georgia 22 Oct. 1738.
56. Baillou, [?]—D. of James Baillou, born in Georgia.
57. Bain, Kenneth—Age 18; servt. to Alex. Tolmie; embark'd 20 Oct. 1735; arrived 10 Jan. 1735-6.
58. Bain, Will., of Thuso—Age 19; taylor; embark'd 20 Oct. 1735; arrived 10 Jan. 1735-6.
59. Baird, Robt.—A new Freeholder at Abercorn 1738 on late Geo. Stephens [lot] who departed.
60. Baker, John, Esq.—He had a grant of 500 acres 2 Oct. 1735, was an eminent man in S. Carolina and great friend to Georgia. Dead 10 Sept. 1736.
61. Ball, Benedict—Son in law to Will. Stephens Esq.; lot 62 in Savannah. His land is cultivated by his father in law. In the Isle of Wight.
62. Bambrech, Jane—Servt. to Elisha Dobree; arrived 30 June 1734. She marry'd Geo. Smith 28 Dec. 1734. Dead 17 May 1735.
63. Bandenoon, *vid*. Aberdaun.
64. Barber, Andrew—Patroon of Demetry's Periagua 1739.
65. Barber, John—Placed on a new settlement call'd Archers point half way between Frederica & Savannah Sept. 1738.
66. Barnard, Jo.—Age 23; nephew to Will. Bradley; embark'd 2 Dec. 1735; arrived 2 Feb. 1735-6. In the Colony the end of the year 1746.
67. Barr, Ambrose.
68. ——, [?], w.
69. Barret, Jonas—In the scout boat; arrived 20 April 1734; lot 160 in Savannah. At first servt. to John Fallowfeild. But in 1736 had this lot granted to him.
70. Bash—Tho.—Servt.; arrived 4 June 1737.
71. Bashter, Mary—Servt. to Peter Baillou; arrived 28 Dec. 1734.
72. Bateman, Will.—Arrived 21 Aug. 1734. He had a grant of 75 acres 13 March 1733-4.
73. ——, Mary, w.
74. ——, Mary, d.—Born in Georgia 8 Sept. 1734; dead 4 Oct. 1734.
75. Bates, Robt.—Servt.
76. Bathurst, Sir Fra., Bt.—Arrived 28 Dec. 1734. He had a grant of 200 acres 7 Oct. 1734, and settled at Westbrook. He marry'd a second wife the widow Pember. Dead Nov. 1736.

77. ———, Frances, w.—Dead 10 Aug. 1736.
78. ———, Eliz., d.—She marry'd Fra. Piercy a gardiner 9 Feb. 1734-5 who ran away to England being concern'd in a fraudulent secreting of Robt. Bathurst's goods. Run away 1738.
79. ———, Martha, d.—She marry'd Willm. Baker 1 Feb. 1734-5. Dead Sept. 1736.
80. ———, Mary, d.—Dead.
81. ———, Robert, son—He ran away to Charlestown to avoid paying his fathers debt to the Trustees and was killed by the Negroes 9 Sept. 1739. Run away; dead 9 Sept. 1739.
82. Bayley, Tho.—Arrived 28 Dec. 1734; lot 206 in Savannah. He had a grant of 500 acres 3 Sept. 1735. A factious man, and quitted the Colony for fear of the Spaniards 30 Aug. 1740. Quitted 30 Aug. 1740.
83. Beal, Hen.—Inmate at Savannah on lot 42. Dead Sept. 1739.
84. Becu, Giles—A baker; arrived 12 Mar. 1733-4; lot 147 in Savannah. Fyn'd 40 shillings for receiving stolen goods 3 Oct. 1734 and again 40 sh. for the same crime 30 Oct. 1734.
85. ———, Hannah, w.
86. ———, Benj., son.
87. ———, Mariane, d.
88. Bedford, Robt.
89. Bell, Andrew—Servt. to Patrick Houston; arrived 1 Aug. 1734; **lot 169 in** Savannah. After his service to Patrick Houston, he had this lot granted in 1736, but the next year left the Colony and in Feb. 1738-9 was in Carolina. Quitted.
90. Bell, Robert—Servt. to Andrew Grant; arrived 1 Aug. 1734. Dead 1740.
91. Bennal, Abrm. — Jews — Arrived 10 July 1733.
92. ———, Sarah, w.
93. ———, Aaron, son.
94. ———, Benj., son.
95. ———, David, son.
96. ———, Jacob, son—Of no visible livlyhood; fled the Colony for fear of the Spaniards 29 July 1740. Run away July 1740.
97. ———, Moses, son.
98. ———, Rachel, d.
99. ———, Sarah, d.
100. Bennet, Elizabeth—D. of Anne Bennet; born in Georgia.
101. ———, Mary—D. of Anne Bennet; born in Georgia.
102. Benskin, Mary—Dead 1 Nov. 1738.
103. Bere, Christopher—Lot 17S. in Frederica. A new Freeholder since 30 Jan. 1737-8. Quitted before Aug. 1741.
104. ———, Mary, w.
105. ———, [?], son—Born in Georgia Oct. 1738.
106. ———, Eliz., d.—Servt. to Edwd. Jenkins.
107. Bernal, Rafael—Jew; arrived 10 July 1735. A very idle fellow settled at Hampstead.
108. Bernal, Rachel
109. Bichly, John.
110. ———, [?], w.—Lot 16S. in Frederica.
111. Bignal, Geo.—Servt. to Jo. Fallowfeild; arrived 16 Dec. 1733.
112. Bird, John—Servt. to Geo. Spencer; arrived 4 June 1737.
113. Bird, Philip
114. Bishop, Joseph—Convicted of Sodomy & enticing servants to run away 1733-4, but escaped justice by flight. Run away Aug. 1738.
115. Bishop, Philip—Arrived 7 July 1733. He had a grant of 500 acres 21 Dec. 1732, which he took up at Thunderbolt. He fled the Colony for felony in Aug. 1738. Ran for felony Aug 1738.
116. ———, Eliz., w.—Run away; dead 1740.

117. ——, Eliz.—Born in Georgia 6 Nov. 1738; dead 8 Nov. 1738.
118. Blair, David—A grant of 500 acres was made him 4 Aug. 1736.
119. Bland, Pet. 1c—Servt. to David Douglass.
120. Bobby, James—Servt. to Elisha Dobree.
121. Bobby, Robert—Servt.
122. Boswell, Edw.—Servt.
123. Bovey, Margt.—Lot 33 in Savannah. See Burnside, Margt. This lot was formerly Tho. Pratt's, who forfeiting, it was granted to her 5 May 1735.
124. A boy Humfrey.
125. A boy Leonard.
126. A boy ——.
127. Boyd, Tho.—A grant of 500 acres was made him 4 Aug. 1736.
128. Bradley, Mary—Bastard of Mr. Will. Bradley's son; born in Georgia 12 Nov. 1738.
129. Breara, John—Age 18; servt. to Will. Horton, Esq.; embark'd 2 Dec. 1735; arrived 2 Feb. 1735-6.
130. Brigham, Geo.—A grant of 100 acres was made him 23 July 1734.
131. Bright, Margt.—W. of Humfrey Bright. Eloped from her husband before 16 Jan. 1737-8 and said to keep company with Joseph Watson.
132. Britain, Cha.—Arrived 31 Oct. 1733; lot 113 in Savannah. On 4 May 1734 he let his house for 7 years to Tho. Neal, and on the 1 Jan. 1736-7 his 5 acre lot to Hen. Moulton for 2 years at 7£ p. ann., and lived inmate on lot 176 afterwds. went to Carolina for debt. Quitted 9 Dec. 1738.
133. ——, Hannah, w.
134. ——, Eliz., d.
135. ——, Will., son.
136. Britain, Francis—Servt. to Adrian Loyer; arrived 12 Mar. 1733-4.
137. Brodie, John—Freeholder at Abercorn where he succeeded to Earl Piercy Hill's lot, 1738, and in 1738 planted 11 acres.
138. Brodie, John—Born in Georgia. Dead 1740.
139. Brooks, Ja. Tho.—Son of Fra. & Anne Brooks; born in Georgia Oct. 1738.
140. ——, Juda—D. of Ditto; twin sister; born in Georgia Oct. 1738.
141. Brooks, Richd.—Servt. to Jo. Vandeplank; arrived 21 Aug. 1734.
142. Brown, Anne — Servt. to Widow Hedges; arrived 1 Aug. 1734.
143. Brown, Jeanne—Servt. to Jo. Houston.
144. Brown, Jo., Esq.—Settled at Highgate on a grant of 100 acres made him 2 Oct. 1735. Try'd for killing his servt. but by managmt. was cleared. In the Colony the end of the year 1746.
145. ——, [?], w.—In the Colony the end of the year 1746.
146. ——, [?], child—Dead 8 Dec. 1738.
147. ——, Archib. Towers—Son of John Brown, Esq.; born in Georgia; dead 8 Dec. 1738.
148. Brown, Mathew—Embark'd 26 Feb. 1736-7.
149. Brown, Saml., junr.—Indian Trader. Inmate at Savannah on lot 51. Son of Saml. Brown of Augusta, Indian Trader, who on 14 June 1736 had orders from Mr. Oglethorp for a 500 acres lot and house in Fort Augusta.
150. Bunkle, George—Servt. to Joseph Wardrope; arrived 21 Aug. 1734; lot 179 in Savannah. After his service under Jos. Wardrope this lot was granted him in 1736 but continued with Wardrope till Aug. 1738. In the Colony the end of the year 1746. Quitted to Carolina May 1742.
151. Burges, [?]—D. of James Baillou; born in Georgia.
152. Burges, Joseph—Embarked 20 Oct. 1735; of Darien: Slayn at the seige

of Augustine June 1740, & left a wife & child at Darien living 6 May 1741. Dead June 1740.

153. ——, Margt., w.—Margt. Burges widow of Joseph. Resident at Darien 6 May 1741.

154. ——, James, son—Born in Georgia. James Burgess their son 4 years & 3 months old 6 May 1741.

155. Burgholder, Michael—Arrived 1735. Settled at Hampstead and very industrious. In the Colony the end of the year 1746.

156. ——, Margt., d.—Servt. to Patrick Houston.

157. ——, Michl., son—His lot improved by his father, the same joyning his. In the Colony the end of the year 1746.

158. ——, [?]—W. of Michl, Junr. & 5 children more. In the Colony the end of the year 1746.

159. Burnes, John—Servt. to Hugh Anderson.

160. Burnes, Robt.—Servt. to Patrick Tailfer.

161. Burnside, Margt. Bovey—W. of Ja. Burnside. Upon the forfeiture of Tho. Pratt Lot 33 was granted her 5 May 1735. She marry'd Ja. Burnside 12 March 1736-7, and lived with him at Rotton Possum. Dead 26 Sept. 1742.

162. Burton, John—Carpenter; arrived 26 May 1734; lot 203 in Savannah. In May 1737 he had fell'd cleard and fenc'd 5 acres yet the hogs destroying his crop, he left his lot same year, and is an inmate on lot 225. A rioter in open court 20 Oct. 1737. Run away to Carolina Aug. 1742.

163. Burton, John
164. Burton, Tho.
165. Bush, Geo.
166. Butler, Lawrence—Servt. to A. Johnson.

167. Byers, Will.—Servt. to Will. & Hugh Sterling; arrived 30 June 1734.

168. Cadman, Hanah—D. of John & Hannah; born in Georgia 8 Jan. 1733-4.

169. Callis, Benj.—Servt. to Cha. Pury.

170. Calloway [?]—Inft. child of Ja. & Eliz.; born in Georgia.

171. Calvin, Ja.—Servt. to Petr. Houston; arrived 1 Aug. 1734; lot 201 in Savannah. Servt. at first to Patrick Houston: afterwds. this lot was granted him. He lives mostly out of the Colony. In May 1737 he had fenced 5 acres & ½, felld and cleard 5, and planted 3½ from whence he had 60 bushels of Ind. corn, 12 of pease.

172. Calwell, Jo.—Son of John; born in Georgia.

173. ——, Constance—D. of John; born in Georgia.

174. Cameron, Alexr.—Embark'd 20 Oct. 1735. Of Darien: Slayn at the seige of Augustine June 1740, & left only a widow of Darien 6 May 1741. Dead June 1740.

175. ——, [?], w.—Wid. of Alexr. In Darien I suppose 6 May 1741.

176. Cameron, Margt.—Servt. to Abrm. Minas.

177. Campbell, Colin, gent.—Age 27; embark'd 20 Oct. 1735; arrived 10 Jan. 1735-6.

178. Campbell, Edwd.—Servt. to Jo. Cundall; arrived 10 Jan. 1733-4. A Dutch woman. Cook on pay at 4£ p ann for the Trust Servts. at Frederica March 1738-9.

179. Campbell, James—Lot 221 in Savannah. He ran away with the Revd. Mr. John Wesley 3 Dec. 1737. This lot formerly belong'd to Will Cookey who resign'd it for lot 9 being swamp and overflow'd. An idle fellow & in debt. He return'd and was in Georgia 7 Jan. 1740/1 and was employd to read prayers for want of a minis-

ter. Run away for debt but returned.
180. Camport, Barbara—Widow employd in the Fort.
181. Camport, Christian — Labourer employd in the Fort.
182. Camuse, Jo. Joseph—Son of Jacob Camuse, Senr.; born in Georgia.
183. ——, Margaret—D. of ditto; born in Georgia.
184. Camuse, Isaac—Son of Ja.; born in Georgia.
185. ——, Jacob, junr.—Son of Ja.; born in Georgia.
186. Canard, David—Servt. to Hugh Sterling.
187. Cannon, Anne—D. of Ri. & Mary; born in Georgia 10 July 1733; dead 7 Aug. 1733.
188. Cardiff, Patrick—Servt. to Tho. Saltar; arrived 17 Dec. 1733.
189. Carpenter, Ri.—Servt. to Tho. Hawkins.
190. Carré, Edwd.—Servt. to Tho. Fletcher; arrived 21 July 1733; run away to Charlestown.
191. Carter, Will.—Servt. to Jos. Hethrington; arrived 7 July 1733.
192. Carteret, Ja., Esq.—Formerly officer in the fr. service. Had a grant of 500 acres 22 March 1737-8 and took it up in the Southern Division near Frederica. Col. Oglethorp paid him 10£ sterl. for cedar posts for the Trustees service 29 May 1739. Qy. might not the Trustees servts. done this? Ret. to England with resolution not to go back April 1741. Run away to Engld. April 1741.
193. ——, [?]—W. of Ja. Carteret, Esq. Return'd to England. Quitted Feb. 1739/40.
194. Carthy, Ja.—Servt. to Tho. Causton; arrived 22 Jan. 1734-5.
195. Carwell, Margt.—D. of James & Margt.; born in Georgia 12 June 1733; dead 7 Sept. 1733.

196. ——, Mary—D. of ditto; born in Georgia 28 July 1734; dead 29 Aug. 1734.
197. Chambers, Jo.—Servt. to A. Johnson; arrived 7 Mar. 1733-4.
198. Chancey, Ri.—Servt. in the Scout boat. For a time servt. to Fra. Delgrass.
199. Chapman, Jo.—Servt. to Phil. Bishop; arrived 7 July 1733.
200. Charles, [?]—Servt.
201. Charles, Charles—Boy.
202. Charles, Jacob—Son of Charles; born in Georgia.
*203. Charnock, Mary—Servt. to Noble Jones; arrived 1 Feb. 1732-3.
204. Chensack, Danl.—Son of James; born in Georgia 21 Dec. 1733; dead 17 June 1734.
205. Chisholme, Alexr. of Invernes—Age 26; servt. to Farqr. Mcgilivray; embark'd 20 Oct. 1735; arrived 10 Jan. 1735-6; run away to Carolina Aug. 1742.
206. Chisholme, Alexr. of Dronach—Age 17; servt. to Mr. Mackay of Scourie; embark'd 20 Oct. 1735; arrived 10 Jan. 1735-6.
207. Chisholme, Margt.—Age 22; servt. to J. Sinclair; embark'd 20 Oct. 1735; arrived 10 Jan. 1735-6.
208. Christe, Maria Christina Eliz.—D. of Jo. & Cath. Eliz. Christe; born in Georgia Nov. 1738. Saltsburger.
209. Christie, Eliz.—W. of Thomas; lot 192 in Savannah. In England. The lot was granted in 1736. Abst. in Engld.
210. Clancey, Ri.—Servt. to Wid. Germain; arrived 10 Jan. 1733-4. Sentenc'd 100 lashes for assault, abusing the constable, & prophaning the Sabbath 16 Sept. 1734; also fyn'd 0.2.6 for assault 31 Sept. 1734.
211. Clark, Donald—Age 23; of Dorris.

* Same as Carnock, p. 11, no. 284.

Farmer; embark'd 20 Oct. 1735; arrived 10 Jan. 1735-6.
212. Clark, Donald—Age 23; of Dorris. Farmer; embark'd 20 Oct. 1735; arrived 10 Jan. 1735-6. [Probably the same as No. 211.]
213. Clark, Donald—Age 42; of Tongie; embark'd 20 Oct. 1735; arrived 10 Jan. 1735-6. Slayn at Augustine June 1740 and left a wife & 4 children living at Darien 6 May 1741.
214. ——, Barbara Grey—Age 40; w. Resident at Darien 6 May 1741.
215. ——, Alexr., son—Age 15; dead as suppos'd.
216. ——, Angus, son—Age 5. Living at Darien 6 May 1746.
217. ——, Barbara, d.—Age 2; dead I suppose.
218. ——, Geo., son—Age 13; dead I suppose.
219. ——, Hugh, son—Age 12. A soldier in the highland Independt. Company, and return'd as such 6 May 1741.
220. ——, Will., son—Age 8. Living at Darien 6 May 1746.
221. Clark, Elias—Son of Hen. & Anne; born in Georgia 13 Mar. 1732-3; dead 28 Oct. 1733.
222. Clark, Eliz.—Child. servt. to Will. Bradley.
223. Clark, Henry—Son of Hen. & Anne; born in Georgia 17 Sept. 1733; dead 9 Sept. 1733 [sic.].
224. Clark, Hugh—Age 21; of Dorris. Farmer; embark'd 20 Oct. 1735; arrived 10 Jan. 1735-6. A soldier in the highland Independt. Company, and return'd as such 6 May 1741. is Serjt. of ye Compy.
225. Clark, Hugh—Born in Georgia. Clark, Hugh 3 years 3 months old 6 May 1741.
226. Clark, John—Born in Georgia; lot 53 in Savannah. Clark, Jo. 3 years 9 months old 6 May 1741. Dead ——.
227. Clark, Will.—Born in Georgia. Clark, Will. 2 years 6 months old 6 May 1741.
228. Clarke, John.—Lot 73 (or 93) in Savannah. He marry'd the widow Dearn and lives on her Lot 29. Appointed Secy. for the Indian affairs 3 May 1738. He went over with Col. Oglethorpe 1738. Died at Frederica. Dead ——.
229. ——, [?], w.
230. Cleamont, Benj.—Servt. to Jo. Coates; embark'd 10 Sept. 1733; arrived 16 Dec. 1733.
231. Clements, Tho.—Servt.
232. Clifford, Edwd.
233. Close, Georgia—D. of Hen. & Hannah; born in Georgia 17 Mar. 1732-3; dead 28 Dec. 1733.
234. Cochran, Ja.—Lt. Col.; arrived 7 May 1738. Grant of 500 acres made him 25 Nov. 1737. He had leave in 1739 to come over & prossecute Capt. Hugh Mackay, and he is not yet allow'd by his majesty to return.
235. Cohen, David—Jew; very idle; arrived 10 July 1733; lot 63 in Savannah.
236. Cohen, David Delmont—Jew; arrived 10 July 1733.
237. ——, Rachel, w.—Jew; dead 29 Mar. 1734.
238. ——, Abigail, d.—Jew.
239. ——, Grace, d.—Jew.
240. ——, Isaac, son—Jew.
241. Collyer, Cha.—Servt. to Rogr. Lacy; arrived 1 Feb. 1733-4.
242. Collyer, Ja.—Servt. to Tho. Fawsset; arrived 19 Jan. 1733-4.
243. Colman, Solomon—Jew.
244. Combs, Saml.—Servt. to Elisha Dobree; arrived 30 June 1734. Bought of Dobree by Tho. Causton. Indictmen of theft found agst. him 2 Oct. 1734.
245. Compass, Isaac—Jew.

246. ——, Rebecca, w.—D. of Tho. Young.
247. Compass, Jacob—Jew.
248. Cook, James—Servt. to Elisha Dobree.
249. Cook, Lawrence.
250. ——, Eliz., w.
251. ——, James, son—Born in Georgia 25 July 1734; dead 29 Oct. 1734.
252. Cook, Will—Majr. to Oglethorps Regimt. Arriv'd May 7, 1738. Grant made him of 500 acres Nov. 25, 1737.
253. Cooksey, Will.—Lot 9 in Savannah. He left this lot being swamp overflow'd, and settled for a time at Grantham. He is indebted to the Trustees and in 1739 went to Carolina where tis supposed he intends to settle & turn mercht. Quitted 1739.
254. ——, Sarah, w.
255. Coole, John—Servt. to Patrick Tailfer; quitted 1740.
256. Cooling, Geo.—Servt. to Patrick Tailfer; embark'd 14 Oct. 1735; arrived 1 Feb. 1735-6.
257. Cooper, [?]—Servt.
258. Cooper, Mary—Wid. of Joseph Cooper; lot 20 in Savannah. Upon her husbands death, she let her lot for 10.7.0 p. ann. and went for England, where she had leave to stay. Abst. 24 Feb. 1736-7.
259. Cornock, Ja.—Plasterer; lot 188 in Savannah; arrived 1 Feb. 1732-3. Went to Carolina. He would have defrauded Bryan Loyer for work done & was cast 7 July 1737. Return'd to Savannah and work'd at the parsonage house in June 1740. Quitted since 9 Dec. 1738 but was ret. June 1740.
260. Cornwall, Tho.—Arrived 16 May 1733; dead 21 July 1733.
261. Courtney, Philip. Recomended by the E of Egmont to Coll. Oglethorp & settled at Frederica, but I know not on what lot. Col. Oglethorp advanc'd him 7.10.0 to set up a shop 29 April 1739.
262. Cox, John — Inmate at Savannah. Found guilty of misprision of treason 10 Mar. 1734-5 & whipt 60 lashes.
263. Cox, Mary—D. of Will. & Frances; born in Georgia 7 Oct. 1733; dead 17 Oct. 1733.
264. Craig, Will.—Servt.
265. Creah, Tho.—Servt. to Will. Millichamp; arrived 15 March 1733-4.
266. Crookshanks, Rob.—Servt. to Farqr. Mcgilivray; embark'd 20 Oct. 1735; arrived 10 Jan. 1735-6. Col. Oglethorp writes July 1739 that he was grown blind in the Trustees service and therefore he allow'd him 5 pence a day subsistence: But he went from Scotland a Servt. to Farquar Macgilivray not on the Trustees acct. and how he came to fall upon the Trust or when I know not. Alive at Darien 6 May 1741.
267. Croom, Benj.—Absent 24 Feb. 1736-7.
268. Cross, Elenor—A child. Daughter I suppose to Tho. & Judith Cross. Inmate at Savannah on lot 22.
269. Cross, John—Servt. to Will Millichamp; embark'd 15 Nov. 1733; arrived 15 Mar. 1733-4.
270. Cross, Thomas—Soldier; lot 22 in Savannah. Marry'd the widow Judith Clark 29 June 1734. He was in Independt. Compy. Soldier at St. Simons Fort, and run away Dec. 1738. Run away Dec. 1738. In the Colony the end of the year 1746.
271. ——, Judith Clark—Wid. his wife; arrived 29 June 1734.
272. Cross, Will.—Lot 217 in Savannah. His lot was swamp overflow'd. Dead 1738.
273. ——, Elizabeth, w.—Re-marry'd to Jo. Teasdale, who lives with her on her lot.
274. Cruise, Edwd.—Servt. to Jo. Vande-

plank; arrived 10 Jan. 1733-4. Whipt 60 lashes for misprision of treason March 1734/5.
275. Cundall, Jo.—Senr.; embark'd 1733; Lot 52 in Savannah. Fyn'd for scandal 3.0.0, Aug. 19th 1734. Run away none knows where. Run away June 1737.
276. Curry, Geo.—Indian Trader; arrived 1736. He had a house and 500 acres mark'd out for him at Augusta 1736 14th June & is an Indian Trader.
277. Cuthbert, Geo.—of Inverness. Farmer; embark'd 20 Oct. 1735; arrived 10 Jan. 1735-6. Settled at Darien. I find him a cattle hunter with 6 servants from 18 Sept. 1738 to 18 June 1739 at the annual expence of 174 £ and Mr. Oglethorp writes that it is absolutely necessary to continue this charge.
278. Cuthbert, Jo.—Run away to Carolina Aug. 1742.
279. Cuthbert, Jo.—Age 31; of Draikes, gent.; embark'd 20 Oct. 1735; arrived 10 Jan. 1735-6. Grant of 500 acres made him 3 Sept. 1735, which he took up at Josephs town, but afterwards abandon'd, and settled at Darien or new Inverness. In 1736 Mr. Oglethorp made him Comander of Fort St. Andrews. Dead 16 Nov. 1739.
280. ——, [?], w.—embark'd 24 June 1737; arrived 20 Nov. 1737.
281. Dadd, Tho.
282. Dalton, John—Lot 3N. in Frederica. He marry'd the wid. Joyce. Germain. Died 1738-9.
283. ——, Joyce Germain, w.—arrived Feb. 1735-6. Upon her 2d. husbands death she came by leave to England with John & Mary her children & tis supposed will not return. Quitted & went to England 1738-9 with her children.
284. ——, Mary, d.—Born in Georgia 1738.
285. Danner, Jacob—Age 35; Tinker. Germ. Swiss; embark'd 21 Sept. 1741; arrived 4 Dec. 1741. Settled on a grant on the S. E. of Hampstead.
286. Dasher, Christr., Senr.
287. ——, Christr., junr.—A boy.
288. Davant, Ja.—Son of John & Eliz.; born in Georgia; 17 Sept. 1733; dead 19 Feb. 1733-4.
289. Davis, Catherine—D. of John & Frances; born in Georgia 22 Jan. 1734-5; dead 22 Jan. 1734-5.
290. Davis, Morgan—Servt. to Rogr. Lacey; arrived 1 Feb. 1733-4; lot 13 in Savannah. He marry'd the widow Amy Johnson 26 March 1735 who dying he deserted the Colony. Dead 1738.
291. ——, Amy Johnson, w.—Dead.
292. Davis, Richard—Lot 210 in Savannah. An inmate on lot 144 in 1738. Dead Jan. 1738-9.
293. ——, Mary, w—Dead Jan. 1738-9.
294. Davison, John—Son of Samuel & Susanna; born in Georgia.
295. Dawson, Tho.—Servt. to Patrick Houston; arrived 1 Aug. 1734; out of his time.
296. Dean, Ellen—W. of Ja. Dean, junr.; lot 139 in Savannah. Fyn'd for defamation 0.6.8. 28 July 1735.
297. ——, Hellena, d.
298. ——, Tho., son.
299. Dearn, John—Arrived 1 Feb. 1732-3; lot 29 in Savannah. Appointed 3 bailif of Savannah 13 Sept. 1735 & took his seat 7 Oct. 1736. Possest of his lot 21 Dec. 1733. Re-marry'd to Eliz. Hotsey 20 May 1735. Dead 1 July 1737.
300. ——, Sarah, 1st w.—Dead 6 July 1733.
301. ——, Eliz. Hotsey, 2d. w.—Re-marry'd

to John Clarke who lives with her on her lot.

302. De Costa, Isaac—Jew; arrived 10 July 1733.
303. De Crasto, Jacob Lopes—Jew; arrived 10 July 1733; Lot 122 in Savannah. Put in possession of his lot 21 Dec. 1733.
304. ——, Sipura, w.—Jew.
305. Delafons, Susana Rivet—W. of Geo. Delafons; dead.
306. Delany, Peter—Trust. Servt.; arrived 10 Jan. 1733-4.
307. Deleneira, David—Jew; arrived 10 July 1733.
308. Delyon, Abrm.—Jew; arrived 10 July 1733; lot 74 in Savannah. Fyn'd for assault and battery 5.0.6. Sept. 28th 1734. An industrous man in 1736 he thoroughly cultivated 4 acres, which produced 50 bushells of Indian corn, 50 of pease & 24 of rice. In 1738 The Trustees lent him 200£ upon security & on certain beneficial conditions for the Province to cultivate vines.
309. ——, Hester, w.—Jew.
310. ——, Rachel, d.—Jew; born in Georgia 2 Aug. 1734.
311. ——, Rebecca, d.—Jew; born in Georgia.
312. Demetry, [?]—Master or owner of a Periagua that for some time was made use of by the Trustees at Frederica.
313. De miranda, David—Jew; arrived 10 July 1733; dead Dec. 1733.
314. De miranda, Jacob—Jew; arrived 10 July 1733. Settled at Hampstead. A very industrious man.
315. Dempster, Geo.—Servt. to Patrick Houston; arrived 1 Aug. 1734; dead Aug. 1738.
316. Denys, Patrick—Tr. Servant; arrived 10 Jan. 1733-4.
317. Derricoat, Jo.—Arrived 2 April 1734. Had possession of his lot 2 April 1734, and settled at Tybee.
318. Dester, Peter—Arrived 1734.
319. Detzer, Anne—Servt. to Will. Cooksey.
320. Detzer, Christr.—Servt. to Will. Cooksey.
321. Detzer, Mathew—Servt. to Will. Cooksey.
322. Deval, Isaac—Jew. Settled at Hampstead. A very idle fellow. He first possest Lot 78 in Savannah which he gave up for another at Hampstead.
323. Dice, [?]—Son of Jacob Dice; born in Georgia; dead 22 Nov. 1742.
324. Dietzius, Andr. Godfrey—Arrived 28 Dec. 1734. He had leave to surrender his grant of 500 acres which was made him 7 Oct. 1734. A Moravian. Quitted to settle in Purysburg with his family.
325. ——, Matalena, w.—Moravian.
326. ——, Anna Amelia, d.—Moravian.
327. ——, Torodea, d.—Moravian.
328. Dixon, Ja.—Joyn'd the Colony, when I know not. He was return'd dead 1740.
329. Dobree, Elisha—Arrived 30 June 1734; lot 13 in Savannah; lot 21S. in Frederica. He came from Carolina & bought the widow Sams lott in Savannah, but afterwards settled at Frederica where he was clerk of the stores until the Trustees shut them up at Michlemass 1739. Quitted Savannah for Fred.
330. Dockharty, Cornel—Indian Trader. On 14 June 1736 Mr. Oglethorp order'd him a 500 acre lot & house in Fort Augusta.
331. Dodding, Jo.—Servt. to Tho. Causton; embark'd 10 Jan. 1733-4.
332. Dormer, James—Arrived 21 Oct. 1733; lot 151 in Savannah. In 1736 he had fell'd & planted 4 acres &

fenced 5 but afterwards neglected his lot & lived inmate on Lot 1.
333. Douglass, David—Lot 170 in Savannah. His lot was granted to him in 1736. Cost in auction of 50£ sterl. debt due to Ja. Muier for 2 years rent 7 July 1737. A factious man: & went to Carolina for fear of the Spaniards 30 Aug. 1740. Quitted 30 Aug. 1740.
334. ——, Jannet, his sister.
335. Douglass, Willm.—Servt. to Patrick Tailfer; arrived 1 Aug. 1734.
336. Downs, Anne—Servt. to Jo. West.
337. Drisdale, James—Servt. to Hugh Anderson.
338. Duché, Andrew—Potter; lot 71 in Savannah. An industrious Potter, and had encouragemt. from the Trustees to carry on his business. The lot belonged formerly to Fra. Lynch who ran away for debt. in 1740 he resignd the place of Constable, and turnd an outragious factioner.
339. ——, Mary, w.—Went to Carolina for fear of the Spaniards 1740. Quitted Sept. 1740 returned.
340. Dun, John—Arrived 28 Dec. 1734. He marry'd Cath. Leak 20 Feb. 1734-5 and afterwards run away. Run away 1734-5.
*341. Dunbar, [?]—W. of Patrick Houston.
342. Dunbar, George, Capt.—He had a grant of 500 acres which he took up at Josephstown: but afterwds. quitted it to settle at Darien. Now Lieut. in Oglethorp's Regiment.
343. Dunbar, John—Age 36; of Inverness. Farmer; embark'd 20 Oct. 1735; arrived 10 Jan. 1735-6; dead 1740.
344. Dunbar, John—Lot 181 in Savannah. He went to England about Dec. 1737. Went to England Dec. 1737.
345. Dunbar, Margt.—Servt. to Will. Bradley.
346. Duncan, John—Servt. to Patrick Houston; arrived 1 Aug. 1734. Servt. at first to Patrick Houston, but afterwards bought by A. Johnson 21 Jan. 1734-5.
347. Duncannon, [?]—Orphan at the Orphan house; quitted to Carolina May 1742.
348. Duncel, Agnese—Servt. to Patrick Graham.
349. Duren, Fra.—Servt. to Edwd. Jenkins; embark'd 15 June 1733; arrived 29 Aug. 1733; dead 1740.
350. Dutton, James—Run away to Carolina Aug. 1742.
351. ——, [?], w.—She dead since.
352. ——, [?]—Child of James Dutton —Dead July 1742.
353. Dutwell, Abrm.—Servt.
354. Elbert, Will.—Servt. to Jos. Wardrope; lot 180 in Savannah. His lot swamp overflow'd. Let to him in 1736. Left ye Colony with his family after ye Spanish invasion of Georgia 1742. Abst. 24 Feb. 1736-7 ret. 1738 but run away to Carolina in Aug. 1742.
355. ——, Sarah, w.
356. ——, Eliz., d.—Born in Ga.—Run away also.
357. ——, [?], d.—Born in Ga.; run away also.
358. Elgar, Fra.—Servt. to Phil. Bishop; arrived 7 July 1733.
359. Ellig, [?], 2 m. old—Son of Tho. Ellig; born in Georgia; dead 27 Sept. 1742.
360. Elliot, Tho.—Servt. Convicted of theft and running away 26 March 1734.
361. Emery, Pet.—Pylot at Tybee. He came from Carolina, & marry'd Anne the widow of Michl. Germain 12 Jan. 1734-5. In right of his wife he cultivated this lot and in 1736 had from 5 acres—35 bushels of Indian corn, 20 of pease, 100 of potatoes, and 20 of rice. In 1739 he was establish'd Pylot at Tybee, and allow'd to keep a pub-

* Same as p. 79, no. 557.

lick house there. A most industrious man. Drownd 1740.

362. ——, Anne, Germain, w.—Lot 78 in Savannah.

363. England, Will.—Servt. to Fra. Lynch; arrived 27 Nov. 1733. Servt. first to Fra. Lynch, afterwards to John Amory.

364. Escobee, Sarah—Servt. to Fra. Lynch; arrived 27 Nov. 1733. At first servt. to Fra. Lynch, then transfer'd to Nuner Henriques, & lastly servt. to Isaac King Clark.

365. Evans, Andrew—Servt.; embark'd 30 Sept. 1733; arrived 16 Dec. 1733; shot himself by accident 26 July 1739.

366. Eyre, Tho.—Lt. in Oglethorpe's Regimant; lot 9N. in Frederica. Agent to the Cherokees.

367. ——, [?], w.—D. of Lt. Ed Cook; quitted to England before Aug. 1741.

368. Fage, Lewis—Son of Peter; born in Georgia.

369. ——, Fra.—Son of Ditto; born in Georgia 30 June 1734; dead 8 July 1734.

370. ——, Peter—Son of Ditto; born in Georgia.

371. Fallowfeild, Jo.—Arrived 15 Feb. 1733-4; lot 136 in Savannah. Fyn'd for defamation four pence 28 July 1735. Naval Officer 3 Feb. 1738/9 & on 30 May 1739 made 3d Bailif of Savanah in Robert Gilberts room. In 1736 he had fully improved 15 acres, from whence he had 95 bushels of Indian corn, 40 of potatoes, & 22 of rice. He let his greatest house, and lived much at a plantation some miles in the country. Succeeded 1st Constable on Noble Jones removel 24 Oct. 1738. Turn'd a violent malecontent 1740. He married about March 1734/5 but I know not who. Quitted to Carolina 1742.

372. ——, Eliz., w.—Quitted to Carolina 1742.

373. ——, [?], son—Born in Georgia; run away with his father.

374. ——, [?], son—Born in Georgia; run away with his father.

375. ——, Sarah, d.—Born in Georgia Nov. 1738; run away to Charlestown—1742.

376. Fanner, Ja.

377. Fawset, Tho.—Gent.; embark'd 21 Sept. 1733; arrived 12 Jan. 1733-4. He had a grant made him of 500 acres 4 July 1733. Dead 14 July 1735.

378. ——, Eliz., d.

379. Ferguson, Tho.—Servt.; arrived 8 June 1737.

380. Ferguson, Will.—Master of the Scout boat.

381. Fernando, Judith—Jew; arrived 10 July 1733. Sister to Abrm. Molina, & lives with him on Lot 69 in Savannah.

382. Fisher, Will.—A minor. An orphan. Has a lot at Hampstead which Michl. Burgholder takes care of.

383. Fitzgerald, Mary—Servt. to Jo. Carwell; arrived 10 Jan. 1733-4.

384. Fitzpatrick, Cath.—Servt. to the Trust. Convicted of a bastard child 26 May 1735.

385. Fletcher, Tho.—Embark'd 4 April 1733; arrived 21 July 1733; lot 98 in Savannah. Qy. if this be the same wch. Hen. Fletcher to whom a grant of 200 acres was past 28 March 1733? Quitted with his family being sick & went to Charlestown.

386. ——, [?], w.

387. ——, [?], d.

388. Flin, John—Servt. to Wid. Thibaut; arrived 10 Jan. 1733-4.

389. Fling, Isaac—Servt.; arrived 10 Jan. 1733-4. Irish Transport servt. condemn'd 100 lashes for stealing 31 May 1735.

390. Fontain, John—Arrived 31 Jan. 1734-5; lot 118 in Savannah. He marry'd Magdalene the wid. of Jeremy Papot 31 Jan. 1734-5. Run away 1737.
391. ——, Magdalene, w.—Embark'd 10 Sept. 1733; arrived 16 Dec. 1733. Run away 1737.
392. Forbes, Hugh—Servt. to Will. & Hugh Sterling; embark'd 20 Oct. 1735; arrived 10 Jan. 1735-6.
393. Forbes, John—Age 26; Sert. to Jo. Cuthbert of Draikes.
394. Foster, Elisha—Embark'd 10 Sept. 1733; arrived 17 Dec. 1733; lot 80 in Savannah. He was made Tything man in 1736.
395. ——, Mary, w.
396. Foster, Geo. — Embark'd 17 May 1737; arrived 20 Nov. 1737.
397. Fowler, Denis—Tr. Servt.; arrived 10 Jan. 1733-4; dead 1 May 1735.
398. Fowler, John—Convicted of enticing servants away 16 March 1733-4.
399. Fox, John—Servt. to Noble Jones; arrived 10 Jan. 1733-4. Irish Transport sentenc'd 60 lashes for stealing 31 May 1735. Also for false imprisonment, and combination to extort money 2.0.0. 12 July 1735.
400. Francis, Will.—P—— at 100£ sterl. *p. ann.* between Savannah & Darien 1738. A Ranger at Fort Arguile at 24£ *p. ann.* as p. Col. Oglethorps acct. he was paid to 19 April 1739, and Col. Oglethorp says these rangers are absolutely necessary. They are employ'd in driving up cattel, & catching run away servants for which tsk they are pd. the pt. of their duty. Made Lt. of Rangers by Col. Oglethorp. He marryd a Dutch woman in 1741.
401. ——, [?], d.—Born in the Colony.
402. Frazer, Donald—Servt. to A. Johnson; arrived 7 May 1734. Sentenc'd 30 lashes for assault 1734.
403. Frazer, Donald of Abercour—Servt. to Patrick Grant; embark'd 20 Oct. 1735; arrived 10 Jan. 1735-6.
404. Frazer, Donald, of Inverness—Age 20; Servt. to Alexr. Mackintosh; embark'd 20 Oct. 1735; arrived 10 Jan. 1735-6.
405. Frazer, Donald of Ditto—Age 22; Servt. to Jo. Cuthbert of Draikes; embark'd 20 Oct. 1735; arrived 10 Jan. 1735-6.
406. Frazer, Donald of Kingussie—Age 25; servt. to Jo. Mackintosh; embark'd 20 Oct. 1735; arrived 10 Jan. 1735-6.
407. Frazer, Thomas — Servt. to Patrick Houston; arrived 1 Aug. 1734. In the Colony the end of the year 1746. Out of his time.
408. Frazer, Will.—Servt. to A. Johnson; arrived 7 May 1734.
409. Free, John—Servt. to Robt. Gilbert.
410. Fretshaw, Hen.—Servt.
411. Fritz, Cath.—D. of Hen. Fritz; born in Georgia; dead; Burnt alive by accident 19 Nov. 1742.
412. Frocis, David—Jew.
413. ——, Hester, w.—Jew.
414. Fullerton, Geo.—Servt. to Hellen Mackay; embark'd 14 Oct. 1735; arrived Feb. 1735-6.
415. Fullerton, Robt.—Servt. to Will & H. Sterling.
416. Furzer, Robt. Senr.—Servt. to Will & Hugh Sterling; arrived 1 Aug. 1734.
417. Fyffe, Rachl.—Servt. to Patrick Houston; arrived 1 Aug. 1734.
418. Gaffney, Michl.—Servt. to ye Wid. Hodges; arrived 10 Jan. 1733-4. Convicted of theft and running away 26 March 1734.
419. Gallant, Cha.—Servt.; arrived 8 Feb. 1733-4. Settled at Tybee.
420. Gallimore, Christr.—Servt. to Alexr. Ross; embark'd 31 Oct. 1734; arrived 28 Dec. 1734; dead 1740.

421. Galloway, James—Lot 173 in Savannah.
422. ——, Eliz., w.
423. Garlant, Geo.—M. El. Peters. He marry'd the widow Eliz. Peters 3 Dec. 1738 & quitted the Colony with her the same month. Quitted 1738.
424. Garret, Hen. M. D.—Lot 127 in Savannah. He became posest of this lot May 1737, but in 1738 flung it up. He still practiceth Physick in Savannah. Lot vacant Feb. 1738-9. Mr. Wesley represented him a direct Deist 17 June 1737. Flung up his lot.
425. Gascoign, Ja.—Capt. of Man of War. A grant of 500 acres made him 24 Sept. 1735, on which he lives being turn'd out of the Kings service for cruelty to his seamen 1738. In 1739 he had leave to sell it to another person for 120£ & ret. to Engld.
426. Gayr, Geo.—Servt. to Anne Morison; arrived 15 July 1734.
427. Gedd, John.
428. Geddes, Ja.—Servt. to Edwd. Jenkins.
429. Germain, Michael — Arrived Feb. 1735-6; dead the day of arrival.
430. ——, Joice, w.—Re-mar. to Jo. Dalton; arrived Feb. 1735-6; lot 3N. in Frederica. Re-marry'd to John Dalton & settled with him at Frederica on Lot 3. After his death 1738/9 she return'd with her children to England where she continues. Quitted 1739.
431. ——, Jo., s.—Of John Dalton her 2d. husb.; born in Georgia; quitted.
432. Germain, Peter — Arrived 1 Feb. 1732-3; lot 78 in Savannah; dead 13 July 1733.
433. Germain, Will.—Br. of Michael; lot 23N. in Frederica. A laborious man on his lot; but I suppose quitted cultivation being Patroon of a Scout boat June 1741.
434. Gibbes, Isaac—Embark'd 19 Nov. 1737; arrived 14 Jan. 1737/8. Settled at Abercorn, but left his land & is an inmate in Savannah.
435. ——, Mary, w.
436. ——, Isaac, son.
437. ——, [?], son.
438. ——, Philip, son.
439. Gideon, Benj.—Jew; arrived 10 July 1733. Settled at Hampstead, but quitted his lot being a very idle fellow. Drown'd 1738.
440. Gilbert, Robt.—Taylor; arrived 16 May 1733; lot 50 in Savannah. 3d. Bailif of Savannah 30 May 1738 but at his own request removed 30 May 1739. He took possession of his lot 21 Dec. 1733. He returnd to England, but on 22 March 1736/7 returnd again to Georgia, and gave a note to the Trustees to repay the expence of his passage. His wife and he turn'd Methodists, and quitted the Colony. Quitted 19 Aug. 1740.
441. ——, Margt., w.—Quitted 19 Aug. 1740.
442. ——, Eliz., d.—Marry'd to Will. Moore July 1733.
443. Giovanoli, Eliz.—D. of Jo. and Maria; born in Georgia; dead Sept. 1742.
444. Givons, [?].
445. Glass, John—Age 18; Servt.; embark'd 20 Oct. 1735; arrived 10 Jan. 1735-6.
446. Glen, Archibald—Servt. to Will & H. Sterling; arrived 1 Aug. 1734.
447. Godleay, Jo.—Servt. to Jos. Hethrington; arrived 7 July 1733; disch. & went to England.
448. Goldwyre, [?]—Son of Jo. Goldwyre; born in Georgia. Car. to Carolina by parents Aug. 1742.
449. ——, [?]—D. of Ditto; born in Georgia. Car. to Carolina by parents Aug. 1742.
450. ——, [?]—D. of Ditto; born in

Georgia. Car. to Carolina by parents Aug. 1742.
451. Goodale, Tho.—Indian Trader; lot 185 in Savannah. His lot was granted him 1736. In the Colony the end of the year 1746.
452. Gordon, Margt. — Servt. to Cha. Pury.
453. Gordon, Phil.—Servt. to Jo. Penrose.
454. Gordon, Robert—Servt. to Tho. Young.
455. Gough, Saml.—Servt. to Harry Buckley; embark'd Oct. 1737; arrived 16 Jan. 1737/8.
456. Gough, Will., Senr.—Arrived 19 June 1733. He had a grant of 80 acres 21 Feb. 1732-3. Dead 6 Sept. 1733.
457. ——, Martha, w.—Dead 23 July 1733.
458. ——, Will., junr.—Arrived 19 June 1733; lot 65 in Savannah. Besides his town lot, he had a grant of 80 acres 21 Feb. 1732-3 but was an idle fellow. His 2d. wife was Susannah widow of Geo. Delafons whom he marry'd 24 Sept. 1735. He was Tything man 1736, but ran to Carolina. Run away 3 Dec. 1737.
459. ——, Mary, w.—Dead 11 July 1735.
460. ——, Bearsly, son—Dead 14 Dec. 1733.
461. ——, Susana, 2d. w.—of William, junr.; embark'd 11 Sept. 1733; arrived 16 Dec. 1733. Widow of Geo. Delafons. Marry'd to Will. Gough junr. 24 Sept. 1735.
462. ——, Will., son.
463. Goulds, Ja.—Goulds (ja.) joyn'd the Colony: when I know not. Return'd. Dead 1740.
464. Graham, Patrick—Apothecary; lot 189 in Savannah. He neglects his own lot and rents lots 137. 211. On 19 May 1736 a grant of 100 acres was past to him. Marry'd Capt. Cuthberts sister 6 March 1739/40.

465. ——, [?], d.—Born in Georgia; dead 27 Sept. 1742.
466. Grant, [?], widow—Lot 9S. in Frederica.
467. Grant, Andrew—Gent.; arrived June 1734. A grant of 400 acres was made him 18 Oct. 1733 which he took up on O'geeky river but neglects it & lives inmate at Savannah. The place was call'd Sterlings bluff, and he and Will Sterling quitted it before Sept. 1737. He went to Carolina for fear of the Spaniards, and was a factious man. In England Jan. 1741/2. Quitted 30 Aug. 1740. Come to Engl. Jan. 1741-2.
468. ——, Joseph, son—Born in the Colony.
469. ——, [?], d.—Born in the Colony.
470. ——, Joseph—Son of Andrew; born in the Colony.
471. ——, [?]—D. of Andrew; born in the Colony.
472. Grant, Archibald—Servt. to Will. & H. Sterling; arrived 1 Aug. 1734.
473. Grant, Daniel—Servt. to Ri. Kirchiner.
474. Grant, Idow—Servt. to Will. Stephens, Esq.
475. Grant, James—Servt. to Will. Stephens, Esq.; out of his time.
476. Grant, John—Age 18; servt. to Patrick Grant; embark'd 20 Oct. 1735; arrived 10 Jan. 1735-6.
477. Grant, Lodowick—A trader in the Cherokee nation.
478. Grant, Margaret—Alive at Darien 6 May 1741.
479. Grant, Peter—Servt. to Tho. Causton.
480. Grant, Patrick—Age 24; of Aberlour. Farmer; embark'd 20 Oct. 1735; arrived 10 Jan. 1735-6; lot 166 in Savannah. A grant of 100 acres was made him 19 May 1736 and this lot was granted him same year, but he neglects both, & has taken 2 other lots in the town at rent from the owners. Tything

man 1738 and a pert sawcy fellow. Kill'd in duel 1740.
481. Grant, Sarah—Born in Georgia. Alive at Darien 6 May 1741 & then 2 years old.
482. Green, Hen.—Lot 158 in Savannah. Convicted of shooting other peoples hogs & converting them to his own use 26 May 1736. His lot was given him Oct. 1736, but not shewn to him till March following.
483. ——, Anne, w.—She came on some occasion to England, but return'd July 1738, and the Trustees pd. her passage back, to be repd. them.
484. Greeney, Abrm.—Labourer at the Fort.
485. Grenier, Andrew—Servt. to Andrew Duche.
486. Grenier, Mary—Servt. to Ditto.
487. Grey, Eliz.—Servt. to Jo. Baillie; arrived 1 Aug. 1734. Discharged her masters service and marry'd Geo. Sims 10 March 1734-5. Disch. Dead 1740.
488. ——, Mary, d.—Born in Georgia 15 Sept. 1734; dead Dec. 1734.
489. Grey, Will.—Agent with the Chickesaw & Utchea Indians.
490. Grimaldi, Cha.—Servt. to Ja. Burnside.
491. Grimshaw, Judith—W. of Jo. Grimshaw, Soldr.; embark'd 16 Aug. 1737; arrived 31 Oct. 1737.
492. Grinter, Jo.—Mason. He did work at the parsons house in June 1740.
493. Groves, Saml.—Lot 4S. in Frederica. A new freeholder, from whence he came I know not. Returnd possess'd of this lot 6 Aug. 1741.
494. Grumace, Hen.—Servt. to Cha. Britain.
495. Gulliver, Jo.—Servt. to Sir Fra. Bathurst Bt.; embark'd 31 Oct. 1734; arrived 28 Dec. 1734; dead 31 Jan. 1734-5.
496. Gun, Will.—Age 30; Servt. to Mr. Mackay of Scourie; embark'd 20 Oct. 1735; arrived 10 Jan. 1735-6; out of his time.
497. Hag, Jo. Ulric—Age 46; Smith; Swiss; embark'd 29 Sept. 1741; arrived 4 Dec. 1741.
498. Hague, Eliz.—Servt. to Ensign Tolson; arrived 4 June 1737.
499. Hamilton, Archibald—Patroon of the Trustees Periagua at Frederica at 18£ p. ann. till 25 April 1739.
500. Hamilton, Paul—Doubted if he went over. Grant of 500 acres made him 24 Sept. 1735.
501. Hanbury, John—Hanbury, Jo. employ'd in the Publick Stores at Frederica June 1739 at 15£ p. ann.
502. Harding, Isaac—Boy to Jo. Harding.
503. Harding, Jo.—Tr. Servt. at Frederica; lot 4N. at Frederica. Succeeded Geo. Spencer (who left the Colony before April 1740) in his lot.
504. ——, [?], w.
505. ——, John, son—Ditto. Both blacksmiths.
506. Harlefoot, Ja.—Arrived 21 Aug. 1734; lot 215 in Savannah. A grant of 150 acres was past to him 27 Feb. 1733-4, and he had leve to part with his town lot 16 Jan. 1735-6 to settle near Skidaway, afterwards he deserted the Colony and is gone none knows where. On 16 Jan. 1735-6 two Trust servants were allow'd him, whom he was to pay for as he should be able. Quitted Jan. 1738-9.
507. Harnet, Derby—Servt. to Elisha Dobree; arrived 30 June 1734.
508. Harris, Fra.—Clerk to Mr. Tho. Jones. He had the care and sallary for one year ending Mich. 1740, allotted for the overseer of ye Tr. Servts.
509. Harris, Will.—Lot 126 in Savannah. This lot was granted him April 1737. Lawrence Mellichamp possest it be-

fore who deserted 3 June 1736. Dead 1737.
510. ——, Anne, w.—On her husbands death she & her son became inmate on Lot 68.
511. ——, Will., son—born in the Colony.
512. Harvey, Jo.—New freeholder 1738-9; lot 20N. at Frederica; quitted before Aug. 1741.
513. Harwood, Danl.—Servt.; arrived 8 Feb. 1733-4; sent to his master in Philadelphia.
514. Hatner, Paul—Age 45; Tr. servt.; dead July 1742.
515. Hatton, Edwd.—Lot 187 in Savannah. Gone to England for debt, since Dec. 1738. He was presented 22 Aug. 1737 for defaming a womans character and confest himself guilty. Quitted to England.
516. Hatton, Will.—Boy.
517. Hay, Jenour—Servt. to Tho. Baillie.
518. Hay, Robert—Arrived 27 June 1737. Grant of 500 acres made him 5 Oct. 1737.
519. Hayes, Owen—Tr. servt.; arrived 10 Jan. 1733-4; run away.
520. Haynes, Gregy.—On 14 June 1736 Mr. Oglethorp order'd him a 500 acre lot and house in Fort Augusta.
521. Headly, Will.—Arrived 20 April 1734. Settled at Skidaway.
522. Headman, Tho.—Servt. to Will. Bradley.
523. Hender, David — Arrived about 1736/7. Settled at Highgate, and a good Improver. He marry'd the sister of Simon Ruviere.
524. ——, Rouviere, w.
525. Henney, John—Cooper to the Tr.; lot 23S. in Frederica. Trust servt. on pay. He marry'd Anne d. of Hen. Meyer.
526. ——, Anne Myers, w.—Dead.
527. ——, [?], d.—Born in Georgia.
528. Herbert, Eliz.—Servt. to Tho. Faw-set; arrived 14 Jan. 1733-4. Marry'd to Tho. Tripp 6 Oct. 1734.
529. Heron, Alexr.—Capt. in Oglethorps 1738 Regiment; arrived 1738. Grant of 500 acres made him 26 April 1738.
530. ——, [?], w.—Embark'd 1738; arrived 1738. Return'd to England Feb. 1739-40. Quitted Feb. 1739/40.
531. ——, [?], d.—Embark'd 1738; arrived 1738. Return'd to England Feb. 1739-40. Quitted ditto time.
532. Heslege, Novel—Boy. Found guilty of misprision of treason 8 March 1734-5 & broke out of jail.
533. Hetherington, Jos.—Arrived 7 July 1733. Settled at Thunderbolt on a grant of 500 acres past him 21 Dec. 1732. He settled himself Sept. 1733, but was convicted of felony in killing Hen. Parkers cattel for his own use and breaking jayl fled the Colony Aug. 1738 he died in Carolina 1740. Run away for felony 1738. Dead 1740.
534. ——, [?], w.—Dead 27 July 1733.
535. ——, [?], d.—Born in Georgia July 1735.
536. Hetherington, Robt.—He had a grant of 250 acres 4 July 1733.
537. Hetherington, Theophilus — He also had a grant of 250 acres 4 July 1733. He fled the Colony for the same felony as did Joseph Aug. 1738. He marry'd the widow Lacy, who ran with him, and died in Carolina 1740 in England Jan. 1741/2. Run away for debt — Mar. 1739-40.
538. Hill, Earl Piercy—Convicted of misprision of treason 8 Mar. 1734-5 and ran away. He was concern'd in the intended insurrection 1734. Run away for misprision of treason.
539. Hislop, Mary—Servt. to Hugh Anderson. Whipt 60 lases March 1734-5 on acct. of the red string plot.
540. Hitchcocks, Jo.—Servt. to Rogr. Lacy;

arrived 1 Feb. 1733-4; dead Sept. 1734.

541. Holmes, Saml.—A grant was made him of 200 acres 18 April 1733. Cast in a debt of 19.11.0 July 1738, and ran to Carolina Jan. 1738/9 probably for debt. He died in Charlestown Sept. 1739. Run away. Dead Sept. 1739.

542. Holsey, Eliz.—Arrived 20 May 1735. Marry'd to John Dearn 20 May 1735.

543. Holstatter, Caspar—Arrived abt. Dec. 1737. Settled at Hampstead, and very industrious.

544. Homer, Ja.—Servt. to Rogr. Lacy; arrived 1 Feb. 1733-4.

545. Hood, Jonas—A boy.

546. Hood, Jonathan—Tr. servt. on pay; arrived 28 Dec. 1734. He marry'd Elizabeth widow of Jo. Warren, and was in England 1737. Qy. if return'd.

547. Hope, Jo.—Servt. to Patrick Tailfer; arrived 1 Aug. 1734.

548. Horn, Jo.—Servt. to Sir Fra. Bathurst Bt.; embark'd 31 Oct. 1734; arrived 28 Dec. 1734; dead.

549. Horn, Will.—Arrived 1 Feb. 1732-3; lot 14 in Savannah. Convicted twice of fraud & cheating; broak jayl and fled the Colony. Run away for stealing.

550. Horris, [?]—Servt. Sentenc'd 50 lashes for deserting, and again attempting to run away 28 April 1734.

551. Horton, Will, Esq.—Ensign to Col. Oglethorp; arrived 5 Feb. 1735-6. A grant was made him of 500 acres 24 Sept. 1735. He had been subsherif of Herefordshire. Settled on Jekyl's Island.

552. Hotchking, Geo.—Labourer; dead 8 May 1737.

553. Houlster, Jo.—New freeholdr.; arrived 1738. Settled at Hampstead, and very industrious.

554. Houston, James—Arrived 1 Aug. 1734. A grant was made him of 500 acres 14 Nov. 1733. Dead 1737.

555. Houston, Ja.—Clerk in the stores to Mr. Causton. Houston, Ja. had a plantation at Skidaway. He fled on Mr. Causton's being removed from store keeper, 2 Nov. 1738 but returned 25th. But again went away abt. Sept. 1739 having made several alterations in the books of acct. Quitted Sept. 1739.

556. Houston, Patrick—Gent. 1740 took a lot in Frederica by mar. to Capt. Dunbars sister; arrived 1 Aug. 1734; lot 3S. in Frederica. Fyn'd 1.0.0 for selling rum 17 July 1735. Convicted of not supplying his servants with necessarys 21 Oct. 1735. A lot of 500 acres was granted him 1 Aug. 1733. But not set out till June 1737. In Oct. 1738 Col. Oglethorp lent him on the Trustees acct. 100£ to enable him to set up a boat to furnish provision cheap to the Colony.

*557. ——, [?] Dunbar, w.

558. Hows, Anne—D. of Robt. Successr. to Henry; born in Georgia 3 Oct. 1733; lot 67 in Savannah.

559. Huff, Will.—Settled at Frederica and employ'd on pay in breaking Oxen June 1739 & then had 20 shill. for breaking 3 payr.

560. Hughes, Percival—D. of Joseph; born in Georgia 4 May 1733; dead 10 April 1734.

561. Hughes, Sarah—D. of Richd.; born in Georgia 25 June 1735.

562. Hunter, Patrick—Apothecary. Inmate at Savannah in 1738 on Lot 18. Apothecary to the orphan house 1740.

563. Hurst, Lancelot—Servt. to Tho. Causton.

564. Hutton, Joseph—Lot 17S. in Frederica.

565. ——, [?], w.

* Same as p. 72, no. 341.

566. Jackson, Edward—Tr. Servant; arrived 10 Jan. 1733-4.
567. Jackson, George—Servt. to Tho. Salter; embark'd Sept.; arrived 17 Dec. 1733.
568. Jackson, Ja.—Arrived 1734. Settled at Highgate. A very industrious man.
569. James, Eliz.—Servt. to Patrick Tailfer; arrived 1 Aug. 1734.
570. Jarvee, David—Servt. to Jos. Wardrope; embark'd 11 April 1734; arrived 21 Aug. 1734; dead 1740.
571. Jecou, David—Inmate at Savanah on Lot 120 Jan. of 1737-8. One David Jewy ret. dead 1740. Qy. if the same.
572. ——, [?], w.
573. Jenkins, Edwd., Senr.—Embark'd 25 May 1733; arrived 23 Sept. 1733; Lot 51 in Savannah. He had a grant of 100 acres made him 17 May 1733, but was uncertain where to take his land, till in April 1737 he pitch'd on an island where he said he would settle. In the meantime he held this lot. Tything man 1736. Quitted 30 Aug. 1740. He went to Carolina with his wife for fear of the Spaniards.
574. ——, Eliz., w. Quitted 30 Aug. 1740.
575. ——, Anne, d.—Arrived 23 Sept. 1733.
576. ——, Edwd., son—A minor; arrived 21 Dec. 1733; Lot 72 in Savannah. He lives with his father. Quitted 30 Aug. 1740.
577. ——, Eliz., d.—Dead 29 Feb. 1733-4.
578. ——, Isaac, son—Dead 29 Jan. 1733-4.
579. Jenkins, Will—Servt.; dead 1740.
580. Jenys, Paul, Esq.—Spr. of ye. Assembly at Charlestown. He had a grant of 500 acres made him 2 Oct. 1735. He died July 1737. Dead July 1737.
581. Jochain, Ri.—Age 26; servt. to Ensign Horton; embark'd 2 Dec. 1735; arrived 2 Feb. 1735-6.
582. Johnson, Anne Sims—Dead.
583. Johnson, Arthur—Arrived 7 May 1734; lot 172 in Savannah. He sold his lot to Joseph Pavie in 1736. See Pavie.
584. ——, Martha, w.
585. Johnson, George—Servt. to Patrick Tailfer. Sawyer; arrived 1 Aug. 1734; out of his time.
586. Johnson, Geo.—Servt. to Will. Sterling; arrived 1 Aug. 1734.
587. Jones, Bridget—Servt. to A. Johnson; arrived 10 Jan. 1733-4.
588. Jones, Inigo—Son of Noble Jones; born in Georgia 26 April 1735.
589. Jones, John—Servt. to Ja. Calloway; arrived 28 Dec. 1734; dead.
590. Jones, Lewis — Jones, Lewis joyn'd the Colony, when I know not. Dead.
591. Jones, Pipe—Servt.
592. Jones, Thomas—Indian Trader; arrived 1 July 1734; lot 44 in Savannah. Half Indian. A Trader among the Indians, and comander of a Party of Rangers in 1739 at the annual expense of 27£ which Col. Oglethorp says is necessary to be continued.
593. Jones, Tho. Wimberly—Son of Noble Jones; born in Georgia; lot 46 in Savannah.
594. Joy, Danl.—Servt. to Noble Jones; arrived 10 Jan. 1733-4; dead 29 Oct. 1734.
595. Kane, Martin—Indian Trader; lot 183 in Savannah. This lot was promised him, but I know not if he took it out. In Feb. 1738-9 vacant. Dead 1738.
596. Kelly, Pet.—Servt. Son of Wid. Kelly; dead Sept. 1742.
597. ——, [?], w.
598. Kelway, Will.—Lot 164 in Savannah. This was a Trust reserved lot on which Kellway settled since 16 Jan. 1737-8, or in March 1739 and resolv'd to keep a ware house. A trader and good interpreter of the Spanish

tongue. 1740 he marry'd the widow of Jo. West, and she died 5 June 1740.
599. Kemp, Nic.—Son of John. Servt. to Hen. Parker.
600. Kennedy, Will.—Age 22; Taylor. Servt. to Jo. Cuthbert of Draikes; embark'd 20 Oct. 1735; arrived 10 Jan. 1735-6. A tailor. Out of his time. Run away with his family to Carolina Aug. 1742.
601. ——, Eliz., w.—Age 24; servt. to Ditto.
602. ——, [?]—Child of above; born in Georgia; run away.
603. ——, [?]—Child of Ditto; born in Georgia; run away.
604. Kent, Ri., boy—Son of Clement Kent Esq. member of Parlt. for Reading in 1722. Settled at Augusta.
605. Kilberry, Will.—Arrived 1 Feb. 1732-3; dead 9 Dec. 1733.
606. Kilcannon, Michl.—Tr. Servt.; arrived 10 Jan. 1733-4.
607. Kinard, David—Servt. to Will. & H. Sterling; arrived 1 Aug. 1734.
608. King, James—Servt. to the Rev. Mr. Quincy; arrived 10 Jan. 1733-4.
609. Kirchner, Ri.—New Freholder; arrived 1737-8; Lot 10S. in Frederica. Formerly Daniel Griffith's lot who quitted the Colony 1736-7. Quitted before Au. 1.
610. ——, Eliz., w.
611. Kirton, Geo.—Sentenc'd 60 lashes for stealing 12 Nov. 1734.
612. Lacey, Saml.—Arrived 28 Feb. 1733-4; lot 60 in Savannah. Master of a Pettiagua & neglects his lot. Abst. 24 Feb. 1736-7 but after in ye town.
613. ——, Eliz., w.—Embark'd 22 March 1736/7; arrived 4 June 1737. Her and her childrens passage was advanc'd by the Trust to be repaid by Saml. Lacy.
614. ——, Eliz., d.—Embark'd 22 March 1736/7.
615. ——, Saml., son—Embark'd 22 March 1736/7.
616. Lacour, [?]
617. Lacy, Elizabeth—Embark'd 28 Sept. 1733; arrived 14 Jan. 1733-4; dead 1 Aug. 1734.
618. ——, Roger, son—Arrived 1 Feb. 1733-4. Settled at Thunderbolt, but by making him Capt. at Augusta, that Plantation sunk. He had a grant of 500 acres 21 Dec. 1732. Dead 3 Aug. 1738.
619. ——, [?], w.—Remarry'd to Theophilus Hetherington, and with him forsook the Colony and went to Carolina where she died 1740. Quitted 8 Mar. 1739/40. Dead 1740.
620. Lacy, James—Arrived 1 Feb. 1733-4. Settled at Thunderbolt on a grant of 500 acres made him 21 Dec. 1732. Dead.
621. LaFosse, Pet.—Servt. to Ri. Mellichamp; embark'd 14 May 1735.
622. Lafour, James—Servt.
623. Lamb, Bullfinch—He had a grant of 500 acres made him 7 Oct. 1734 wch. he forfeited by not going over and keepg. the conditions and accordingly it was declared void 2 June 1736. Went not over and forfeited.
624. Lane, Mary—Servt. to Elisha Dobree; arrived 30 June 1734. Convicted of Felony 24 April 1734. Dead.
625. Lang, Abraham—Age 46; smith; Swiss; embark'd 29 Sept. 1741; arrived 4 Dec. 1741.
626. Langford, Jo.—Boy.
627. Langford, John—Servt. to the Tr. at Augusta. Fyn'd 2.0.0 for unlawfull imprisonment & combination to extort money 12 July 1735. Also convicted of extortion in selling flesh meat 14 July 1735. Also convicted of keeping a bawdy house 9 Oct. 1735. Dead.

628. ——, [?], w.
629. Lawley, Ri.—Embark'd 14 Oct. 1735; arrived Feb. 1735-6; lots 25N. & 26N. in Frederica. Hard at work on his 5 acre lot. Afterwards kept a boat & then quitted April 1740 & came for England. Quitted in April 1740.
630. Laws, Holly Day—A lot of 50 acres in Frederica was orderd him 3 May 1738.
631. Leary, Timothy — Arrived 1 Aug. 1734; lot 154 in Savannah; dead.
632. Ledesma, Moses—Jew; arrived 10 July 1733; Lot 59 in Savannah. Took possession of his lot 21 Dec. 1733. In 1736 he had fell'd cleard & planted 2 acres, which produced 14 bushells of Indian corn. He since neglected his lot.
633. ——, Hester, w.—Jew.
634. ——, Abraham, son—Jew; born in Georgia 27 July 1733.
635. ——, Rachel, d.—Jew; born in Georgia.
636. ——, Rebecca, d.—Jew; born in Georgia.
637. ——, Samuel, son—Jew.
638. Levally, Jo., senr.—Embark'd 14 Oct. 1735; arrived Feb. 1735-6; lot 6S. in Frederica. Appointed Tything man in case of vacancy 7 Oct. 1735.
639. ——, Anne, w.
640. ——, Mary, d.
641. ——, John, son—Embark'd 2 Dec. 1735; arrived 2 Feb. 1735-6; lot 9S. in Frederica. Went with Jo. Levally the husband and father to Carolina Dec. 1740. Quitted Dec. 1740.
642. ——, Sarah—W. of Jo. Levally junr.; embark'd 2 Dec. 1735; arrived 2 Feb. 1735-6. Went with Jo. Levally the husband and father to Carolina Dec. 1740. Quitted Dec. 1740.
643. ——, Mary—Born in Georgia. Went with Jo. Levally the husband and father to Carolina Dec. 1740. Quitted Dec. 1740.
644. Levi, John—Servt. to Paul Amatis; quitted.
645. Levi, John, junr.—Son of Hanah Brittain; arrived 31 Oct. 1733; lot 204 in Savannah. Came with his brothers from Carolina, and deserted with Benjamin. Quitted 24 Feb. 1736-7.
646. ——, Benj.—His brother; arrived 31 Oct. 1733; lot 205 in Savannah. Quitted 24 Feb. 1736-7.
647. ——, Tho.—His brother; arrived 31 Oct. 1733; lot 215 in Savannah. Abst. 24 Feb. 1736/7.
648. Lichliege, Hans Henrich—Age 34; farmer.
649. Lobb, Richd. — Apothecary; arrived 15 Feb. 1733-4; lot 90 in Savannah. Fyn'd double the value for killing a chicken 18 May 1734. Also fyn'd for defamation 0.3.4 26 May 1735. He quitted the Colony, but on the change of tenure put in his claym to be restored to his lot Oct. 1739. He became possest of this lot by the death of Tho. Chewter without heirs—male. In 1736 he had fenced 5 acres and fell'd and cleard 3½ from which he had 55 bushells of Indian corn. But in 1738 he cultivated only 3 acres. In Engld. 24 Feb. 1736-7.
650. ——, Hodges Eliz., w.—She marry'd Ri. Lobb 8 May 1734. Dead 4 Aug. 1735.
651. Logie, Andrew—A lot of 50 acres in Savannah was orderd him 3 May 1738.
652. Lopes de Crasto, Jacb.—Jew; arrived 10 July 1733; lot 122 in Savannah. His lot swamp overflow'd, & so cultivated nothing.
653. ——, Sipura, w.—Jew; widow of David.
654. Lopes de Pax, David—Jew; arrived 10 July 1733; dead 7 Feb. 1733-4.

655. ——, Sipura, w.—Re-marryd to Lopes de Crasto. She remarry'd Jacob Lopes de Crasto 1735.
656. Lowl, Josiah — of the Rangers Compy.; arrived 1 Feb. 1732-3; Lot 101 in Savannah. His lot supposed vacant Feb. 1738-9.
657. Loyd, Joseph—Son of Henry; born in Georgia.
658. Lynch, Fra.—Arrived 22 Nov. 1733. He ran away from his creditors.
659. Lyndal, Jo.—Arrived 8 May 1734; lot 173 in Savannah. In 1738 he had fell'd & clear'd 5 acres & ½ but cultivated only one. He was Pyndar 1739.
660. Macbane, Lachlans—Indian trader. On 14 June 1736 Mr. Oglethorp order'd him a lot of 500 acres & a house in Fort Augusta. In the Colony at the end of the year 1746.
661. Macbean, Archibald—Age 26; of Aberlaur. Farmer; embark'd 20 Oct. 1735; arrived 10 Jan. 1735-6. Return'd dead 1740. Dead 1740.
662. ——, Cath. Cameron, w.—Age 21.
663. ——, Alexandr., son—Dead 1740.
664. Macbean, Duncan—Age 21; servt. to Jo. Mackintosh, Holmes son; embark'd 20 Oct. 1735; arrived 10 Jan. 1735-6.
665. Macbean, McWillie, Jo.—Age 27; servt. to Jo. Spence; embark'd 20 Oct. 1735; arrived 10 Jan. 1735-6.
666. Macbride, Ant.—Servt. to Will. & H. Sterling; arrived 1 Aug. 1734.
667. Macbride, Hen.—Servt. to Will. & H. Sterling; arrived 1 Aug. 1734.
668. Macdermot, Barrow—Tr. Servt.; arrived 10 Jan. 1733-4.
669. Macdonald, Donald—Age 22; embark'd 20 Oct. 1735; arrived 10 Jan. 1735-6. Living at Darien. Still a servant 6 May 1741.
670. ——, Alvine Wood, w.—Age 20. Alias Winwood Macdonald. Alive at Darien 6 May 1741.
671. Macdonald, Donald—Born in Georgia. Alive at Darien 6 May 1741 and then 6 months old.
672. Macdonald, Ja.—Servt. Fynd 19.0.0 for enticing and carrying away servants 23 June 1734.
673. Macdonald, Jo.—Born in Georgia. Alive at Darien 6 May 1741 & then 2 years 3 months old.
674. Macdonald, Jo.—Servt. to Jo. Baily; arrived 1 Aug. 1734. At first servt. to John Baily: afterwards to Andrew Grant.
675. Macdonald, John—Age 19; servt. to Donald Macdonald.
676. Macdonald, Mary—W. of Alexr; a Soldier; embark'd 16 Aug. 1737; arrived 31 Oct. 1737.
677. Macdonald, Rachel—Servt. to Will. Stephens, Esq.
678. Macdonald, Rainold—Age 18; Servt. to Jo. Mackintosh of Kingussie junr.; embark'd 20 Oct. 1735; arrived 10 Jan. 1735-6. Of Darien of the highland company of Rangers 6 May 1741. There was one of both names kill'd or made prisoner at Moosa June 1740 who left a wife & 4 children at Darien 6 May 1741. Qy if this be he.
679. Macer, Alexr.—Servt. to Hugh Anderson.
680. Macferline, Danl.—Servt. to Will. & H. Sterling; arrived 1 Aug. 1734.
681. Macgilivray, Archibd.—Age 15. He had a grant of 50 acres made him 3 Sept. 1735, and on July 9 same year a town lot in Savanah but I believe he took it not.
682. Macgilivray, Farquar—Age 30; servt. to J. Cuthbert of Draikes; embark'd 20 Oct. 1735; arrived 10 Jan. 1735-6.
683. Macgilivray, Lachlan—Age 16; servt.

to Jo. Mackintosh, Holmes son; embark'd 20 Oct. 1735; arrived 10 Jan. 1735-6.
684. Macgowran, Pet.—Tr. servt.; arrived 10 Jan. 1733-4.
685. Macgregor, Jane—Servt. to Will. & H. Sterling; arrived 1 Aug. 1734.
686. Mac-Inver, Murdow—Servt. to J. Cuthbert of Draikes; embark'd 20 Oct. 1735; arrived 10 Jan. 1735-6.
687. Mackay, [?]—of Scourie. Gent.; embark'd 20 Oct. 1735; arrived 10 Jan. 1735-6.
688. Mackay, [?]—of Strothie. Gent.; embark'd 20 Oct. 1735; arrived 10 Jan. 1735-6.
689. Mackay, Cha.—Age 17; of Tar; embark'd 20 Oct. 1735; arrived 10 Jan. 1735-6. Ensign to the highland Independt. Company, & so returnd by Col. Oglethorpe 6 May 1741.
690. Mackay, Hugh, Lt.—Now Capt. in Oglethorps Reg. He had a grant of 500 acres made him 24 July 1735. He quitted the Colony and Regiment upon not being promoted to Major of the Regiment 1740. Quitted 1740.
691. ——, Hellen, w.—Embark'd 14 Oct. 1735; arrived Feb. 1735-6.
692. Mackay, Hugh—Born in Georgia. Alive at Darien 6 May 1741 & then 1 year old.
693. Mackay, James—Age 17; of Tar; embark'd 20 Oct. 1735; arrived 10 Jan. 1735-6. Of Darien; Slayn at the Seige of Augustine June 1740.
694. Mackay, Ja.—Age 40; of Durnes. Farmer; embark'd 20 Oct. 1735; arrived 10 Jan. 1735-6. Slayn or made prisoner at Moosa June 1740. Left a wife & 4 children.
695. ——, Barbara McLeod, w.—Age 36. Alive at Darien with her 4 children 6 May 1741.
696. ——, Barbara, d.—Age 17. Alive at Darien 6 May 1741 but said then to be only 11 years old.
697. ——, Donald, son—Age 9. Alive at Darien 6 May 1741.
698. ——, Jeanne, d.—Age 6.
699. Mackay, John—Age 56; of Durnes. Farmer; embark'd 20 Oct. 1735; arrived 10 Jan. 1735-6.
700. ——, Jannet, w.—Age 32.
701. ——, Eliz., d.
702. ——, Hugh, son—Age 18.
703. ——, John, son—Age 3.
704. ——, Mary, d.
705. ——, Will., son—Age 6.
706. Mackay, John, Esq.—Arrived 1 Feb. 1732-3. He had a grant of 500 acres made him 3 Sept. 1735, & took it at Josephstown, but dying, that settlement in a little time disperst. Dead 25 July 1736.
707. Mackay, Jo.—Age 50; of Lairg; embark'd 20 Oct. 1735; arrived 10 Jan. 1735-6.
708. ——, Jannet Mackintosh, w.—Age 40. Alive at Darien 6 May 1741.
709. ——, Donald, son—Age 6.
710. ——, Jeanne, d.—Age 2.
711. ——, Patrick, son—Age 7.
712. Mackay, Patrick—Fled Scotland for Felony. He had a grant of 500 acres made him 3 Sept. 1735, and keeps servts. on it: But has also a plantation on Carolina side of the River Savannah, on which he keeps Negroes, which is of bad example to our Planters.
713. ——, [?], w.—Mrs. Montagut— She was wid. of Mr. Montagut & remar. 1740.
714. ——, Will., son—Arrived 1 Feb. 1732-3; lot 55 in Savannah. Took possession of his lot 21 Dec. 1733 his father quitting Josephs town his country grant, lives here with his son. Abs. 24 Feb. 1736-7.

715. Mackay, William—Age 18; servt. to Mackay, [?] of Strothie.
716. Mackay, Will.—Age 21; of Lavig; servt. to Mackay, [?] of Scourie. A Soldier in the Independent Company of highlanders & so return'd by Col. Oglethorp 6 May 1741.
717. Mackdonald, Georgia—Born in Georgia. Alive at Darien 6 May 1741 and then abt. 6 years old.
718. Mackdonald, Janet—Born in Georgia. Alive at Darien and then 2 years old.
719. Mackenzie, Cath.—Servt. to Noble Jones.
720. Mackimmie, Alexr.—Age 50; labourer; embark'd 20 Oct. 1735; arrived 10 Jan. 1735-6.
721. Mackintosh, Anne—Born in Georgia. Living at Darien and then 4 years old.
722. Mackintosh, Benj.—Age 50; of Dorris. Farmer; embark'd 20 Oct. 1735; arrived 10 Jan. 1735-6.
723. ——, Cath., w.—Age 45. Alive at Darien 6 May 1741.
724. ——, Eliz., d.—Age 20.
725. ——, Jannet, d.—Age 18.
726. ——, Lachlan, son—Age 12. Living at Darien 6 May 1741 but said to be only 13 years old at that time.
727. Mackintosh, Donald—Age 17; servt. to John Mackintosh of Inverness. Living at Darien still a servt. 6 May 1741.
728. Mackintosh, Donald—Age 20; of Inverness. Servt. to Alexr. Mackintosh; embark'd 20 Oct. 1735; arrived 10 Jan. 1735-6.
729. Mackintosh, Eneas—Capt. at Fort St. George. Afterwards at Fort Polachocolas. Capt. at Fort St. George at 37.10.0 p. ann. till 16 May 1739. He was Capt. of 10 Rangers, which Coll. Oglethorp reduced 16 Dec. 1738. But continued him ½ a year longer to hunt up the Trustees wild cattel, which is generally done in May. He afterwards was Comandr. at Fort Palachocolas, but in Feb. 1739-40 return'd to Scotland where an estate fell to him. Quitted 27 Feb. 1739/40.
730. Mackintosh, Geo.—Age 21; of Durnes; taylor; embark'd 20 Oct. 1735; arrived 10 Jan. 1735-6.
731. Mackintosh, Geo.—Born in Georgia. Two years old May 1741.
732. Mackintosh, Hugh—Born in Georgia. Alive in Georgia 6 May 1741 & then 2 years old.
733. Mackintosh, Jo.—Age 50; Senr. of Dornes. Farmer; embark'd 20 Oct. 1735; arrived 10 Jan. 1735-6. Alive at Darien 6 May 1741.
734. ——, Cath., w.—Age 47.
735. ——, Alexr., son—Age 8. Living at Darien 6 May 1741.
736. ——, Beatrix, d.—Age 5. Living at Darien 6 May 1741.
737. ——, Will., son — Age 12. Of the highland Compy. of Rangers & so return'd by Col. Oglethorpe 6 May 1741.
738. Mackintosh, Jo.—Age 15; farmer; embark'd 20 Oct. 1735; arrived 10 Jan. 1735-6. Of the Highland Company of Rangers, and as such return'd by Col. Oglethorpe 6 May 1741.
739. Mackintosh, Jo.—Age 21; of Dorris. Farmer; embark'd 20 Oct. 1735; arrived 10 Jan. 1735-6. Mackintosh, Jo. Holmes went to settle in Carolina. Dec. 1740. Quitted Dec. 1740.
740. Mackintosh, John—Age 24; of Inverness. Farmer; embark'd 20 Oct. 1735; arrived 10 Jan. 1735-6. Son of Holmes. One of both names was killd at Moosa, or made prisoner June 1741. Qy. if this be he. The man left a wife & child at Darien 6 May 1741.
741. Mackintosh, Jo.—Age 36; Junr. of

Kingussie Farmr.; embark'd 20 Oct. 1735; arrived 10 Jan. 1735-6.

742. ——, Margt., w.—Age 30. Alive at Darien 6 May 1741.

743. ——, John, son—Age 8. Alive at Darien 1741.

744. ——, Lachlan, son—Age 9.

745. ——, Margt., d.—Age 18.

746. ——, Phineas, son—Age 3. Alive at Darien 1741.

747. ——, Will., son—Age 10.

748. Mackintosh, John—Age 50; of Dornach; embark'd 20 Oct. 1735; arrived 10 Jan. 1735-6.

749. Mackintosh, Moor Jo. — Gent.; Chief of Darien. See his family [Nos. 741-747 in this list]. Keeper of the Store at Darien 1739. Taken at Moosa in 1740 & now a prisoner in Spain Nov. 1741, where if he dies he will leave a widow & 6 children in Darien. At the seige of Augustine Col. Oglethorpe made him Capt. of the Highland Company. Has a wife & 6 children at Darien 6 May 1741. [Same as No. 741.]

750. ——, [?], w.—Resident at Darien with her 6 children 6 May 1741.

751. Mackintosh, Lachner—Age 26; servt. to Benj. Mackintosh.

752. ——, Margt., w.—Age 23; servt. to Benj. Mackintosh.

753. Mackintosh, Laghlan—Ranger at Fort Arguile the middle way between the Darien & Savannah. When Col. Oglethorp dismist the 15 Rangers there he was obliged as he writes to keep on two at 24£ p. ann. each. They were paid by him till 19 April 1739, but thinks to reduce them also when the German servants have got in their crop. He had the charge of Fort Arguile in 1740.

754. Mackintosh, Robt.—Servt. to Saml. Davison. Employ'd in the Scout boat 1738 and another servant promised Davison in his room.

755. Mackintosh, Robt. of Moy—Age 20; servt. to Ja. Maqueen; embark'd 20 Oct. 1735; arrived 10 Jan. 1735-6.

756. Mackintosh, Roderick—Age 19; farmer; embark'd 20 Oct. 1735; arrived 10 Jan. 1735-6. Of the Highland Company of Rangers, & so return'd by Col. Oglethorpe 6 May 1741.

757. Mackintosh, Sarah—Servt. to David Douglass.

758. Mackintyre, Will.—Servt. to Will. & H. Sterling; arrived 1 Aug. 1734.

759. Maclean, Allan—Age 21; of Inverness. Farmer; embark'd 20 Oct. 1735; arrived 10 Jan. 1735-6.

760. Maclean, Alexr.—Age 32; of Inverness. Farmer; embark'd 20 Oct. 1735; arrived 10 Jan. 1735-6; dead Mar. 1739/40.

761. Maclean, George—Age 30; of Ardelack. Farmer; embark'd 20 Oct. 1735; arrived 10 Jan. 1735-6.

762. Maclean, John—Age 19; of Inverness. Servt. to Allan Maclean. Of the Highland Company of Rangers & so return'd by Col. Oglethorpe 6 May 1741.

763. Maclean, John—Age 20; servt. to Robt. Macpherson of Alvie; embark'd 20 Oct. 1735; arrived 10 Jan. 1735-6.

764. Maclean, Simon—of Inverness; servt. to Allan Maclean.

765. Macleod, Angus of Hawnick—Age 17; weaver; servt. to Mackay of Strothie; embark'd 20 Oct. 1735; arrived 10 Jan. 1735-6.

766. Macleod, Donald of Tar—Age 18; labourer; servt. to Mackay of Strothie; embark'd 20 Oct. 1735; arrived 10 Jan. 1735-6. Of the Highland Independt. Company, and so return'd by Col. Oglethorpe 6 May 1741.

767. Macleod, Donald of Tar—Labourer;

servt. to Mackay of Strothie; Embark'd 20 Oct. 1735; arrived 10 Jan. 1735-6.
768. Macleod, George—Age 17; labourer; servt. to Mackay of Strothie; embark'd 20 Oct. 1735; arrived 10 Jan. 1735-6.
769. Macleod, Hugh—Scots Minister at Darien; embark'd 20 Oct. 1735; arrived 10 Jan. 1735-6. A grant of 300 acres to him & his successors as ministers at the Darien for religious uses was made out 1739. Quitted the Colony 1741. Quitted 1740 [sic.].
770. Macleod, Hugh—Age 21; labourer; servt. to Mackay of Strothie; embark'd 20 Oct. 1735; arrived 10 Jan. 1735-6. Of the Highland Independt. Company, & so return'd by Col. Oglethorpe 6 May 1741.
771. Macleod, Hugh—Age 18; labourer; servt. to Mackay of Strothie; embark'd 20 Oct. 1735; arrived 10 Jan. 1735-6. Of the Highland Independt. Company & so return'd by Col. Oglethorp 6 May 1741.
772. Macleod, John—Age 18; labourer; servt. to Mackay of Strothie; embark'd 20 Oct. 1735; arrived 10 Jan. 1735-6. Of the Highland Company of Rangers and so return'd by Col. Oglethorpe 6 May 1741.
773. Macleod, Mary—Servt. to Tho. Causton.
774. Macmurrwick, Alexr.—Age 20; servt. to Colin Cambel; embark'd 20 Oct. 1735; arrived 10 Jan. 1735-6.
775. Macoul, Alexr.—Age 30; servt. to Mr. Mackay of Scourie; embark'd 20 Oct. 1735; arrived 10 Jan. 1735-6.
776. Macoul, Alexr.—Servt. to Mr. Mackay of Scourie; embark'd 20 Oct. 1735; arrived 10 Jan. 1735-6. [Same person?].
777. Macpherline Duncan—Servt. to Will. & H. Sterling; arrived 1 Aug. 1734.
778. Macpherson, Ja.—A minor; son of Capt. Patrick; arrived 1 Feb. 1732-3; lot 61 in Savannah. He went to Carolina, and is with his Father. Abst. 29 Feb. 1736-7.
779. Macpherson, Norman—Age 24; labourer; embark'd 20 Oct. 1735; arrived 10 Jan. 1735-6.
780. Macpherson, Robt.—Age 24; of Alvie; farmer; embark'd 20 Oct. 1735; arrived 10 Jan. 1735-6.
781. Macqueen, Ja.—Age 19; of Inverness; embark'd 20 Oct. 1735; arrived 10 Jan. 1735-6.
782. Macqueen, James—Age 19; his servt.; embark'd 20 Oct. 1735; arrived 10 Jan. 1735-6.
783. Main, Geo.—Age 23; servt. to Donald Steward; embark'd 20 Oct. 1735; arrived 10 Jan. 1735-6.
784. Malcome, Jane—Servt. to A. Grant; arrived 1 Aug. 1734.
785. ——, [?]—Her child.
786. Mallier, Peter
787. ——, Jane, w.—Dead 29 Oct. 1742.
788. Manly, Hen.—Arrived 1 April 1734; lot 104 in Savannah. He never cultivated: and on shutting up the Publick Stores went away to Carolina. Quitted Jan. 1738/9.
789. ——, Sarah, w.
790. ——, John, son—Born in Georgia.
791. ——, Peter, son—Born in Georgia 17 Oct. 1734.
792. Marauld, Stevan—Arrived abt. Dec. 1735; lot 229 in Savannah. He cultivated nothing, his lot being swamp overflow'd. On shutting up the stores he went to Carolina. Quitted Jan. 1738/9.
793. Mariot, Thomas—A Bailif of Frederica; lot 25S. in Frederica.
794. Marks, Hugh—Jew; arrived 10 July, 1733.
795. ——, Anne, w.—Jew; arrived 10 July 1733. Dead 27 Nov. 1738.

796. Marks, Isaac—Jew; arrived 10 July 1733; lot 92 in Savannah. Jacob Yowil who died 18 Sept. 1736 left him this lot by will wch. was allow'd of.
797. Marsh, Ja.—Shoemaker at ye Orphan house; run away to Carolina May 1742.
798. Martino, Erno—Servt. to Jos. Hethrington; arrived 7 July 1733; dead.
799. Masterson, Tho.—Servt. to Hugh Anderson.
800. Mathews, Jacob—Age 27; 2d. husb. of Mary Musgrove; dead 6 June 1742.
801. Mathewson, Jo.—Servt. to Jos. Hethrington; arrived 7 July 1733. Servt. to Jos. Hethrington, afterwards to Walter Augustin. Dead.
*802. Mauve, [?], w. of Mathew.
803. ——, [?], d.
804. Maxwell, Primrose—Lot 8S. in Frederica.
805. Mears, Andrew—Servt. to Cha. Pury.
806. Mears, Willm., Senr.—Sawyer; arrived 15 June 1734; lot 58 in Savannah. Marry'd Eliz. Gilbert July 1733.
807. ——, Elis. Gilbert, w.
808. ——, Jo., son—Born in Georgia Nov. 1738.
809. ——, Mary, d.—Born in Georgia.
810. ——, Will., son—Born in Georgia 7 Aug. 1734; dead 7 Aug. 1734.
811. Mellichamp, Ri.—Arrived 21 Oct. 1734; lot 81 in Savannah; after absent.
812. ——, Hanah Willoughby, w.—Arrived 16 Dec. 1733. The widow of James Willoughby who died 17 Oct. 1734. She marry'd Ri. Mellichamp 31 Aug. 1736.
813. Mellichamp, Will.—Gent.; arrived 15 Mar. 1733-4. Fyn'd 200£ 0.0 for devising to get unlawfull possession of goods 12 July 1735. Kept to bail but fled. Run away for forgery.
814. ——, Sarah, w.
815. ——, Cha., son—A minor; lot 75 in Savannah; abst. 24 Feb. 1736/7.
816. ——, Eliz., d.
817. ——, Fra., d.
818. ——, Jonathan, son—Abst. 24 Feb. 1736/7.
819. ——, Lawrence, son—Run away with his father.
820. ——, Tho., son—Indicted for counterfeiting with his father Carolina bills & fled for it. Abst. Run away with his father.
821. Mellichamp, Willm.—A minor; lot 79 in Savannah; abst. in Carolina.
822. Mendoza, David—Jew.
823. Merrick, Tho.—Servt.; arrived 10 Jan. 1733-4; run away or lost.
824. Merrifield, Mark
825. Meyer, Tho.—Son of Hen. Meyer; born in Frederica.
826. Michel, Mary—Servt. to Jo. Vandeplank; arrived 21 Oct. 1734.
827. Miers, Rodolf—Boy.
828. Milledge, Aaron—Son of Tho. & Eliz.; born 9 Aug. 1733; dead 3 Oct. 1733.
829. Miller, David—Age 26; servt. to Mackay of Strothie; embark'd 20 Oct. 1735; arrived 10 Jan. 1735-6. Of the highland Independt. Company, & so return'd by Col. Oglethorpe 6 May 1741.
830. Miller, James—Age 18; servt. to Ja. Anderson; embark'd 20 Oct. 1735; arrived 10 Jan. 1735-6.
831. Miller, Jo.—Private storekeeper. A private store keeper at Augusta.
832. Miller, Michl.—Arrived 11 Mar. 1733-4. Mostly at Tybee.
833. Miller, Richd.—Arrived 11 Mar. 1733-4. Settled at Tybee, and in possession of his lot there 2 April 1734.
834. Minas, Abrm.—Jew; embark'd 10 July 1733; arrived 10 July 1733; lot 94 in Savannah. Possest of his lot 21 Dec. 1733. In 1736 4 acres of his garden lot & 1 of his farm were culti-

---

* *See*: Mathew More, p. 90, no. 878.

vated, & produced 36 bushells of Indian corn.
835. ——, Abigail, w.—Jew.
836. ——, Edwd., son—Jew; born in Georgia 14 July 1734.
837. ——, Hester, d.—Jew.
838. ——, Leah, d.—Jew.
839. ——, Philip, son—Jew; born in Georgia 12 July 1733.
840. Minas, Simon, Boy—Jew; arrived 10 July 1733. Settled at Hampstead, where after 4 years & ½ he cleard 5 acres, but planted little, & built only a hut.
841. ——, [?], d.—Jew; born in the Colony 10 July 1733.
842. Miranda, Jacob—Jew.
843. Mitchel, Andrew—Son of Andrew Mitchel; born in Georgia. Carry'd to Carolina by his father Dec. 1740. Quitted Dec. 1740.
844. ——, Jo.—Son of ditto; born in Georgia Feb. 1738/9. Carry'd to Carolina by his father Dec. 1740. Quitted Dec. 1740.
845. Mittin, Eliz.—Servt. to Will. Sale.
846. Molina, Abrm.—Jew; arrived 10 July 1733; Lot 69 in Savannah.
847. ——, Sarah, w.—Jew.
848. ——, Hester, d.—Jew.
849. Molina, Isaac—Jew; arrived 10 July 1733.
850. ——, Rachel, w.—Jew.
851. Molton, Hen.—Arrived 1 Feb. 1732-3; lot 143 in Savannah. He marry'd Frances widow of Loyd Gibbons 7 Sept. 1736, and this lot goes at his death to Mary Gibbons his daughter in law. He lives an Inmate on Lot 109.
852. Monro, Alexr.—Age 30; of Inverness; farmer; embark'd 20 Oct. 1735; arrived 10 Jan. 1735-6. Return'd dead 1740.
853. ——, Margt., w.—Age 27.
854. ——, Isabel, d.—6 m. old.
855. Monro, Alexr.—Age 24; of Dornoch; labourer; embark'd 20 Oct. 1735; arrived 10 Jan. 1735-6; dead 1740.
856. Monro, Donald—Age 45; of Alnit Rossit; labourer; embark'd 20 Oct. 1735; arrived 10 Jan. 1735-6.
857. Monro, John—Age 16; of Alnit Rossit; labourr.; embark'd 20 Oct. 1735; arrived 10 Jan. 1735-6.
858. Monro, John—Age 21; of Kiltairn; labourr.; embark'd 20 Oct. 1735; arrived 10 Jan. 1735-6.
859. Monro, Robt.—Age 17; of Dornoch; labourer; embark'd 20 Oct. 1735; arrived 10 Jan. 1735-6.
860. Monro, Will.—Age 12; of Dornach; labourr.; embark'd 20 Oct. 1735; arrived 10 Jan. 1735-6.
861. Monro, Will.—Age 40; of Durnes; farmer; embark'd 20 Oct. 1735; arrived 10 Jan. 1735-6. Of the highland company of Rangers and so return'd by Col. Oglethorpe 6 May 1741.
862. ——, Eliz., d.—Age 17.
863. ——, Margt., d.—Age 14.
864. Montagut, Saml.—A private storekeeper. The widow Montagut marry'd Patrick Mackay 1740. Dead 7 Nov. 1739. [i.e., Samuel].
865. ——, [?], w.
866. Montfort, Steven—Arrived 1734. Settled at Highgate about 5 years, and planted 12 acres. He marry'd the widow Ruviere, whose husband Paul Ruviere died 2 Sept. 1734.
867. ——, Wid. Rouviere, w.
868. ——, [?]. Born in Georgia.
869. ——, [?]. Born in Georgia.
870. ——, [?]. Born in Georgia.
871. Montsonte, Abrm.—Jew; arrived 10 July 1733.
872. Montsonte, Bernal Rafael—Jew; arrived 10 July 1733.
873. ——, Rachel, w.—Jew; arrived 29 Aug. 1733; dead.

874. Montsonte, Melino—Jew; arrived 10 July 1733.
875. Moore, George—He had a grant of 400 acres past to him 1 Aug. 1733.
876. Moore, M. Oglethorp—D. of Robt. Moore; born in Georgia 24 Sept. 1733; dead 15 Dec. 1733.
877. Moore, Tho.—Servt.
878. More, Mathew—Shoemaker.
879. Morel, Peter—Embark'd 14 Jan. 1733-4; arrived abt. 12 Mar. 1733-4. An industrious man. In 1738 he cleard & planted 12 acres with corn, rice, pease & potatoes, & built convenient housing.
880. ——, [?], w.
881. ——, [?], child.
882. ——, [?], child.
883. ——, [?], child.
884. ——, [?], child.
885. ——, [?], d.—Born in Georgia.
886. Morent, Jo.—Jew; servt. to Hugh Marks; dead 1 Dec. 1738.
887. Morgan, Anne — Servt.; arrived 4 June 1737.
888. Moris, Tho.—Servt. to Tho. Fawsset; arrived 14 Jan. 1733-4. Sentenc'd 50 lashes for deserting & again attempting to run away 28 April 1734.
889. Morison, Ambrose—Arrived 8 Feb. 1733; lot 105 in Savannah. This lot was not surveyd to him till 1737. He marry'd Anne the wid. of Will. Alfingston 26 Mar. 1734. The lot is his wifes and was given her on her quitting Skidaway. Run away 1736.
890. ——, Wid. Anne Alfinston, w.—Arrived 14 Jan. 1733-4. A drunken woman. Dead 26 June 1737.
891. Morison, Cath. of Durnes—Age 22; servt. to Will. Monroe; embark'd 20 Oct. 1735; arrived 10 Jan. 1735-6.
892. Morison, Cath.—Servt. to Jos. Coles; afterwd. to Isaac Nuner; arrived 10 Jan. 1733-4.
893. Morison, Hugh—Age 23; farmer; embark'd 20 Oct. 1735; arrived 10 Jan. 1735-6. A Highland Ranger, and so return'd by Col. Oglethorpe 6 May 1741.
894. Muir, Mary—2d. w. of Ja. Muir; arrived 16 Dec. 1733. She went over servt. to Anne Hainks, but Ja. Muir bought & marry'd her 25 Dec. 1734. Her name, Woodman.
895. ——, Sara, d.—Born in Georgia.
896. Murray, Alexr.—Age 17; labourer; embark'd 20 Oct. 1735; arrived 10 Jan. 1735-6.
897. Murray, Jo.—Age 25; servt. to Mackay of Scourie; embark'd 20 Oct. 1735; arrived 10 Jan. 1735-6; out of his time.
898. Musgrove, Jo. — Indian Interpreter; arrived 1 Feb. 1732-3; Lot 45 in Savannah. Indian Interpreter. Joyn'd the Colony from the first, and was possest of his lot 21 Dec. 1733. Dead 12 June 1735. [Did not come from England.]
899. ——, Mary, w.—On 24 Sept. 1735 a grant of 500 acres was made her it having been promised her deceased husband, and she took up her land at Grantham. She is the best Interpreter in the Trustees service and in good circumstances. In 1736 she marry'd Jacob Mathews who lived with her on her country lot. and died 1742. [A native—not from England.]
900. ——, Benj., son—Dead 9 Feb. 1733-4.
901. ——, Edwd., son—Dead.
902. ——, James, son—Dead.
903. ——, Jo., son—Dead 29 Dec. 1733.
904. Myrhover, Hen. — Labourr. at the Fort of Frederica 1738.
905. An orphan boy.
906. Neal, Tho.—2d. husb. of Wid. Amatis; lot 14 in Savannah. He marry'd Catherine the widow of Paul Amatis April 1737. Quitted. Lives in Carolina.

907. Nelson, Alexr.—Servt. to Tho. Salter; arrived 17 Dec. 1733.
908. Nelson, Jane—Servt. to Hugh Anderson.
909. Newman, Tho.—Servt. to Will. Sale; arrived 12 Mar. 1733-4.
910. Noah, Shem—Jew; servt. to Abrm. Minas; arrived 10 July 1733.
911. Noble, Ja.—Servt. to Sr. Fra. Bathurst Bt.; arrived 23 Dec. 1734. At first servt. to Sr. Fra. Bathurst. Afterwds. to Ja. Burnside.
912. Noe Costa, Saml.—Jew; servt. to Saml. Nuner; arrived 10 July 1733.
913. Noel, Danl.—Servt.
914. Norwood, Ri.—Servt. to Fra. Delgrass; arrived Jan. 1733-4. Convicted of assault: prophaning the Sabbath, & abusing the Constable 16 Sept. 1734. Marry'd to Jane Papot 5 Nov. 1734.
915. Nunez, Hen. Isaac—Jew; arrived 10 July 1733; lot 57 in Savannah. Possest of his lot 21 Dec. 1733.
916. ——, Abigail, w.—Jew.
917. Nunez, Saml., M.D.—Jew; arrived 10 July 1733; lot 43 in Savannah. Went to Carolina for fear of the Spaniards. Quitted 30 Aug. 1740.
918. ——, Rachel, 1st. w.—Jew; dead.
919. ——, Danl., son—Jew; lot 47 in Savannah. His lot swamp overflow'd. Went to Carolina for fear of the Spaniards. Quitted Sept. 1740.
920. ——, Moses, son—Jew; lot 49 in Savannah.
921. ——, Rebecca, 2d. w.—Jew. Went to Carolina for fear of the Spaniards. Quitted 30 Aug. 1740.
922. ——, Sypera, d.—Jew; quitted 30 Aug. 1740.
923. Nyson, Benj.—Servt. to Ja. Burnside.
924. Obryen, Jo.—Tr. Servt.; arrived 10 Jan. 1733-4.
925. Obryen, Kennedy—Indian Trader. A supplyer of Indian Traders with goods, and settled at Augusta. A grant was past to him of 500 acres 4 July 1739, which he had occupied 3 years before. His rent commenceth 4 July 1747.
926. Oldner, Ri.—Planter & new Freeholder; arrived 1737-8; lot 42N. in Frederica. An experienced Planter, but employed 2 years in the Scout boat: In 1738 Col. Oglethorp made him overseer of the soldiers at annual pay to teach them to cultivate their lands.
927. Olivera, Jacob—Jew; arrived 10 July 1733; lot 73 in Savannah.
928. ——, Judith, w.—Jew.
929. ——, David, son—Jew.
930. ——, Isaac, son—Jew; shot by accident 16 Nov. 1734.
931. ——, Leah, d.—Jew.
932. Ongy, Cath.—Servt. to Robt. Potter; arrived 10 Jan. 1733-4. She marry'd Michl. Welsh 16 Feb. 1734-5.
933. Ord, Walter—Servt. to Andrew Grant; arrived 1 Aug. 1734.
934. Ormiston, Tho.—A grant of 200 acres was past to him 31 March 1736. Dead Carolina Aug. 1742.
935. ——, [?], d.—Born in Georgia.
936. Overstreet, Hen.—Settled at Augusta. In the Colony the end of the year 1746.
937. ——, [?], w.
938. ——, [?], child.
939. ——, [?], child.
940. ——, [?], child.
941. Owens, Ri.—Servt. to ——; lot 177 in Savannah. This lot was granted him in 1736. Vacant Feb. 1738-9. Dead 1738.
942. Palmer, Tho.—Servt. to Roger Lacy; arrived 1 Feb. 1733-4.
943. Papot, [?]—Born in ye Colony.
944. Papot, Jane Robe—2d. w. of Ja. Papot.
945. ——, [?], son—Born in ye Colony.

946. ——, [?], son—Born in ye Colony.
947. Parker, Anne—D. of Hen. & Anne; born in Georgia.
948. ——, Hen. Will.—Son of Ditto; born in Georgia 25 Jan. 1733-4.
949. Parker, (Wid. Sale)—W. of Robt. Parker; arrived 12 March 1733-4; lot 76 in Savannah. Her former husband Will. Sale who died 8 July 1734 had a grant of 300 acres past to him 18 Oct. 1733, which he took up at Skidaway. She remarry'd to Robt. Parker. Run away with him July 1737.
950. Parnel, [?]—W. of Danl. Parnel; Lot 20 in Frederica. Quitted with her husband Jan. 1738-9.
951. Paterson, Alexr.—Son of Robt. Paterson. Supposed dead before Aug. 1741.
952. ——, David—Son of Ditto. Supposed dead before Aug. 1741.
953. ——, Patrick—Son of Ditto. Supposed dead before Aug. 1741.
954. Paulo, Antonio—Servt. to Tho. Causton.
955. Paulo. Frederick—Servt.
956. Pauvre, Jo.—Servt. to Andrew Michel. He had a lot in Frederica, but I know not the number. Deserted before April 1740.
957. ——, Eliz., w.
958. Pavey, Joseph—Victualler; embark'd 1736; lot 172 in Savannah. He had lycense to keep a publick house 2 Dec. 1736. He had leave to purchase this lot of Arthur Johnston 16 Aug. 1736, and paid 3 negroes with 10£ sterl. for it: valued at 73£ sterl. In 1738 he left the town to settle at Augusta, where 14 June 1736 Mr. Oglethorp orderd him a lot of 500 acres.
959. Pell, Hen.—Servt. to Jo. Roberson.
960. Pendrick, Will—Servt. to Andrew Grant; arrived 1 Aug. 1734.
961. Penner, Eliz.—Age 2; bastard of Mr. Norris; born in Georgia.
962. Pennifeather, Jo., Esq.—Arrived 21 July 1733. A grant was past to him of 300 acres 21 Feb. 1732-3, but quitted the Colony and died at Purysburg and took up no land. Quitted & died at Purysburg.
963. Pensyre, Fra. Joseph—Son of Saml. Pensyre; born in Georgia 10 Sept. 1734.
964. ——, Tiberius—Son of Ditto; born in Georgia 10 Oct. 1733; dead 7 Nov. 1733.
965. Pensyre, Tho.—Inmate at Savannah on Lot 40 in 1738.
966. Periam, [?]—Arrived Jan. 1739/40. A follower of Mr. Whitfeild, & taken out of a Madhouse in London.
967. Phelps, [?]—An Inmate at Savannah. A keeper of stores at Savannah. A factious fellow. Went to Carolina for fear of the Spaniards, and arrived in England Dec. 1740. Quitted Sept. 1740.
968. Piercy, Ma. Bathurst—W. of Fra. Piercy. Daughter of Sr. Fra. Bathurst. Marry'd to Fra. Piercy 9 Feb. 1734-5. Run away with her husband 1738.
969. Pitt, Henry—Carpenter. A grant of 100 acres was past to him 19 May 1736, but I know not if he went over.
970. Pluviant, Cha.—Servt. to Phil. Bishop; arrived 7 July 1733.
971. Polhill, Nathanl.—He had a grant of 150 acres past to him 21 Nov. 1733, but lives an Inmate with Edward his elder brother & his sisters on Lot 194 at Savannah with his mother Sarah Retford, now Goldwyre. Dead July 1737.
972. ——, Sarah, w.
973. ——, Anne, d.
974. ——, Edwd., son—Dead I suppose.
975. ——, Grace, d.

976. ——, Nathaniel, son—Orphan.
977. Polwart, Jo.—Servt. to Will. & H. Sterling; arrived 1 Aug. 1734. Boat man to Jo. Latter. Died at Frederica. Dead 1738.
978. Port, [?]—Age 51; widow; dead Oct. 1742.
979. Pouvroy, Jo.—Servt. to Ja. Houston; arrived 1 Aug. 1734.
980. ——, Martha—Servt. to Ditto; arrived 1 Aug. 1734.
981. Powel, Alderman—Servt.
982. Powel, Jane—Servt. to Robt. Williams.
983. Powell, Henry—Lot 16N. in Frederica.
984. ——, [?], w.
985. ——, [?], d.
986. Preston, Geo., junr.—Esq. A grant of 500 acres was past to him 25 Nov. 1737. He had leve not to go over, sending 10 servants.
987. Prevost, Danl.—Storekeeper. Lot 16 in Savannah; Lot 20S. in Frederica. This lot was granted him 31 May 1738 at the desire of John West & Eliz. Huges his wife. It was her former husband's Joseph Hughes [sic.] who died Sept. 30, 1733. In 1739 he resolv'd to keep a ware house & built it. Afterwards settled at Frederica.
988. Price, Ruth.—Servt. to Jo. Tesdale. One Reece Price is set down for a grant of 150 acres past 31 March 1736. Qy. if it be this man?
989. Price, Turner—Servt.
990. Price, Will.—Servt. to Ja. Calloway.
991. Priest, Will.—Servt. to Ja. Burnside.
992. Proctor, Eliz.—D. of Thomas Proctor, Senr.; born in Georgia.
993. Proctor, Steven—Return'd dead 1740. Joyn'd the Colony, but I know not when. Dead 1740.
994. Purdee, Jo.—Servt. to A. Grant; arrived 1 Aug. 1734.

995. Pury, Charles—A private Storekeeper. Inmate & a private Storekeeper at Savannah on Lot 16.
996. Pye, Eliz.—D. of Jo. & Eliz. Pye; 10 months old; born in Georgia; dead Sept. 1742.
997. ——, Mary—Age 4; d. of ditto; born in Georgia; dead Aug. 1742.
998. Pyka, Ri.—Lately a Tr. Servt.; lot 14S. in Frederica. Formerly at Amelia in the Trustees service, but in 1738 busie improving his 5 acre lot, till taken off by Col. Oglethorp to settle at a watch house 3 myles by water and 1½ by land from Frederica on the river to stop runaways. He marry'd a freeholders daughter and is allow'd 6 p. of meat & 6 p. of bread p week. He was maim'd in the Trustees service.
999. ——, Eliz., w.
1000. Pytt, Rowland—A grant of 500 acres was past to him 2 Oct. 1735. But excused going over. Had leave not to go over.
1001. Rantowl, Alexr.—Lot 168 in Savannah. He went to Charlestown, and was not return'd in Jan. 1738-9. His lot was gv. him 1736. Quitted Feb. 1736-7.
*1002. Rea, John Mastr. of the Scout boat at Amelia; arrived 8 May 1734; lot 176 in Savannah. Master formerly of the Scout boat at Amelia, afterwards (June 1741) Patroon of a trading boat. In the Colony the end of the year 1746.
1003. Ready, Tho.—Servt. to Patrick Houston; arrived 1 Aug. 1734; dead 1 Sept. 1738.
1004. Reid, Will.—Servt. to Patrick Tailfer.
1005. Retford, Robt.—Servt. to Jos. Wardrope; arrived 1 Aug. 1734; Lot 194 in Savannah. On expiration of his service, this lot was granted to him April 1737. His widow marry'd John

* See: p. 95, no. 1042, Roy.

Goldwire who lives with her on this lot. Dead June 1738.

1006. ———, Sarah, w.—Re-marry'd to Jo. Goldwyre; run away to Carolina Aug. 1742.
1007. Reynolds, Alexr.—Servt. to Will. Wardrope.
1008. Rigden, [?]—Born in Georgia 1737; dead 18 June 1737.
1009. Rigler, Leonard—Age 25; butcher; Swiss; embark'd 29 Sept. 1741; arrived 4 Dec. 1741. He paid his and his wife's passage.
1010. ———, Catharina, w.—Age 19.
1011. Ring, Agnese—Servt. to A. G. Dietzius; afterwards to Tho. Causton. German.
1012. Ring, Anne—Servt. to A. G. Dietzius; afterwards to Tho. Causton. German.
1013. Ring, Jo.—Servt. to A. G. Dietzius; arrived 28 Dec. 1734. German. Quitted 28 May 1735.
1014. ———, Cath., d.—Servt. to Ditto. German.
1015. ———, Jo. Christr., son—Servt. to Ditto. German.
1016. ———, Jo. Peter, son—Servt. to Ditto. German.
1017. Ring, Mary—Servt. to A. G. Dietzius; afterwards to Tho. Causton. German.
1018. Roach, Sarah—Servt. to the Widow Cox; arrived 10 Jan. 1733-4. The Widow Cox assign'd her to Jo. Musgrove.
1019. Roan, George—Arrived April 1734; Lot 145 in Savannah. Bound over for assault 8 April 1734. Again fyn'd for assaulting an Officer on duty 1 June 1734. Again fyn'd for assault 20 Feb. 1734-5. A beggar by his drunkenness. Kept a licentious tipling house. Run away 1738.
1020. ———, Eliz. Andrews, w.—Arrived 4 Jan. 1733-4. She marry'd George Roan 10 Aug. 1734.
1021. Robe, Alexr.—Servt.
1022. Robe, Jack—Servt.—Out of his time.
1023. ———, [?], w.
1024. ———, [?], d.—Born in Georgia.
1025. Robe, Jane—2d. w. of Ja. Papot. Jane Robe mar. to Ja. Papot & 2d. wife Jan. 1734-5.
1026. Roberson, Hen.—Placed on a new settlement call'd Archers Point half way between Frederica & Savannah Sept. 1738.
1027. ———, [?], w.—Placed there with her husband.
1028. Roberson, Ri.—Son of Jo. & Hannah; born in Georgia.
1029. ———, [?]—D. of Ditto; born in Georgia.
1030. Robinson, Will.—Boy.
1031. Rogers, Cha. Philip—A minor; son of Judith Cross; lot 48 in Savannah. His lot granted 21 Dec. 1733. In 1738 there was only 1 acre fell'd. He lives with his mother Judith Cross on Lot 22.
1032. Rone, Hen.—Servt.; arrived 10 Jan. 1733-4. Fyn'd 5 shillings for stealing clapboards & selling them 4 July 1734.
1033. Rone, Joseph—Servt.; arrived 10 Jan. 1733-4. Fyn'd same time for the same crime.
1034. Rone, Ri.—Servt.; arrived 10 Jan. 1733-4. Fyn'd same time for the same crime.
1035. Ross, Alexander—Arrived 28 Dec. 1734; lot 220 in Savannah. He had a brother living in Edinburgh May 1737, but he is supposed dead since, & that the lot is vacant. Out of his time.
1036. Ross, Hugh—Servt. to Will. & H. Sterling; arrived 1 Aug. 1734. Carpenter & labourer.
1037. Ross, Hugh of Drenach—Age 36; servt. to Mr. Mackay of Scourie; embark'd 20 Oct. 1735; arrived 10 Jan. 1735-6. Living at Darien still a serv-

ant 6 May 1741 but said to be 54 years old.
1038. Ross, James—Servt. to Patrick Houston; arrived 1 Aug. 1734.
1039. Ross, James—Miller; of Waffin; embark'd 20 Oct. 1735; arrived 10 Jan. 1735-6.
1040. Roth, Ja. Fred—Son of Geo. Bartholmew; born in Georgia 10 April 1734. At Ebenezar.
1041. Rottray, Alexr.—Servt. to Patrick Houston; arrived 1 Aug. 1734.
1042. Roy, John, a boy—Arrived 8 May 1734; Lot 176 in Savannah. In the Colony the end of the year 1746. Abst. 24 Feb. 1735-6.
1043. Rutlidge, [?]—Tr. servt. Employ'd in the Tr. Periagua boatman at Frederica, with an annual sallary of 13£ .10.0. 1739.
1044. Rutterford, Jo.—Servt. to Andrew Grant; arrived 1 Aug. 1734.
1045. Ryley, Alice—Servt. to Ri. Cannon; arrived 10 Jan. 1733-4. An Irish Transport. Condem'd for the murder of Will. Wise her master 1 Mar. 1733-4. Hang'd 20 Jan. 1734-5.
1046. ——, James, son—Born in Georgia 21 Dec. 1734; dead 15 Feb. 1734-5.
1047. Ryley, James—Arrived 4 May 1735. He marry'd Deborah Potter 4 May 1735. Dead 1740.
1048. Ryley, John—Servt. to the Trustees; arrived 10 Jan. 1733-4. Sentenc'd 30 lashes for breaking open a door being drunk 19 May 1734.
1049. Sale, Will.—Arrived 12 Mar. 1733-4; Lot 76 in Savannah. He had a grant of 300 acres 18 Oct. 1733, and took it at Skidaway. Dead 8 July 1734.
1050. ——, Eliz., w.—Re-marry'd to Robt. Parker 30 Sept. 1734 and ran away to England with him. Run away 9 July 1736.
1051. ——, Joseph, son—Born in Georgia 12 April 1734; dead 24 June 1734.
1052. Sallie, Ant.—Sallie, Ant. joyn'd the Colony, when I know not. Dead.
1053. Salomon, Salomon—Jew; arrived 10 July 1733.
1054. Salter, Tho.—Bricklayer; arrived 17 Dec. 1733; lot 68 in Savannah. A rioter in open court 20 Oct. 1737. He marry'd Anne the Wid. of Jos. Coles 9 Sept. 1736. A Tything man in Sept. 1739.
1055. Samms, Mary—W. of Jo. Sams; lot 9 in Savannah. Had leave to sell her interest 2 Mar. 1734-5. Sold her Ints.
1056. Sandford, Cornelius—He had a grant of 500 acres 11 May 1733. Of Bristol: but went not over.
1057. Sarsfeild, Will.—Servt. to Tho. Causton; arrived 22 Jan. 1734-5.
1058. Savy, John—Convicted of defaming the Trustees 1 April 1735. He fled to the Spaniards, and laid a scheme for their invading Georgia, then repented and cast himself upon the Governor for pardon, and is now a prisoner at large in London. Afterwards his majesty made him a Lieut. and he is in the American Service 1741.
1059. Scot, James—Servt. to A. Grant; arrived 1 Aug. 1734; out of his time.
1060. Scot, Hamilton—An Inmate under some criminal prossecution 7 Oct. 1736, but how it ended I know not.
1061. Scot, John—Servt. to Andrew Grant; arrived 1 Aug. 1734.
1062. Scot, Thomas—Son of John the blacksmith; born in Georgia.
1063. ——, William—Son of ditto; born in Georgia.
1064. Searls, Ja.—Mastr. of a Periagua. Master of a Periagua at Frederica or in the Southern division of the Province 1739. On his own acct. retir'd to Carolina where he was arrested for debt, and by the gout has lost the use of him limbs. Quitted 1739.

1065. Secore, Samuel—Jew; embark'd 10 July 1733.
1066. Sellier, John—Swiss; bricklayer; lot 39 in Savannah. He marry'd the widow of Danl. Thibaut, & lives with her on her Lot 39. He came from Purysburg, turned Methodist and abandon'd cultivation 27 March 1740. At work at the Orphan house 1741.
1067. Serrier, Peter—Sentenc'd 50 lashes for assault: prophaning the Sabbath: & abusing the constable 16 Sept. 1734. Also fyn'd 10 shillings for assault 31st of same month.
1068. Shale, William—Shipwright; servt. to Noble Jones; arrived 10 Jan. 1733-4; run away to Carolina Aug. 1742.
1069. Sharrer, James—Servt.
1070. Shaw, John—He lately joyn'd the Colony, at Frederica, and Col. Oglethorp lent him 19 April 1739 5£ on the Trustees acct. to set up the trade of a hatter.
1071. Sheftel, Benj.—Jew; arrived 10 July 1733; Lot 64 in Savannah. He had possession 21 Dec. 1733.
1072. ——, Eliz., w.
1073. ——, Sheftel, son—Born in Georgia 3 Aug. 1734.
1074. ——, [?], son—Born in Georgia.
1075. Shillity, John—Servt. to Jo. Roberson; arrived 4 June 1737.
1076. Simms, [?]—Arrived Jan. 1739-40. Follow'd Mr. Whitfeild from London, and performer of church offices in his absence. Said to have been a butcher in Clare Market.
1077. Simms, Alexr.—Servt. to Will. Williamson.
1078. Simons, [?]
1079. Simpson, Saml.—Servt. to Robt. Williams.
1080. Sinclair, Archibald—Servt. to Patrick Houston; arrived 1 Aug. 1734.
1081. Sinclair, Archibald—Lot 24S. in Frederica. Tything Man in the South division of Frederica town 1738-9.
1082. ——, Isabel, w.
1083. ——, James, son—Dead before Aug. 1741.
1084. ——, Margt., d.
1085. Sinclair, John—Servt. to Jo. Mackintosh of Dorres; arrived 10 Jan. 1735-6.
1086. Sinclair, Will.—Servt. to Will Bradley.
1087. Slowly, John—Servt. to Tho. Fawsset; arrived 14 Jan. 1733-4; dead 9 Aug. 1734.
1088. Smith, [?]—Employ'd in the Trustees Periagua 1739 at Frederica.
1089. Smith, Anne Skideway—D. of Tho. & Frances; born in Georgia 22 April 1734.
1090. Smith, George—Arrived 1734. Sentenc'd 60 lashes for stealing 12 Nov. 1734. Marry'd to Jane Bambrick 28 Dec. 1734.
1091. Smith, James—Arrived 27 Jan. 1733-4; lot 40 in Savannah. Marry'd the Widow Close 8 Feb. 1733-4, and lived with her on this her lot. Abt. May 1740 they both quitted the Colony to settle in Scotland on an estate fallen to him, and had leave to sell his lot to Capt. W. Thompson. Quitted May 1740.
1092. Smith, John—Arrived Dec. 1735; lot 228 in Savannah.
1093. Smith, Mary—Servt. to Tho. Fawsett; arrived 22 Jan. 1734-5.
1094. Smith, Philip—Servt. to Phil. Bishop; arrived 7 July 1733.
1095. Smith, Will—Keeps a Periagua of his own. His residence and business in the Southern division of the Province 1739.
1096. Smith, William—Servt.; arrived 4 June 1737.
1097. Somers, Joseph—Servt. to Will. Sale; arrived 12 Mar. 1733-4. His lot at Abercorn, but not occupied in 1738.

It was before the lot of Will. Curtis who died 26 May 1734. In Carolina.

1098. Spence, John—Age 36; Servt. to Jo. Cuthbert of Draikes; arrived 10 Jan. 1735-6.
1099. Spencer, Sarah—D. of Geo. & Mary; born in Georgia; dead before Aug. 1741.
1100. Squires, Botham—Arrived 16 May 1733. He quitted at his own desire: afterwards return'd, but could not obtain another grant. Quitted 14 Aug. 1733.
1101. Stabler, John—Son of David; born in Georgia.
1102. ——,Tho.—Son of Ditto. New Freeholdr.; at Frederica; lot 15N. at Frederica. A new Freeholder at Frederica 1738-9. I know not yet his lot.
1103. ——, Will.—Son of Ditto; born in Georgia.
1104. ——, Eliz.—D. of David; born in Georgia.
1105. Stammer, Ja.
1106. Stammer, Tho.—Arrived 1737; Settled at Highgate, and good Improver.
1107. ——, [?], w.
1108. ——, [?], child.
1109. Stanton, Geo.—Arrived 25 Feb. 1733-4. Marry'd to A. Willoughby 29 Jan. 1734-5.
1110. Stephens, Donald—Age 53; of Lange; labourer.
1111. Stephens, Geo.—Servt. to Will. Sale; arrived 12 Mar. 1733-4. His service being expired he had a lot given him at Abercorn, but deserted the Colony. Quitted 1738.
1112. Stephens, Newdigate—A younger son of Col. Stephens; embark'd 1741; arrived 1741.
1113. Sterling, Hugh — Gent. — Arrived 1 Aug. 1734. 14 Nov. 1733 he had a grant of 500 acres. Hugh & William settled at Sterlings Bluff on the Ogykee river, but after some years cultivation abandon'd their improvmts. to live in Savannah, where they wasted their substance; they quitted before Sept. 1737. Dead 1740.
1114. ——, Will.—Gent.; arrived 1 June 1734. 14 Nov. 1733 he had a grant of 500 acres. On 26 May 1739 he & Andrew Grant wrote they had lost 906.2.9 by cultivating with white servants and desired consideration for it. Went to Carolina for fear of ye Spaniards. Quitted 30 Aug. 1743.
1115. Steward, [?]—Servt. to Tho. Causton.
1116. ——, [?], w.
1117. ——, [?], son.
1118. ——, [?], son.
1119. ——, [?], d.
1120. ——, [?], d.
1121. Steward, Cha.—Servt. to Andrew Grant; arrived 1 Aug. 1734.
1122. Steward, Donald—Age 48; of Inverness; mariner; embark'd 20 Oct. 1735; arrived 10 Jan. 1735-6; Lot 207 in Savannah. Master of a sloop. Drowned in sailing within Portroyal Sound. Drown'd April 1740.
1123. ——, Jeanne, w.—Age 35.
1124. ——, [?], son—Age 8.
1125. ——, Anne, d.—Age 8.
1126. ——, Isabel, d.—Age 5; born in Georgia.
1127. ——, John, son—Age 11.
1128. Steward, Donald—Age 23; servt. to Donald Steward of Inverness.
1129. Steward, Tho.—Boy.
1130. Stewart, Anne—Alive at Darien 6 May 1741.
1131. Stewart, Anne—Alive at Darien 6 May 1741 and then 8 years old.
1132. Stewart, David—Age 23; of Cromdale; surgeon; arrived 10 Jan. 1735-6.
1133. Stoll, Ezechiel—Age 30; smith; Swiss; embark'd 29 Sept. 1741; arrived 4 Dec. 1741. Paid his own pass-

age. Settled on a grant S. E. of Hampstead with his family.
1134. Storey, Robt.—Servt. to Wid. Bowling; arrived 10 Jan. 1733-4; dead 3 Mar. 1733-4.
1135. Stringer, Josua—Servt. to Will. Sale; arrived 12 Mar. 1733-4. After his service was out he had a lot at Abercorn, and afterwards deserted the Colony. The lot had been John Thompson senrs. He afterwards left the Colony. Quitted 1738.
1136. Stronach, Priscilla—D. of Michl. Stronach; born in Georgia.
1137. ——, Will.—Son of Ditto; born in Georgia.
1138. Sullivan, Jo.—Servt. to Jo. West; arrived 10 Jan. 1733-4.
1139. Sumner, Tho.—New Freeholdr. 1738; lot 18S. in Frederica. A new Freeholder at Frederica since 30 Jan. 1737-8. By trade a carpenter. Built a good house in 1740.
1140. ——, Mary, w.
1141. ——, Benj., son—Born in Georgia 1737.
1142. —— (Servt.)
1143. —— (Servt.)
1144. —— (Servt.)
1145. —— (Servt.)
1146. —— (Servt.)
1147. Sutherland, Alexr.—Age 30; servt. to Mr. Mackay of Scourie; embark'd 20 Oct. 1735; arrived 10 Jan. 1735-6.
1148. Sweeny, [?]—Lot 15S. in Frederica. He ran away from his family, and left a helpless wife with 3 children. It is not said what is become of them. Run away from his family.
1149. ——, [?], w.
1150. ——, [?], son.
1151. ——, [?], son.
1152. ——, [?], d.
1153. Tailfer, Patrick—Surgeon; arrived 1 Aug. 1734. Settled at first on the river Nese, but quitted to practice surgery in Savanah. He had a grant of 500 acres 18 Oct. 1733. A proud saucy fellow and a Ringleader for allowance of Negroes & change of tenure. Went away to Carolina for fear of the Spaniards 31 Aug. 1740. Quitted 30 Aug. 1740 [sic.].
1154. ——, Mary, w.—Quitted.
1155. Tanner, Eliz.—Belong'd to the orphan house; run away to Carolina Aug. 1742.
1156. Tarrel, Geo.—Servt. to Roger Lacy; arrived 1 Feb. 1733-4.
1157. Tatzner, Ambrose—See Tuckner.
1158. Taylor, Abraham—Servt. to Will. Bradley.
1159. Taylor, Alexr.—Servt. to Will. & H. Sterling; arrived 1 Aug. 1734; out of his time.
1160. Taylor, Anne—Servt. to Jo. Musgrove Senr.; arrived 28 Dec. 1734; dead 3 June 1735.
1161. Tebbut, James—Son of Tho. & Anne; born in Georgia 1 Aug. 1733; dead 6 Aug. 1735.
1162. Terrian, Stephen—Cooper; lot 154 in Savannah. This lot formerly belong'd to Tim. Leary who arrived 1 Aug. 1734 & died at Savanah.
1163. ——, Mary, w.
1164. Terry, Willm.—He had a grant of 200 acres past to him 18 Oct. 1733.
1165. Thickness, Philip—Servt.; arrived Sept. 1736.
1166. Thompson, Daniel—Servt. to Hugh Anderson.
1167. Thompson, George—Servt. to Tho. Christie; arrived 10 Jan. 1733-4. On the expiration of his service in 1738 a lot was granted him at Abercorn wch. formerly belong'd to Will Box. Dead.
1168. Thompson, Jo.—Servt. to Jo. Baillie; arrived 1 Aug. 1734.
1169. ——, Thomas—Son of John Thompson, Senr.

A LIST OF EARLY SETTLERS OF GEORGIA

1170. Thompson, Will.—Servt. to Patrick Graham; ret. to Engld. Nov. 1736.
1171. Thornwell, Eliz.—A soldiers wife; arrived 4 June 1737.
1172. Tillison, John—Servt. to Rogr. Lacy; arrived 1 Feb. 1733-4.
1173. Timberman, Jo.—Servt. to Tho. Millidge; arrived 10 Jan. 1733-4; dead 13 Feb. 1733-4.
1174. Tinley, John—Servt. to Patr. Graham; afterwds. to Will. Bradley. In the Colony the end of the year 1746.
1175. Todd, Andrew—Servt. to Will. & H. Sterling; arrived 1 Aug. 1734.
1176. Togler, Joannes—Age 27; farmer; Swiss; embark'd 29 Sept. 1741; arrived 4 Dec. 1741. He paid his own passage but not his wife's. Settled on a grant S. E. of Hampstead.
1177. Tolmie, Alexr.—Age 36; Farmer; embark'd 20 Oct. 1735; arrived 10 Jan. 1735-6. Lot vacant he died without heirs. Dead 16 Nov. 1736.
1178. Tolson, [?]—Ensign; embark'd 22 March 1736/7; arrived 4 June 1737.
1179. ———, [?], w.
1180. ———, [?], son.
1181. ———, [?], d.
1182. Tomi, Samuel—Servt.
1183. Tondee, Pet., Senr.—Arrived 16 May 1733; Lot 70 in Savannah. In possession of his lot 21 Dec. 1733; dead 19 July 1733.
1184. ———, Cha., son—Servt. to Hen. Parker.
1185. ———, Peter, son—Servt. to Hen. Parker; minor & orphan.
1186. Townsend, Edwd.—Arrived 8 Feb. 1733-4; lot 17 in Savannah. Fynd one shilling for assault 28 July 1735. Eliz., widow of Ri. Hodges was possest of this lot 2 April 1734. He had a lycense to keep victualling house which recall'd 2 Dec. 1736. He marry'd the widow Hodges 22 Feb. 1734-5, and deserted the Colony on shutting up the stores Dec. 1738. Master of a periagua at ye Siege of Augustine July 1740. Run away Dec. 1738 but returned & has a periagua 1740 but went away again Aug. 1742.
1187. Trent, Eliz.—Dead 29 Oct. 1738.
1188. Trip, [?]—Son of Tho. Trip & Eliz. Herbert; born in Georgia.
1189. ———, [?]—D. of ditto; born in Georgia.
1190. ———, [?]—D. of ditto; born in Georgia.
1191. Truan, David—He and Jacob Truan were inmates at Savannah on Lot 116 in 1738.
1192. Truan, Jacob
1193. Trumbull, Ja.—Servt. to Will. & H. Sterling; arrived 1 Aug. 1734.
1194. Tuby, Ja. Moore—Arrived 31 Mar. 1734.
1195. Tuckner, [?]—Son of Ambrose; born in Georgia; dead before Aug. 1741.
1196. Tuckwell, Jo.—He had a grant past to him of 50 acres 2 Oct. 1735, but was excused going over.
1197. Turner, Eliz. Carrol—D. of Ja. & Eliz.; born in Georgia 7 Jan. 1733-4; dead 29 Jan. 1733-4.
1198. Tyrril, Geo.
1199. Tyrry, Tho.—Servt. to Will. Stephens, Esq.
1200. Upsal, Oliver—Servt. to Jo. Amory.
1201. Upton, Tho.—Gent. He had a grant of 150 acres 11 May 1737 and took it in the Southern division of the Province near the town of Frederica, where he built a good house and clear'd about 8 acres of land, but in 1739 Col. Oglethorp agreed with him to buy it and the improved land for the ministers use, and made him a new grant on the Island Alkony a little South of Skidaway.
1202. ———, [?], w.

1203. Uré, Rachel—Servt. to Patrick Tailfer; arrived 1 Aug. 1734; quitted; dead 1741.
1204. Valatin, Jeremy—Servt.; french.
1205. ——, Anne, w.—Dead Oct. 1742.
1206. Venables, Jo.—Upholster; embark'd 22 March 1736/7; arrived 3 June 1737. Went to Carolina a week after he landed in order to return to England. Went to Carolina 10 June 1737.
1207. Vicary, [?]—W. of Ambrose Vicary. She is with her children in England, but One Dart of Charles Town acts for her. In Engld. with her children.
1208. Villaroel, Isaac—Jew. Settled at Hampstead.
1209. Votican, Cath.—Servt. Sentenc'd 100 lashes for thieving and running away 10 Aug. 1734.
1210. Vowel, Jacob—He was in possession of a lot in Savannah Dec. 21, 1733, but where I know not, or what became of him.
1211. Wade, Edward—A broken cheesmonger. He had a grant of 100 acres 7 Oct. 1734.
1212. Wade, John—Servt. to Hugh Frazer; arrived 10 Jan. 1733-4.
1213. Wagner, Saml.—Settled at Hampstead. He died without heir male or female, & his next relations had leave to sell the lot. Dead 1738.
1214. Wakefeild, John—Lot 15S. in Frederica. A new Freeholder in Sweeny's room since 30 Jan. 1737-8. Quitted before Aug. 1741.
1215. ——, Sarah, w.—Quitted before Aug. 1741.
1216. Walker, [?], D. of Tho. & Mary; born in Georgia.
1217. ——, Saml.—Son of Ditto; born in Georgia; supposed dead before Aug. 1741.
1218. Wall, Tho.—Servt. to Capt. Scot; embark'd 4 April 1733; arrived 21 July 1733. From Capt. Scot's service he devolv'd to Capt. Macpherson's.
1219. Wallis, Will.—Servt. to Saml. Mercer; arrived 10 Jan. 1732.3. [Sic.].
1220. Walman, Will.—Servt. to Isaac Gibbs.
1221. Walser, Andrew—Lot 33S. in Frederica.
1222. ——, Barbara, w.
1223. ——, Anne, d.
1224. ——, John, son.
1225. Walsmley, Margt.—Servt. to Jo. Fallowfield; arrived 15 Feb. 1733-4. Assign'd by her master to Joseph Watson.
1226. Ward, Anne—D. of Saml. Ward; born in Georgia Oct. 1738.
1227. Ward, John—Servt.
1228. Wardrope, Jos.—Age 35; carpenter; arrived 21 Aug. 1734; lot 211 in Savannah. He had a grant of 150 acres 30 Jan. 1733-4. In 1738 he let this town lot Patrick Graham, who off of 5 acres had 20 bushells of Indian corn, 10 of potatoes, and 100 of rice. A rioter in open court 20 Oct. 1737. Quitted with his family to Carolina May 1742.
1229. ——, Jane, w.—Age 42.
1230. ——, Elenor, d.—Age 13.
1231. Waterman, Geo.—Shoemaker; arrived 7 Dec. 1733; lot 112 in Savannah. Prossecuted and obliged to give security for assault, prophaning the Sabbath, and abusing the Constable 16 Sept. 1734. Again fyn'd half a crown for assault 31 of same month. Quitted 16 Jan. 1737-8.
1232. ——, Sarah, w.
1233. Wathy, Samuel—Embark'd 19 Nov. 1737; arrived 14 Jan. 1737/8. Went over to settle at Frederica, but was seduced to remain at Charlestown at his arrival.
1234. Watson, Hugh—Age 18; servt. to Tho. Baillie; embark'd 20 Oct. 1735;

arrived 10 Jan. 1735-6; murd. at sea June 1739.

1235. Watson, Joseph—An insolent vile man: tis said he has a grant of 500 acres, but I don't find when, or when taken up. Twice fyn'd for scandal; again fyn'd for assaulting an Indian, and afterwds. capitally convicted of killing one, but brought in lunatick. Is now out on good behavior. In the Colony the end of the year 1746.

1236. Watten, Joseph—Prossecuted and obliged to give security for assault: prophaning the Sabbath: & assaulting the Constable 16 Sept. 1734.

1237. Wattle, Tho.—Servt. After his service he became land holder at Abercorn, but in 1737 that settlement was deserted. He marry'd Eliz. widow of Tho. Smith of Skidaway 15 July 1735, & lives inmate with her at Savannah.

1238. ——, Eliz. Smith, w.—The widow of Tho. Smith of Skidaway who died 16 May 1735.

1239. Webb, Tho., Senr.—Weaver at ye orphan house; run away to Carolina Aug. 1742.

1240. ——, Eliz., d.—Run away with her father.

1241. Webster, Will—Servt. to Hugh Anderson.

1242. Wedd, Jo.—Joyn'd the Colony but I know not when. Return'd dead 1740. Dead 1740.

1243. Wedge, Tho.

1244. Welsh, Eliz.—D. of John & Anne; born in Georgia.

1245. Welsh, Michl.—Idle vagabond. Sentenc'd to be whipt for stealing 31 May 1735.

1246. Welsh, Mary—Idle vagabond. Sentenc'd 39 lashes for the same 31 May 1735.

1247. Welsh, Simon—Servt. to Rogr. Lacy; arrived 10 Jan. 1732-3 [sic.]. Condemn'd to be hang'd for robery 6 Oct. 1733 but broak jayl and fled the Colony. Run away 1733.

1248. Welsh, Steven—Servt. to Jos. Close; arrived 10 Jan. 1732-3 [sic.].

1249. West, Joseph—Son of John & Eliz. Hughes; born in Georgia 26 Dec. 1734.

1250. Weston, [?]—W. of Willes Weston; dead.

1251. ——, (woman servant)

1252. ——, (woman servant)

1253. Weston, Hanah—D. of Willes Weston; born in Georgia Feb. 1737-8.

1254. Whey, Hen.—Servt. to Donald Steward.

1255. White, James—Servt. to Edwd. Jenkins; embark'd 15 June 1733; arrived 29 Aug. 1733. An Irish Transport servt. hang'd for murdering Will. Wise in his bed. Mistake it was Nic. White. Dead 24 Nov. 1742.

1256. White, John—Servt. to Widow Willoughby; arrived 10 Jan. 1732-3.

1257. White, Nics.—Servt.; arrived 10 Jan. 1733-4; hang'd for murder.

1258. White, Richd.—Servt.; arrived 10 Jan. 1733-4. Irish Transport, hang'd for murdering Will. Wise 20 June 1734-5. Hang'd for murder.

1259. Wicks, Fra.—Arrived 17 April 1733. Settled at Fort Arguile. He came from Carolina, and marry'd Mary Hicks servt. 17 April 1733, he came from Carolina.

1260. Wicks, Nehemiah—Hang'd himself 14 Dec. 1733-4.

1261. Wierley, Hans Caspar—Age 45; weaver; Swiss; embark'd 29 Sept. 1741; arrived 4 Dec. 1741. Hans Caspar Wierley pd. his own passage.

1262. Wigan, Joseph—Sentenc'd 150 lashes for Adultery with an Indian 8 April 1734.

1263. Wiggin, Tho.—Indian Trader; lot 184 in Savannah. A Trader to the

Creek nation. This Lot was granted him in 1736. Dead 5 July 1742.

1264. Wilkee, Tho.—Servt. to Patrick Tailfer; arrived 1 Aug. 1734.

1265. Wilkins, Hannah—Servt. to Fra. Lynch; arrived 27 Nov. 1733. Servt. at first to Fra. Lynch. Afterwds. to Jo. West.

1266. Wilkins, Richd.—Sentenc'd to give security for good behavior being convicted of disorderly lewd living 24 Nov. 1736.

1267. Williams Anne — Servt.; embark'd 4 June 1737.

1268. Williams, Griffith—Lot 2N. in Frederica.

1269. Williams, James—Mercht.; arrived 1736; lot 167 in Savannah. A Bristol man of substance who traded before to the W. Indies, this lot was granted him in 1736. He is younger brother to Robt. Williams, Senr.

1270. Williams, John—He had a grant of 500 acres 11 May 1733.

1271. Williams, Misael—Servt. to Robt. Williams, Senr.

1272. Williams, Robt.—Senr. mercht. He had a grant of 500 acres 11 May 1733, and went from Bristol. He was a great clamourer for change of Tenure, and for introduction of Negroes, that he might furnish the Planters & get their lands in his hands.

1273. ——, Robt., son—Lot 182 in Savannah. A Minor in England, and never went over. Abst. 1739.

1274. Williamson, Will.—Attorney. Made Recorder of Savannah in Tho. Christies room. He marry'd Miss Hopkey, niece to Mrs. Causton. 25 March 1740 the Trustees determind he should not be Recorder he insisting on conditions that were not fit to allow. He went to Charlestown in 1739 & there abides. Quitted 1739.

1275. Wilson, Amelia Moore—W. of Ja. Wilson; arrived 29 Aug. 1733; quitted wth. her husbd.

1276. Wilson, Clement—Son of Michl. & Alkey; born in Georgia.

1277. ——, Sarah—D. of do.; born in Georgia.

1278. Willy, Ant.—Indian Trader; shot himself Inne 1742.

1279. Wood, James—Lot 10 in Frederica. In England. Abst. 24 Feb. 1736-7. Quitted ret. England.

1280. Wood, Jonathan.

1281. Wood, William—Capt. in Oglethorps Regimt. He had a grant of 500 acres 21 Dec. 1737.

1282. Woodhouse, Mary—Placed at a New Settlement call'd Archers point half way between Frederica & Savannah Sept. 1738.

1283. Woodrofe, Will. — Haberdasher of Small wares; lot 125 in Savannah. This Lot was given him in 1736. He had before a Grant of 50 acres 24 July 1735. He neglects & lives an Inmate on Lot 9. This Lot belong'd before to Lewis Bowen who D. in Aug. 1734. He has a ware house well furnished 1739.

1284. ——, [?], w.—Embark'd 21 Oct. 1740; arrived 4 March 1740-1.

1285. Woodward, [?]—Servt.

1286. Woolley, [?]—Embark'd 16 Aug 1737; arrived 31 Oct. 1737. Went over to settle at Frederica, but was seduced to remain at Charlestown at his arrival. Stayd in Carolina when arrived in his way to Georgia.

1287. Wright, Jo.—Servt.

1288. Wrightnour, Laurence—Lot 27N. in Frederica.

1289. ——, [?], w.

1290. Wurwick, Laurence—Patroon of the Trustees Periagua at Frederica since April 1739 at 18£ a year.

1291. Yoakley, James—Embark'd 28 Sept. 1733; arrived 14 Jan. 1733-4; lot 131 in Savannah. Supposed dead and his Lot supposed vacant. Quitted 1736 & supposed dead.

1292. Youghal, Jacob—Jew; arrived 10 July 1733.

1293. Young, Danl.—Lot 20 in Frederica. He succeeded Danl. Parnel in this lot when the latter deserted the Colony in Jany. 1738-9. Dead or quitted before Aug. 1741.

1294. Young, Geo. — Age 45; Tr. servt.; dead Aug. 1742.

1295. Young, Isaac, Senr.—Bricklayer; arrived 21 Aug. 1736. He had a grant of 100 acres 2 June 1736. But on 4 May 1737 complain'd he had no land which was his own fault, as Mr. Causton inform'd the Trustees. At last he chose it at Pype makers creak, but was allow'd only 50 acres.

1296. ——, Sarah, w.

1297. ——, Isaac, son—Lot 195 in Savannah. This lot was granted him April 1737.

1298. ——, Eliz., w.—Dead 29 Oct. 1742.

1299. ——, Eliz., d.—Born in Georgia; dead 1740.

1300. ——, John, son.

1301. ——, Nathl., son—Quitted to Carolina & dead 1740.

1302. ——, Thomas, son—Age 15; a minor; bricklayer; lot 200 in Savannah. Isaac Young Senr. his father who has no Town lot of his own lives with this his son on this Lot. Run away to Carolina Aug. 1742.

1303. Young, Mary Box—W. of Thomas the wheelwright.

1304. Ct. Zinzendorf, Nic. Louis; Moravian Bishp. He had a grant of 500 acres 18 Jany. 1734-5, and sent Moravians over. Excused going over.

[Reprinted from *The Georgia Historical Quarterly*,
XXXI, 4 (December, 1947, 282-88).]

A List of the First Shipload of Georgia Settlers

Edited by E. MERTON COULTER

The original of the document which appears below is in the Egmont Manuscripts of the famous Phillipps Collection. John Percival (1683-1748), the first Earl of Egmont (a title which no longer exists), was one of the original trustees of Georgia and was as active in the establishment of the new colony as was Oglethorpe. Undoubtedly, many of the Egmont Manuscripts are in the Earl's handwriting and the others are either originals or contemporary copies made by others. These manuscripts, consisting of twenty-one volumes, were until recently a part of the immense collection of manuscripts made by Sir Thomas Phillipps, Bt., of Middle Hill, Worcestershire, and Thirlestaine House, Cheltenham. In 1946, the University of Georgia purchased the Egmont Manuscripts through the agency of Sotherby & Company, London. The document here presented is included in the volume (serial number 14207) entitled "Letters, papers, & Accts &c Sent to Georgia or post in England from 9 June 1732 to 9 June 1735" (pp. 61-63). Information on the subsequent career of these original settlers is given in another volume of the Egmont Manuscripts (serial number 14220) entitled "A List of Persons who went from Europe to Georgia On their own account, or at the Trustees charge, or who joyned the Colony, or were born in it distinguishing Such as had Grants there or were only Inmates." This information is included here in the footnotes, which accompany the document.

As neither document is dated there is no way to determine with absolute certainty the time when each was written; but, of course, there is every reason to suggest that both were made in colonial times. It can be shown, however, that the second List was composed not earlier than 1752. In that year the calendar was changed to make the year begin on January 1, instead of March 25, which was the usage before that time. Subsequently, in referring to dates which came between January 1 and March 25 before the change, to prevent a misunderstanding as to whether it was Old Style or New Style reckoning, the simple device of giving both years was used, as for instance "8 Feb. 1733-4", as is recorded in footnote 26.

A LIST OF THE PERSONS SENT TO GEORGIA ON THE CHARITY BY THE TRUSTEES FOR ESTABLISHING THE COLONY THERE. 16 Novbr. 1732.

By CAPT. THOMAS [of the *Anne*].

	No. of Persons
Paul Amatis[1] aged [blank space] understands the Nature & Production of Raw Silk	1.
Timothy Bowling[2] Aged 38. Potashmaker	1.
Wm Calvert[3] Trader of Goods aged 44, Mary[4] his Wife aged 42 Wm Greenfield[5] aged 19 & Charles Greenfield[6] aged 16 his [i. e. Calvert's] Nephews, Sarah Greenfield[7] aged 16 his Neice & Elizabeth Wallis[8] aged 19 his Servant	6.
Richard Cannon[,][9] Calendar & Carpenter aged 36, Mary[10] his Wife aged 33, his Sons Marmaduke[11] aged 9 & James[12] aged 7 months, his daughter Clementine[13] aged 2½ & His Servant Mary Hicks[14] aged [blank space]	6.
James Carwell[15] Peruke maker aged 35 & Margaret[16] his Wife aged 32	2.

---

1. "Italian silk man." "Brought from Piedmont to introduce silk in Georgia, but took a disgust and settled chiefly at Charleston, where he died [December, 1736]." His brother, Nicholas, was "brought from Piedmont for the same purpose, [arriving July 21, 1733] but proved an idle troublesome fellow & quitted the colony. In Aug. 1735, his Brother discharg'd him." These facts and all information in subsequent footnotes were taken from the volume of the Egmont Collection, entitled "A List of Persons who went from Europe to Georgia On their own account, or at the Trustees charge, or who joyned the Colony, or were born in it distinguishing Such as had Grants there or were only Inmates." The information about Amatis is on page 9. Hereafter, this volume will be cited as List
2. He died November 5, 1733. List, 19.
3. "Said to be a land holder at Fort Arguile, 16 Jan. 1737-8, but I don't find him in the list. Would have denyd a note of hand to Ja. Dormer. Acct was cast 7 July 1737." He received lot number 7 in Savannah. List, 29.
4. She died July 4, 1733. List, 29.
5. He settled at "Fort Arguile." List, 73.
6. The list gives nothing further about him. List, 73.
7. "Marry'd to Will Elbert 22 June 1734 and lived mostly in Carolina." List, 73.
8. "Became wife of Lawrence Cook." List, 229.
9. "He marry'd to his 2nd. wife the widow of Daniel Preston 24 Oct. 1734." He received lot 5 in Savannah. He died May 27, 1735. List, 31.
10. She died July 22, 1733. List, 31.
11. He afterwards became a servant to Thomas Causton. List, 31.
12. He died on shipboard on the way to Georgia. According to the record here he was 1 year old. List, 31.
13. According to the record she was 3 years old. List, 31.
14. "Discharged by consent and marry'd Fra. Wicks 17 April 1733." List, 85.
15. "Keeper of the Workhouse 1737 but of very bad character. In July 1739 Mr. Oglethorpe appointed him Provost Marshal and Jailer at Savannah wth. a sallary of 20 pounds." He received lot 4 in Savannah. List, 31.
16. She died September 7, 1733. List, 31.

Thomas Causton[,][17] Callicoe Printer aged 40 .... 1.
Thomas Christie [,][18] Merchant aged 32 & Robert
Johnson[Johnston,][19] his Servant aged 17 .... 2.
Robert Clark [Clarke,][20] Taylor aged 37, Judith[21]
his Wife aged 29, & his Sons Charles[22] aged 11, John
aged 4, Peter[23] aged 3 and James[24] aged 9 months .... 6.
Henry Close [,][25] Clothworker aged 42, Hannah[26]
his Wife aged 32 & Ann[27] his daughter aged under 2   3.
Joseph Coles [,][28] Miller & Baker aged 28, Anna[29]
his Wife aged 32, Anna[30] his daughter aged 13, &
Elias Ann Wellen[31] his Servant aged 18 .... 4.
Joseph Cooper[,][32] Writer aged 37 .... 1.
Wm Cox [,][33] Surgeon aged 41, Frances[34] his Wife
aged 35, Wm. his Son aged above 12. Eunice[35] his
daughter aged 2¾ and Henry Lloyd [Loyd][36] his
Servant aged 21 .... 5.

---

17. "At first appointed 3d Bailif, then 2d & lastly 1st Bailif in 1735. He was also Publick Store-Keeper on Hughes death 30 Sept. 1733, but turn'd out of both Offices 1739 for abusing his Trust." He received lot 24 in Savannah. List, 31.
18. "Recorder of Savannah till made 1st Bailif in Hen. Parkers room 20 June 1739. But removed 25 March 1740 by letter from the Trustees, & likewise suspended from being Recorder till an acct. he had made with the stores be made up. He lives in open adultery wh. Turners wife & he is guilty of other faults. 26th April 1740 he left Georgia, & in June following came for England, where he proposed to stay, but returned." He received lot 19 in Savannah. List, 35.
19. "He marry'd Anne d. of Geo. Syms. His lot was granted him 20 Dec. 1733, and is supposed vacant." He received lot 13 in Savannah. He died July 23, 1734. List, 97.
20. He received lot 22 in Savannah. He died April 18, 1734. List, 33.
21. "Re-marry'd to Tho. Cross 29 June 1734 and quitted the colony with him [December, 1738]." List, 33.
22. He soon died but no date of his death is given. List, 33.
23. The records do not show anything further about these boys. List, 33.
24. He died on shipboard on the way to Georgia. The record here gives his age as 1 year. List, 33.
25. He received lot 40 in Savannah. "His lot was Swamp overflow'd." He died Dec. 14, 1733. List, 35.
26. "Re-marry'd to Ja. Smith a Carolinian 8 Feb. 1733-4 who lived here on her lot. Abt. May 1740 they both left the colony to settle in Scotland on an estate, and sold their loc to Capt. Thompson for 20£." List, 26.
27. She died April 2, 1734. List, 35.
28. He received lot 27 in Savannah. He died March 4, 1734-5. List, 35.
29. "Re-marry'd to Tho. Salter 9 Sept 1736 & lives with him on his lot 68." List, 35.
30. Nothing in this record about her.
31. "Sent back to England." List, 225.
32. He received lot 20 in Savannah. He died March 29, 1735. List, 37.
33. He received lot 6 in Savannah. He dfed April 6, 1733. List, 37.
34. "Re-marr'd to Ja. Watts Lieut. 1 June 1734 who died the same month. She afterwd. [1734] went to England wth. her two children." List, 35.
35. William and Eunice returned to England in 1734. List, 35.
36. "He bought out his time, & had lycense to keep a publick house 2 Dec. 1736. He marr'd Phobe—He went to Carolina to get work—His wife return'd to England wth. Capt. Thompson & arriv'd 2 May 1740." He received lot 171 in Savannah. He absconded February 6, 1738-9 but returned. List, 111.

Joseph Fitzwalter [,]³⁷ Gardener Aged 31 _____ 1.
Walter Fox [,]³⁸ Turner aged 35 _____ 1.
John Gready³⁹ understands Farming Aged 22 _____ 1.
James Goddard [,]⁴⁰ Carpenter & Joyner Aged 38, Elizabeth⁴¹ his Wife aged 42, John his Son aged under 9 & Elizabeth⁴² his Daur. aged 5 _____ 4.
Peter Gordon [,]⁴³ Upholsterer aged 34 & Katherine⁴⁴ his Wife aged 28 _____ 2.
Richard Hodges [,]⁴⁵ Basketmaker aged 50, Mary⁴⁶ his Wife aged 42, & his daughters Mary⁴⁷ aged 18, Elizabeth⁴⁸ aged 16 & Sarah⁴⁹ aged 5 _____ 5.
Joseph Hughes⁵⁰ in the Cyder Trade & understands Writing & Accompts aged 28 & Elizabeth⁵¹ his Wife aged 22 _____ 2,
Noble Jones [,]⁵² Carpenter aged 32, Sarah⁵³ his Wife aged 32, Noble⁵⁴ his Son aged 10 months

---

37. "He marry'd Molly an Indian d. of Capt Tukance [Tuscanee?] 8 Aprl. 1735 who ran from him, a Rambler. He went over 1. Constable of Savannah. He was Publick gardiner till 1736. Mr Oglethorpe removed him for insufficiency [inefficiency?] 21 Oct. 1738." He received lot 8 in Savannah. List, 59.
38. "Made Tything Man 23 Nov. 1736. In all his time he only fell'd one acre of land." He received lot number 2 in Savannah. List, 61.
39. "Frequently in Carolina. Try'd & conv. [convicted] for breach of Covent. with Geo. Smith 9 July 1737." He received lot number 3 in Savannah. List, 73.
40. He received lot number 1 in Savannah. He died July 1, 1733. List, 71.
41. She died July 28, 1733. List, 71.
42. John and Elizabeth were servants to Thomas Christie. List, 71.
43. "Bailif of Savannah, but removed — 1738. He thereupon return'd & remain with his wife in England, & by leave parted with his lot to the daughters of Major Will. Cook, 12 April 1738." He left Georgia April 12, 1738 and died in 1740. He received lot 23 in Savannah. List, 71.
44. Nothing in this record about her.
45. "He was 2d Bailif of Savannah: and succeeded by Tho. Causton 16 Oct. 1734." He received Lot 17 in Savannah. He died July 20, 1733. List, 85.
46. "In possession of the lot design'd her husband. She marry'd Edwd. Townsend 22 Feb. 1734-5. She was fyned 20 shill. for retailing liquours without lycence 2 Oct. 1734, a vile foul mouthed Malecontent, & fled the colony 21 July 1740 with her young daughter." She ran away July 29, 1740, to Carolina and there died. List, 85.
47. Nothing in this record about her.
48. "She marry'd Ri. [Richard] Lobb 8 May 1734." She died August 4, 1735. List, 85.
49. She ran away July 29, 1740. List, 85.
50. "Storekeeper to the Trust while he lived." He received lot 16 in Savannah. He died September 30, 1733. List, 87.
51. "Re-marry'd to Jo. West, and at both their desires this lot was granted to Danl. Prevost 31 May 1738. She marry'd John West 20 April 1734, who dying 1739 She lived with Will. Kelleway as wife with the character of a lewd woman." She died June 5, 1740. List, 87.
52. "Employ'd to Survey the peoples lots, but removed for negligence. He took possession of this lot 21 Dec. 1733, and afterwards improved land at some distance from the town. He was I think a Constable also, and Officer for executing the Rum act. He now resides mostly at his new plantation abt. 10 miles from Savannah. On 21 Oct 1738 Mr Oglethorp removed him from being Surveyor and first Constable, but afterward gave him the comand of the Narrows." He received lot 41 in Savannah. List, 97.
53. Nothing in this record about her.
54. He received lot 46 in Savannah. List, 97.

[years?], Mary[55] his daughter aged 3 & his Servants
Thomas Ellis[56] aged 17 & Mary Cormock[57] aged 11   6.
Wm Littell [Littel][58] understands Flax & Hemp
aged 31, Elizabeth[59] his Wife aged 31. his Son
Wm.[60] aged under 2 & Mary[61] his daughter aged 5__   4.
Thomas Millidge [,][62] Carpenter & Joyner aged 42,
Elizabeth[63] his Wife aged 40, his Sons John[64] aged
11, Richard[65] aged 8, & James[66] aged 1½ & his
daughters Sarah aged under 9 and Frances[67] aged 5__   7.
Francis Mugridge[68] Sawyer aged 39_____   1.
James Muir [,][69] Peruke maker aged 38, Ellen[70] his
Wife aged 38, John[71] his Son aged 18 months &
Elizabeth Satchfield[72] his Servant aged 25_____   4.
Joshua Overend[73] aged 40_____   1.
Samuel Parker[74] a Heelmaker & understands Car-
penter's Work aged 33, Jane[75] his Wife aged 36, &
his Sons Samuel[76] aged 16 & Thomas[77] aged under 9   4.
John Penrose [,][78] Husbandman aged 35 & Eliza-

---

55. Nothing in this record about her.
56. "He had first lot 54, but exchanged it with Will. Mackay for this. Afterwards deserted the Colony. As late as 14 June 1737 he was a servant and consequently had then no lot." He received lot 55 in Savannah. He left Georgia December 1738 but returned. List, 55.
57. Nothing in this record about her.
58. He received lot 37 in Savannah. He died July 12, 1733. List, 111.
59. "Re-marry'd to John West 28 Aug. 1733, and had possession of the lot intended her husband Will. Littel 31 Dec. 1733." She died September 26, 1733. List, 111.
60. The record here states that he was born in Georgia. List, 111.
61. She died July 12, 1733. List, 111.
62. He received lot 36 in Savannah. He died July 29, 1733. List, 119.
63. She died June, 2, 1734. List, 119.
64. He received lot 91 in Savannah. His age here is stated as twelve. List, 119.
65. Nothing in this record about him.
66. He died November 4, 1734. List, 119.
67. Nothing in this record about Sarah and Frances. List, 119.
68. "Possest of his lot 21 Dec. 1733. Doubted if he left not a Minor in England." He received lot number 12 in Savannah. He died July 1, 1735. List, 123.
69. "Possest of his lot 21 Dec. 1733. Re-marry'd to Mary Woodman 29 Dec. 1734. No cultivated of land. Ran to Carolina in 1739 and died there Sept. 1739." He received lot 18 in Savannah. List, 123.
70. She died July 10, 1733. List, 123.
71. He left Georgia in March, 1733. List, 123.
72. Nothing in this record about her.
73. He was a mercer and received lot 11 in Savannah. "The Lot supposed vacant Feb. 1738-9." He died June 23, 1733. List, 155.
74. "He lived not to take up his lot, which was possest by his widow. He went over 2. Constable of Savannah." He received lot 38 in Savannah. He died July 20, 1733. List, 159.
75. "She took possession of the lot intended her husband 21 Dec. 1733. Re-marry'd to Sml. Mercer 6 May 1734." She died August 9, 1742. List, 159.
76. He was a smith, received lot 93 in Savannah, and died in 1741. List, 159.
77. Nothing in this record about him.
78. "Fyn'd thrice for retayling spirituous liquors with out lycence. And twice for Assault and defamation. His lot swamp overflow'd. He went over 2d Tything man of Savannah." He received lot 15 in Savannah. He ran away to South Carolina in August, 1742. List, 161.

beth[79] his Wife aged 46.. 2.
Thomas Pratt[80] [occupation unknown] aged 21...... 1.
John Sammes [Samms,][81] Cordwainer aged 42......... 1.
Francis Scott[82] a reduced Military Officer aged 40
& his Servt John [Richard] Cameron[83] aged 35......... 2.
Joseph Stanly [Stanley,][84] Stockingmaker & can
draw & reel Silk aged 45, Elizabeth[85] his Wife aged
35, & John Mackoy [Mackay,][86] his Servant aged 25   3.
George Symes [,][87] Apothecary aged 55, Sarah[88]
his Wife aged 52, & Ann [Anne][89] his daughter
aged 21.. 3.
Daniel Thibaut[90] understands Vines aged 50, Mary[91]
his Wife aged 40, James[92] his Son aged under 12 &
Diana[93] his daughter aged under 7............................. 4.
John Warrin [,][94] Flax & Hemp Dresser aged 34,
Elizabeth[95] his Wife aged 27, his Sons Wm.[96] aged
6, Richard[97] aged 4, John [98] aged 1½ & one to be
baptized aged 3 weeks & his daughter Elizabeth[99]
aged 3.. 7.

---

79. "Found guilty of the same things, and also of keeping a bawdy house 26 May 1736. Went to Carolina for fear of the Spaniards." She left Georgia in September, 1740. List, 161.
80. "Possest of his lot 21 Dec. 1733. His lot was given to Mrt. [Margaret?] Bovey, he forfeiting it By returning to England without leave 23 April 1735, contrary to Covenant." List, 163.
81. "Had possession of his lot 21 Dec. 1733." He received lot 9 in Savannah. He died August 21, 1733. List, 189.
82. He died January 2, 1734. List, 191.
83. Absconded at Palacholas. List, 29.
84. "Possest of his Lot 21 Dec. 1733, and had fell'd fenc'd & cleard 4 acres, which by his sickness were neglected: he left the Colony 29 July 1740 being superannuated and past labour." He received lot 21 in Savannah. He left Georgia in 1740. List, 197.
85. "Publick midwife of Savannah. She return'd to England to ly in Octbr. 1736." List, 197.
86. He died July 25, 1733. "He left neither wife nor child." List, 117.
87. "Possest of his Lot 21 Dec. 1733. Re-marry'd to Eliz. Gray 10 Mar. 1734-5. His lot supposed vacant." He received lot 7 in Savannah. List, 197.
88. She died July 21, 1733. List, 197.
89. "Marry'd 1st to Robt. Johnston [Johnson]. 2dly. to Morgan Davis 26 Mar 1735." She died in 1739. List, 197.
90. He received lot 39 in Savannah. He died October 24, 1733. List, 213.
91. "Put in possession of the Lot designed her husband 21 Dec. 1733. She re-marry'd Jo. Cellier of Purysburg [S. C.] 17 March 1734-5 who lives with her on this lot." List, 213.
92. He became a servant to William Bradley. List, 213.
93. Nothing in this record about her.
94. "He landed with a child born on shipboard whose name I know not." He received lot 10 in Savannah. He died August 11, 1733. List, 223.
95. "She went to England on her husbands death in 1733-4 but marryed again to Jonathan Hood and return'd." List, 223.
96. He died September 5, 1733. List, 223.
97. "Went to England with his mother 1733 but his lot kept for him." List, 223.
98. He died June 12, 1733. According to this record he was two years old. List, 223.
99. Her name is not mentioned in this record.

Wm Waterland[100] late a Mercer aged 44 .... 1.
John West [,][101] Smith aged 33, Elizabeth[102] his
Wife aged 33, & Richard[103] his Son aged 5 .... 3.
James Wilson [,] [104] Sawyer aged 21 .... 1.
John Wright [,][105] Vintner aged 33, Penelope[106] his
Wife aged 33, John his Son aged 13 & Elizabeth[107]
his daughter aged 11 .... 4.
Thomas Young [,][108] Wheelwright aged 45 .... 1.

16 Novr. 1732 Muster'd on board the Ann at
 Gravesend. Total 114
 The Freight of which Passengers amoted. to 91 Heads.[109]
  By Capt Smyter on board the Volant
Samuel Grey [,][110] Silk Throwster aged 30 & his
Apprentices Chetwin Furzer [Chetwyn Furzend,][111]
aged 16 & Cornelius Jones[112] aged 15 .... 3.
John Vanderplank[113] bredd at Sea aged 48 .... 1.

Total 4.

---

100. "2nd Bailif of Savannah for a time but turned out 2 Aug. 1733 for misbehaviour, and afterwd went to Carolina & never returned. Brother to Dr. Waterland the Kings chaplain, who for his drunkenness would take no notice of him." He received lot 34 in Savannah. He left Georgia February 4, 1734. List, 223.
101. "Appointed 3d Bailif 13 Oct. 1733, which he some years later resign'd. On 7 Oct. 1735 he had a grant of 500 acres, and 11 May 1737 was permitted to alienate this lot. He marry'd Eliz. Little his 2. wife 28 Aug. 1733 and Eliz. Hughes his 3d wife 24 April 1734. In June 1739 he had leave to sell his Interest and quit the Colony by reason of ill health, but died of the consumption before he could set out. His wife remarry'd to Will. Kelleway." He received lot 31 in Savannah. He died in 1739. List, 225.
102. She died July 1, 1733. List, 225.
103. He died July 31, 1733. List, 225.
104. "Bound in recognizance for assaulting the guard on duty 30 July 1734. Convicted of extortion in selling flesh meet [meat] 14 July 1735. Fyn'd 5 shillings for wilfully destroying other mens hoggs 28 July 1735. m. Mildred d. of Robt. Moore 1 Feb. 1734-5." He received lot 32 in Savannah. He was absent for some years but returned in 1740. List, 227.
105. He received lot 30 in Savannah. "His lot swamp over-flow'd." He died in December, 1737. List, 227.
106. "Remarry'd to Joseph Fitzwalter, and lives on his lot No. 8." List, 227.
107. No information on John and Elizabeth in this record.
108. He received lot 26 in Savannah. "Possest of his lot 21 Dec. 1733. He marry'd the Widow Box of Abercorn July 1734." List, 235.
109. The remainder of this document refers to passengers arriving on another ship, who logically should not have been included in this list.
110. He was expelled from Georgia, June 17, 1733. List, 73.
111. "After discharge from his Service he took this lot, but went to Serve in the Scoutboat 1736." He received lot 152 in Savannah. He absconded in February 1736-7. List, 61.
112. "Apprentice to Saml. Grey. Discharged by his mother." List, 97.
113. "Made Naval Officer 7 Oct. 1735." He received lot 25 in Savannah. He died in 1737. List, 214.